Moved and Seconded

OTHER BOOKS BY REBECCA RULE

Headin' for the Rhubard: A New Hampshire Dictionary (well, kinda)
Islandport Press, 2010

Live Free and Eat Pie: A Storyteller's Guide to New Hampshire
Islandport Press, 2008

Could Have Been Worse
Plaidswede Publishing, 2006

The History of the Concord Music Club
Town and Country, 2004

True Stories: Guides for Writing from Your Life
with Susan Wheeler, Heinemann, 2000

The Best Revenge
University Press of New England, 1995; released in paperback, spring 2004

Creating the Story: Guides for Writers
with Susan Wheeler, Heinemann, 1993

Wood Heat,
Nightshade Press, 1992

Moved *and* Seconded

TOWN MEETING IN NEW HAMPSHIRE
the Present, the Past, and the Future

Rebecca Rule

with contributions from

Susan Bruce
Jere Daniell
Elizabeth Dubrulle
Neil English
Gary Evans
Garth Fletcher
Justine "Mel" Graykin
Donald Hall
Marie Harris

Jack Hutchinson
Ronald Jager
Jane Kenyon
Dudley Laufman
Charles V. Moser
Gary Patton
Susie Riley
Ken Sheldon
Jody Wells

PLAIDSWEDE PUBLISHING
Concord, New Hampshire

Designed and composed at Hobblebush Books,
Brookline, New Hampshire (www.hobblebush.com)

Printed in the United States of America

ISBN 978-0-9837400-5-6
Library of Congress Control Number: 2011945247

Cover illustration by Marc Sutherland, first published in
New Hampshire Magazine

Published by:

PLAIDSWEDE PUBLISHING
P.O. Box 269 · Concord, New Hampshire 03302-0269
www.plaidswede.com

For David Emerson, 1949–2009, who loved New Hampshire history, town meeting, and Susan Bruce. And, gawd, wa'n't he funny!

Special thanks to John K. Rule for reading the manuscript with an engineer's eye to be sure my i's were dotted and t's crossed (most of them) and for his constancy and support.

Acknowledgments

Thanks for the information, guidance, enthusiasm, songs, photos, and stories:
Rick Agran, Dave Anderson, Joann and Bob Bailey, Peter Beard, Susan Bruce,
Dorothy Campbell, Rodney Campbell, Frank Case, Carole Anne Centre, Andrea
Cheeney, James Cheeney, Alvin Clark, John Colburn, Chris Cote, Caroline Cross,
Pat Cummings, Jere Daniell, Elizabeth Dubrulle, Neil English, Lucy Edwards, Gary
Evans, Garth Fletcher, Ken Forbes, Richard Gale, Katie Holmes Gallagher, Justine
"Mel" Graykin, John and Rita Gulardo, Bill Hall, Donald Hall, Sid Hall, Zak Harris,
Dave Henry, Joey Holmes, Jack Hutchinson, Ronald Jager, Julia King, Millie Kmiec,
Marion Knox, Jean Lane, Dudley Laufman, Inez McDermott, Maura McNeil,
Maureen Mann, J. P. Marzullo, Dennis McClary, Buddy McDougall, Charles V.
Moser, Dave Nagel, Howard O'Dell, Jim O'Donnell, Gary Patton, Ashley Paul, Peter
E. Randall, Eric Reitter, Susie Riley, Sue and Robbie Robertson, Deb Schulte, Ken
Sheldon, Frumie Selchen, Arthur Slade, Linda Smith, Richard Snow, Marilyn
Stuller, Nancy Taylor, Bruce Tribolini, Chaloe Tyler, Eleanor Vanderpool, Dick
Wakefield, Jody Wells, and Paul Yelle. Thanks to Susan Kennedy for her careful edit-
ing and to Sid Hall for his inspired design.

And for anyone inadvertently left out, I'm sorry. So many people helped with
this book in person or through their writings, I know I've missed naming some of
you. Still, your contributions are greatly appreciated. Town meeting belongs to all
of us.

Contents

Unity town meeting, March 17 2007

"*Very obviously the town meeting is not apart from us, it is not above us . . . Three of us together in official assembly make a unit of wisdom that is greater than the sum total of our separate capacities, but at the same time this new element comes from within us. Yes, the town meeting is unmistakably from and of us. It is not put over us by a beneficent father or social order apart from ourselves; we do not elect it; it could not exist without us—it is us.*"

CLARENCE M. WEBSTER, *TOWN MEETING COUNTRY*

Let's Get This Meeting Started:
How This Book Came to Be

S usan Bruce came up with the idea. She explains what she calls her Inspiration Flash this way: At a four-day workshop, she met a Brooklyn man who had a friend from Franconia. The friend had told him a little bit about town meeting. After each workshop session, the Brooklyn man would pump her for information about town meeting. He was fascinated. Susan tried to explain the language and the process, but he didn't quite get the picture until she loaned him a town report. Evidently, the town report became his bedtime reading, because the next day he was all fired up. He finally understood what we do at town meeting. "You vote on streetlights," he said. "The whole town gets together to make nuts and bolts decisions!"

"Yes," Susan said. "That's what we do, once a year. We all meet, and make those decisions together."

"Could we do this in Brooklyn?" he asked.

Susan said, "You do know that the population of Brooklyn is three times that of the entire state of New Hampshire—I don't think this would work in Brooklyn."

He laughed, and said, No, he guessed it wouldn't.

But she could tell he was jealous.

Once the idea emerged for a book explaining this institution, unique to New England, it was a case of "Why didn't anyone think of a New Hampshire town meeting book before?"

Originally, Susan and I planned to write the book together, but life intervened, and Susan was unable to participate as fully as she'd hoped. Nevertheless, over the three years—give or take—it took to bring the book into being, Susan stayed close to the project, always available to read a draft of a chapter, quick to contribute fresh ideas. I couldn't have written it without her.

George Geers at Plaidswede Publishing supported the project from the beginning. He'd published my book, *Could Have Been Worse: True Stories, Embellishments and Outright Lies*, so he knew I could meet deadlines. (My two greatest skills, developed over a long career, are meeting deadlines and showing up.) George loves all things New Hampshire—especially history. When presented with the book proposal, he said something like: This will be the quintessential, comprehensive, authoritative, be-all and end-all work on New Hampshire town meeting.

"Kinda like Peter Wallner's two-volume biography of New Hampshire's only U.S. President, Franklin Pierce?" I said.

"Yuh, kinda like that," he said.

(Those last two lines may have taken place only in my head.)

Let me be the first to acknowledge that this is not, in fact, the quintessential, comprehensive, authoritative, be-all and end-all work on New Hampshire town meeting. The topic is both broad and deep—too broad and deep to cover fully in one plump volume. But on these pages:

You'll find the rules of the game—how town meeting works and some of the thinking behind it.

You'll learn the history of town meeting in New Hampshire, and how it has evolved over the last couple hundred years. Esteemed Dartmouth historian Jere Daniell has allowed his previously unpublished historical overview "Town Meeting: Symbol for a Nation" to be included in its entirety, saving me a ton of work.

You'll meet the characters—from silent knitters to rabble rousers—who play their parts in the theater of town meeting.

You'll listen in on some olde-time town meetings to learn what the issues were way back when.

You'll listen in on current town meetings, to see what's changed (technology) and what's stayed the same (human nature).

You'll hear the stories and the funny, wise, thoughtful, thought-provoking, and outrageous comments from members of the legislative body as well as town officials.

You'll dip into the literature of town meeting—the poems, the novels, the short stories, the essays—some by famous writers, some by writers who may be new to you.

And most of all, I hope you'll find a colorful portrait of town meeting, drawn from many sources. I hope, too, that this portrait will help you understand why town meeting is a New England treasure.

About the Stories

I've been collecting town meeting stories for years. All the stories here have a kernel of truth. Some I can, with confidence, attribute to certain people in certain towns and even trace to certain dates. Others are a bit more fluid. If I am not sure of (and can't document) the veracity of a story—but it rings true—I'll tip you off by introducing it with something like "They say . . ." or "I heard that . . . " or "So-and-so recalls the time when . . ."

Sometimes I have an inkling of where a story took place, but no concrete evidence (like a reference in a town report), in which case I'll set the story in Woodford. There is no Woodford, New Hampshire. It's a made up name representing many real places. Some will read these Woodford stories and say, "I know that happened here in New Boston." And be right. Same thing, or something similar, probably happened in Pittsburg, Alstead, and Rye. Each town is unique, but not *that* unique.

Caution

As you read, you may come to the conclusion—as I did—that town meeting is an endangered species. You may feel discouraged—as I did—about its future. What can be done, you may ask, to keep town meeting strong? A growing population, declining attendance, and a state-sanctioned option to eliminate town meeting (SB 2) threaten not only its vitality but its very existence.

We can't do much about population growth. People will move to New Hampshire, young folks will have babies, and the population may continue to grow. Or, maybe, level off. That'd be good. Once a town gets to be bigger than, say, 10,000 residents, traditional town meeting becomes cumbersome, and other options (representative town meeting, town council) may be needed.

The state-sanctioned option to eliminate town meeting (SB 2) could itself be eliminated by a vote of the House and the Senate. That'd be good.

But you may also conclude, as I did, that the best thing any of us can do for town meeting is to participate. Step up. Run for office. Serve on committees. Get involved. It takes smart, organized, committed town officials to plan town meeting and carry out the will of the voters. It takes an animated, involved, committed legislative body (we, the voters) to turn out in force, generate lively discussion, and together decide the fate of our community.

Oh, and some homemade pies, beans, ham—a good feed—wouldn't hurt either. Come to town meeting for the apple pie, stay for pure democracy.

"The chance to have our voices heard—that's central to town meeting. Whether or not the vote goes our way, there's satisfaction in voicing our side, laying out our perspective. Sure, most people have their minds made up before they enter the hall, but because we are all in a hall together there exists the possibility that somebody might change somebody's mind. Oh, it's happened. A nudge and a wink from someone you respect; a quiet 'slow down, let's think this over' from someone who seems wise and logical; a passionate 'you may not think you're hurting anyone with this, but you're hurting me,' and the ground you thought was so firm beneath your boots shifts just a little. Maybe you won't vote for it. But maybe you won't vote against it either. Maybe you'll just sit with your hands folded this once, because you're not as sure which side is right as you were when you walked through the door. These are the small miracles of town meeting."

REBECCA RULE

Moved and Seconded

The Northwood checklist, 2010

"In a town meeting the great secret of political science was uncovered, and the problem solved, how to give every individual his fair weight in government. . . . Here the rich gave council, but the poor also; and, moreover, the just and the unjust. . . . In this open democracy every opinion had utterance; every objection, every fact, every acre of land, every bushel of rye, its entire weight."

RALPH WALDO EMERSON

1

A Primer on Town Meeting: The Basics, the Law, and the Language

In the school auditorium at the Bow Town Meeting 2010, I sat in the non-voter section taking in the spectacle. The section was clearly marked, but voters kept trying to sit with us. Because there were so few of us, I guess, our section looked like a good place to stretch your legs, lean back, have a little nap if needs be. It was an evening meeting and folks were tuckered out. The moderator's helpers—wearing orange vests—shooed the interlopers away. Voters had to sit together so show-of-hands votes could be efficiently counted. And god-forbid a nonvoter (nonresident, unregistered, or under age) should raise her hand and sway the vote. That wouldn't be legal. Or fair. Or right. Or constitutional!

Behind me sat a group of high school girls who'd clearly been assigned to experience democracy in action. They were chatty. Trying to figure out what the heck was going on. I pointed them to the warrant on page 171 of the town report. This seemed to help. One said, "Do they have town meeting every month?"

"No," I said, "just once a year." I didn't get into the subject of school meetings or special town meetings. That would have taken too long to explain. (And the meeting was about to begin.)

And so this chapter was inspired. It's amazing what people don't know about town meeting. (It amazed me how much I didn't know once I got knee-deep in research.)

First, a review of the basics then and now. Then comes a primer on the technicalities, fundamentals, and laws—just what a person needs to know to understand what's going on and participate with confidence. And finally, a glossary of associated terms. Whether you're an old hand who feels like a brush up, or new to the subject with just a hazy idea of what town meeting entails, you may find this chapter useful.

The Basics

The more things change the more they stay the same in the essentials. More than 250 years have passed since town meeting's wilderness beginnings. Folks still gather at a central location, though these days it's more likely to be a school gymnasium or auditorium than a town hall or, in the early days, a tavern or someone's front room. Warrant articles go up for vote. People choose sides. Arguments pro and con are presented, questions posed, both real and rhetorical. Sometimes jaws set. Sometimes tempers flare. Invitations to step outside and settle differences in the town hall yard seem less freely offered than in the old days. Not necessarily because passions run cooler; more likely due to the looming possibility of lawsuits.

Food is usually available for purchase as a fundraiser for one group or another—though the bounty of comestibles ain't, generally, what it used to be. Instead of a full supper of beans, ham, and fixings, you're more apt to find coffee, soda, sandwiches, and baked goods from the women's club or friends of the library. In some places it's just a few Girl Scouts selling cookies. I speak from experience when I say a box of Thin Mints, delicious as they are, will not sustain a person over the course of a meeting that lasts several hours. At one lengthy meeting, desperate voters sent out for pizza, followed by confusion over who ordered the pepperoni, who wanted plain cheese or mushroom, and who owed what on the tab.

Used to be school business and town business were discussed at one meeting, with the election of town officers ongoing at voting booths in the back (or front) of the hall. Joann Bailey, Northwood Town Historian, recalled: "Some people came and stayed at the meeting. But some came just to vote, so there was a perpetual line of interruption, if you will."

As school budgets grew and town business became more complicated, most opted to deal with school issues at one meeting and town issues at another. In Northwood—and surely Northwood is not the only place to experiment in this way—for some years school and town meeting were held at the same time in different buildings. Voters had to choose which to attend, or shuttle themselves back and forth if particular issues were of interest. This was how it was when Joann Bailey moved to town in 1952. "School and town meetings ran simultaneously," she said. "I couldn't believe it. Town meeting was in town hall and school meeting was over in the Center School building (next door), so you had to choose which one you'd go to. It didn't go on like that for very many years."

The modern town meeting is divided into two parts. Part One takes place at the polls on the second Tuesday in March. Voters collect a ballot, go into a voting booth, and vote for their favorite candidates. Zoning ordinances also, by state law, must be approved or disapproved at the polls, which are open all day as in state and federal elections. Part Two takes place in the evening or a few days later, say, on the following Saturday. This is the part most people think of as town meeting—the community gathers, discussion ensues on a series of warrant articles, and votes are taken on the spot by voice, show of hands, or secret ballot. Most towns address the needs of the school at one sit-down meeting called school district meeting, and the needs of the town at another session called town meeting.

One newly elected school board member got the low-down right off quick: "We always schedule school meeting *before* town meeting," she was told by the other board members. "That way we're apt to get more money. After town meeting, people are always feeling much poorer. Pssst: Don't tell the selectmen! Don't want to give them any ideas."

Some towns hold tight to tradition for its own sake. And why not? No harm in continuity. Dunbarton has elected hog reeves (people traditionally charged with rounding up pigs escaped from the farms in town) annually for almost 250 years. It's an official town position with the honor going to the most recently married couple. They don't even have to campaign.

Prior to both town and school meetings, the costs to run the town and its various departments have been calculated by the selectmen and, in some towns, by the Municipal Budget Committee in conjunction with the selectmen. Same deal with the school meeting, only it's the school board or the Municipal Budget Committee in conjunction with the school board. Warrant articles that begin "To see if the Town will vote to raise and appropriate . . ." propose specific amounts to be raised by taxes for the coming fiscal year. Since the fiscal year typically starts in July, there's a lot of guess work. How much will it cost to heat the school nine months from now? How many students will attend? How many of those will need special education? How much money do we need to set aside for salting and sanding the roads? How many police officers must we employ? Will the pumper truck last another year? What about the furnace at town hall? Should we patch it, or is that throwing bad money after good? If we don't give the administrative assistant a raise, will she leave us for a better offer?

School Meeting Versus Town Meeting: What's the Difference?

A selectman explained that in his town the school district meeting opens at 9:00 a.m. with about ten people in attendance (in a good year). The votes go fast and the meeting's usually over by 10:00 a.m., when the moderator closes the school district meeting and opens town meeting. By then the hall is full of voters raring to go. Here's the puzzlement: The costs to run the school account for about 80 percent of the tax burden. The town part accounts for a measly 20 percent. Yet people turn out for the town and not the school. Seems they'd rather argue about the roads, the library, the cemeteries, and the new fire truck than schools.

I've observed the same phenomenon. Unless there's a new school on the warrant or a new teacher contract, attendance at school meeting is, in general, considerably lower than at town meeting.

Why is that?

Maybe it's because town meeting discussions get down to the nitty-gritty, and we revel in the nitty-gritty. We do (or don't) need a stop light at this intersection. We know this because we drive through it twice a day. Or we live across the road. We do (or don't) need a new dump truck. We know about trucks. We've owned them. We know about transmissions because we've burned out a few ourselves, or we work repairing autos, or our cousin Sid does, so we know a good price or a jacked-up one when we see it. The police chief doesn't (or does) deserve a raise because she did (or didn't) give us a ticket and some lip when she pulled us over.

School business is somehow more remote. We all went to school. Most of us had, have, or will have kids in school, but we don't live in the school like we live in the town. We can complain that test scores have gone down when cost per pupil has gone up—but most of us don't really know what those test scores mean exactly. Or if the tests are any good in the first place. We grouse that music (or art or physical education or foreign language) classes are frills. But some opera singer, architect, marathoner, or delegate to the UN is bound to dispute that. We complain that teachers work just 180 days a year from 8 a.m. to 2:30 p.m. (though teachers claim different) while real working people work eight hours a day (or more) all year round. How come they're getting raises and benefits when we haven't seen a raise since Christ wore knickers, and our benefits are being cut? Plus they don't have to work summers! We want good educations for the kids, but throwing money at schools doesn't necessarily mean they'll get that good education.

The comments at school meeting are spirited, but fairly general. One memorable exchange from a long-ago meeting:

"Heck, we don't need those fancy computers. You put a kid and a teacher on a log. That's education."

A teacher sitting next to me whispered in my ear: "How much is it going to cost for all those logs, not to mention all those teachers?"

School meeting and town meeting tend to differ in tone and tenor. Discussion at school meeting tends to be more abstract, less openly vitriolic—though the undercurrents can be strong indeed, and downright mean, too. I recall one meeting when a photocopied sheet was circulated (no one admitted to printing it) accusing the principal of having an affair with a teacher and favoring that teacher with extra classroom supplies. Far as I know, neither accusation was true—but the real message, that the women in question were gay, tainted the meeting and caused so many hard feelings that both the teacher and the principal quit and moved to less homophobic locales.

That kind of personal attack is the exception, not the rule, thank goodness. Usually at school meeting, we speak of concepts: student/ teacher ratios, top-heavy administration, and the sweets vs. the meat and potatoes of education. Throw the SAU (superintendent's office), the SAU's lawyer, and the teachers' union into the mix with a five-year negotiated contract, and it's hard to get your teeth into anything substantial.

Town meeting provides more substance. The legislative body simply knows more (or thinks it does) about town affairs. We go to the dump once a week, so we are familiar with the inefficiencies—and we know from our own close encounters that the dumpmaster is a sweetheart (or a stickler). We drive the roads. We register our cars. We frequent the beaches and fish the lakes. We were rescued by the rescue squad or harassed by the building inspector. The dog officer has it in for our darling Bobo. Town affairs affect our everyday lives: "If that Class 6 road is designated a nature trail, does that mean I can't run my ATV on it? What the hay do you people have against ATVs? Yuh, well, I'd go cross-country skiing too, if I didn't have two fake knees and a hip on its way south."

One farmer's explanation for his no vote encapsulates the earthy tenor of town meeting. He said: "I could support this new fire truck if it was an International."

Over the years, town and school budgets have evolved from, say, a nice round $100 for annual support of schools to pages of small print listing anticipated expenses line by grueling line. These grueling lines explain what is usually the largest money item on the warrant: the operating budget. Besides warrant articles developed by the select board, school board, and Municipal Budget Committee, additional articles may be petitioned by anybody in town, with the signatures of at least twenty-five residents. That's changed. Used to be ten. Petitioned articles could address anything from installing a street light on Potter's Lane (it's awful dark on Potter's Lane) to eliminating the police commission (which had been voted in two decades earlier on account of alleged corruption in the PD).

And that's it in a nutshell. Part One, voting for town officials and zoning ordinances. Part Two, a sit-down gathering to debate and vote on the rest. The warrant lists the items to be voted on. The moderator guides the meeting. The Girl Scouts provide cookies.

For more details, logistics, and laws, read on.

When and Where

By tradition town meeting is held annually on the second Tuesday of March. Some towns hold their meetings on other evenings or on a Saturday in March. Some towns with large contingents of snow birds wait until June when more people are around. By law the selectmen are responsible for choosing the place where town meeting will be held and specifying it in the warrant. A town may hold its meeting in an adjacent town if there is no facility large enough within the town. If so, the selectmen must arrange transportation between the regular polling place and the site for the out-of-town meeting.

The Warrant

The warrant is prepared by the selectmen in advance of the meeting. It lists the articles or topics to be taken up. Some years a warrant might be ten articles long. Other years it might be thirty. Depends on how many items town officials want to pull out of the general operating budget to be voted on separately. Or how many big items—trucks, renovations, expanding the sewer system—must be addressed. Also, how many petitioned articles pop up.

Selectmen may add articles right up until the warrant is posted, at least fourteen days before the meeting. They cannot, however, add articles requiring an appropriation of funds unless they were discussed at budget hearings.

The warrant must be posted at the site of the meeting and in at least one other public place in town. It specifies the day, time, and the location of the meeting, and specifies when the polls will open and close for Part One, as well as where the ballot voting will take place.

The subjects of all business to be discussed must appear in the warrant. Articles may be amended from the floor, so long as the fundamental subject remains unchanged. For example, an article to build a baseball field on town land may not be amended to, instead, dig out and repair the septage lagoon. All amendments to that article must be baseball related.

The moderator may postpone the meeting due to bad weather up until two hours before the scheduled start. A date, or in town meeting lingo a *date certain*, for the postponed meeting must be set. The moderator informs the citizens of the postponement and rescheduling through radio, television, or newspaper announcements.

In addition to articles from the selectmen, as previously mentioned, petitioned articles may be included in the warrant. Anybody in town can petition an article with the signatures of twenty-five or more voters from the town or 2 percent of registered voters. The petition must be submitted no later than the fifth Tuesday before town meeting, and placed on the warrant with only minor changes, like corrections to spelling or grammar. If the selectmen fail to include a legally petitioned article, they are subject to criminal prosecution. Selectmen are not required to post a petitioned article if what it proposes is patently against the law. No sense voting on something if it can't legally be implemented.

Most warrants include a final article: "To transact any other business which may legally come before this meeting." Not much ever comes of this article; not much can with the rules about posting subject matter in advance. Though a formality, this final article signifies that the end is coming. Next up: "Motion to adjourn." And we're done!

What a Warrant Looks Like

DALTON TOWN WARRANT

You are hereby notified to meet at the Municipal Building in Dalton, NH on Tuesday, the 8th day of March 2011 to act upon the itemized subjects to follow. The polls will open at 8 a.m. in the forenoon and will close at 7 p.m. The business meeting will be held in the gymnasium and will be opened at 7 o'clock in the evening.

To elect all necessary officers for the year.

To see if the Town will vote to raise and appropriate the sum of Seven Hundred Sixteen Thousand Eight Hundred Eight Dollars ($716,808) for general Town operations.

To see if the Town will vote to raise and appropriate the sum of Twenty-five Thousand Dollars ($25,000) to be added to the Highway Department Heavy Equipment Capital Reserve Fund. Selectmen recommend this article.

To see if the Town will vote to raise and appropriate the sum of Twenty-five Thousand Dollars ($25,000) to be added to the Paving Capital Reserve Fund. Selectmen recommend this article.

To see if the Town will vote to raise and appropriate the sum of Ten Thousand Dollars ($10,000) to be added to the Fire Department Vehicle Equipment Capital Reserve Fund. Selectmen recommend this article.

To see if the Town will vote to raise and appropriate the sum of One Thousand Dollars ($1,000) to be added to the Sewer Pump Renovation and Replacement Capital Reserve Fund. Selectmen recommend this article.

To see if the Town will vote to raise and appropriate the sum of Five Thousand Dollars ($5,000) to be added to the Police Cruiser Capital Reserve Fund. Three Thousand Dollars to come from the unexpended fund balance. Selectmen recommend this article.

To see if the Town will vote to raise and appropriate Three Thousand Dollars ($3,000) to be added to the Pay Per Bag Replacement Expendable Trust Fund previously established for the repurchase of bags for the "Pay Per Bag" system. The source of these funds will be 25 cents from each bag sold. No taxes will be raised with this appropriation. Selectmen recommend this article.

To see if the Town will vote to raise and appropriate the sum of Two Hundred Twenty Thousand Dollars ($220,000) for the purchase of a new grader and to authorize the withdrawal of One Hundred Thirty Thousand

Dollars ($130,000) from the Highway Department Heavy Equipment Capital Reserve Fund and to authorize the Selectmen to borrow Ninety Thousand Dollars ($90,000) from long term notes and bonds. A 2/3 ballot vote is required. The Selectmen recommend this article.

To see if the Town will vote to establish an expendable trust fund for the purpose of purchasing a new assessing / tax software system for the Town and to raise and appropriate the sum of Eight Thousand Dollars ($8,000) to be placed in this fund. Also to see if the Town will appoint the Selectmen as agents to expend from this account. The Selectmen recommend this article.

To see if the Town will vote to register and disseminate to all concerned its objection, opposition and commitment to stop the construction of any portion of the 1200 Megawatt High Voltage Direct Current Transmission Line in the Town of Dalton as presently proposed by Northeast Utilities, NStar and Hydro-Quebec since such a huge scar constructed and erected through and above the Town's treasured residential and scenic private properties will cause inestimable damage to the orderly economic development of the Town, its economy, and the health and well being of its residents; or to take any other action relative thereto. Petitioned article.

To transact any other business that may legally come before the meeting.

Reading between the Lines of a Warrant Article

Here's how a typical article might appear in the warrant:

Article 4: To see if the Town will vote to raise and appropriate the sum of Thirty Thousand dollars ($30,000) for repairs to the town hall foundation. (Majority vote required.) (Recommended by the Board of Selectmen 2–1) (Not Recommended by the Budget Committee 2–9–1) (Impact on the tax rate is $0.09).

Translation: Two selectmen favor fixing the foundation for $30,000. One doesn't. Maybe she thinks $30,000 is too much or too little. Maybe she thinks the repair can wait. Nine members of the budget committee oppose the appropriation. Two don't. One abstains. Maybe he's in the foundation business and hopes to nab the job. If the article passes, the cost to the individual property owner will be nine cents per $1000 of property value (an estimate), so someone who owns a $200,000 house will pay $18 in property taxes.

The Town Report or Annual Report

To learn the history of any town, a good place to start is the annual town report. Often compiled by the town manager or selectmen's assistant, town reports are printed shortly before town and school meeting and made available to voters at those meetings.

Various commissions, boards, and committees report on their activities and accomplishments. The library trustees summarize activities at the library. The supervisor of the transfer station lets people know how much trash is passing through and how recycling efforts are faring. The principal says a few words about how great the school is. The names and positions of town officials are listed, as are the names of those who graduated from the local schools, those born in the preceding year, those who were married, and those who died.

Each report includes the minutes of the town and school meetings of the previous year.

But the most important part, the pages citizens pour over and mark up, are those for the warrant and proposed budget, listed separately for the town and school. Most budgets include side-by-side comparisons of the money approved for the preceding year, the amount actually spent, and the suggested appropriations to be voted on for this next fiscal year. In towns that have an official budget committee, an elected group of budget watchers, the recommendations of the selectmen or school board are listed side-by-side with the recommendations of that committee. It's a lot to look at, a lot to take in, a lot to discuss, but year after year we buckle down and vote in a budget we think will work for our community, and not tax us out of hearth and home.

2010 PHOTO BY THE AUTHOR

Deerfield Supervisors of the Checklist Cherie Sanborn, Diane Valade, and Meredith Briggs

The Moderator

A moderator is chosen in even-numbered years by ballot at the polls. He or she presides over town meetings, sets the pace, keeps discussion on track, and announces voting results. The moderator is also in charge of elections—town, state, and national. Most towns have a back-up moderator, appointed by the moderator, who can stand in if the moderator is indisposed or disposed to step away from the lectern and speak to an issue as a private citizen.

State law authorizes moderators to establish rules governing the meeting. It also gives voters the power to overrule the moderator. If a voter believes the moderator has made a questionable ruling, the voter may ask the house to overrule the moderator's decision. Then comes a vote on the matter.

The New Hampshire Local Government Center publishes an annual *Town Meeting and School Meeting Handbook*, with guidelines for running town meeting. A number of the moderators interviewed for this book say they use a combination of suggestions from the handbook, *Robert's Rules of Order*, and their own rules.

Moderating is an art. Good moderators control procedure without letting procedure control them. They keep meetings on track without being pompous or heavy handed. Good moderators know when to cut off a blabbermouth and when to let someone take her time getting to her point. Good moderators cut tension with humor. Many moderators serve for years, even decades, which creates a level of comfort and continuity for the voters, who know what to expect every year, allowing them to educate new voters in the whys and wherefores of their town meeting's particulars, peculiarities, and idiosyncrasies.

The Rules

Some moderators read their rules aloud at the start of the meeting. Others publish them in the town report. Some remind voters of a few of the rules and address others when questions arise. But be certain of this: each moderator has a strict set of rules that keep the meeting in check. Without them the meeting would, indeed, be in danger of devolving into chaos.

Here, from the minutes of the 2010 meeting, are the rules that Jack Hutchinson uses to control Deerfield's deliberative session. His rules are

A Brief History of the Position of Town Moderator and How It Evolved

Distilled from *Town Government in New Hampshire: The New Hampshire Historical Records Survey Project*, 1940:

As early as 1641 the Massachusetts Bay Colony's "Body of Liberties," laws governing the colonists, mentioned a president or moderator for assemblies, which undoubtedly included town meetings. In Exeter, two years earlier, residents designated that "Isack Grosse *Ruler*, Augustine Storr and Anthony Stanyon, shall have the ordering of all Town affairs . . ." In 1695, the title "Ruler" changed to "Moderator" on official documents.

By 1718 the position of moderator was made official across the state. The moderator was to be elected by the people for every town or proprietary meeting. Atkinson, according to its *Town Minute Books*, elected a moderator at its first town meeting in 1767.

By an act of 1771, any justice of the peace "upon the application of ten freeholders" could call a town or parish meeting and run that meeting until a moderator was chosen. In 1844 a second ballot for the election of a moderator was authorized in cases where no candidate received a majority on the first ballot vote.

Selectmen were authorized to choose a moderator in 1846, but if no selectmen were present, the people voted. This law was repealed in 1847. Evidently the people wanted their say in such an important matter. From then on moderators would be elected by the legislative body. Beginning in 1847, provision was made for the moderator to step down in mid-meeting to speak to an issue. In this case a selectman or town clerk would preside until a new moderator was selected. The new moderator could be anybody in town *except* a selectman or a supervisor of the checklist.

A 1795 ruling gave moderators the right to charge a constable with ejecting troublemakers. This practice continues. I've seen just a couple people asked to leave over the years, but several threatened with ejection if they didn't simmer down. Usually they simmered down.

On voting day once the polls close, the moderator must count the ballots—with the help of ballot clerks—in the presence of other town officials. The moderator is also responsible for marking defective ballots.

modified to accommodate the SB 2 format of "talk now, vote another day," as he explains in the third bulleted section. (More on SB 2 in Chapter 18.)

PURPOSE, RULES, & DECORUM

- Each member who wishes to vote in this meeting should have checked in with the ballot clerks, and should have received a voting card and a sheet of ballots. If you are a registered voter and have not checked in yet, please do so now. Are there any individuals present who are not registered voters of the Town of Deerfield? Though you are not permitted to vote, by Deerfield tradition you are permitted to participate in debate.

- The rules for this meeting will be *Robert's Rules of Order* as modified by the moderator in accordance with the laws of the State of New Hampshire.

- Our meeting today is "for the transaction of all business other than voting by official ballot." This first session "shall consist of explanation, discussion, and debate of each warrant article." Our business today is to consider each warrant article and, within the limits of the law, determine the details of those articles to be voted by official ballot at the March 9th second session. Amendments to articles are in order and will be voted at this meeting. However at the conclusion of our deliberation on each article we will not vote. Instead, the chair will instruct the town clerk to place the article on the official ballot.

- Our order of the day is the Town Warrant. The chair will read each article, then request a motion to place it on the official ballot and a second for that motion. The maker of the motion will have the first opportunity to speak. Then the floor will be open to all. If you wish to address the meeting, please approach one of the microphones. The chair will recognize members at the microphones in turn. When it is your turn to speak, please step up to the microphone and speak directly into it. The microphone is voice activated, and your remarks are recorded so that the clerk may make an accurate record of this meeting.

- All remarks must be confined to the merits of the pending question, or to questions of order or privilege, and all remarks must be addressed to the chair. When you are recognized, please state your name. Each speaker will be allowed three minutes to express his or her views. You may speak as many times as you wish, but all members who wish to speak will have a first turn before any has a second. The overriding principle in all cases is fairness.

- A speaker may address the currently pending question or he may move to close debate, but he may not do both in the same turn. This means that if a speaker argues for or against a motion, he may not then conclude his remarks with "and I move the previous question." We adopted this rule a number of years ago and, with the support of the assembly, will follow it in this meeting.

- A secret ballot will be conducted when requested by five members in writing prior to a hand vote. Such request must be for a specific vote, not for "all votes in this meeting" or "all amendments to this article." The secret ballot provision exists to offer secrecy, and is not intended to be used as a tactic of delay. If you wish to request a secret ballot, please approach a microphone, and, when recognized, make the request. Then pass the written request to the moderator. Otherwise votes will be by a show of voting cards.

- If the Chair cannot judge a clear majority, he will move to a Division. Likewise if a member is not satisfied that the result announced by the Chair is correct, he should request a Division. Division will be a count of the raised cards.

- Seven members who question any non-ballot vote immediately after it is announced may request a written ballot vote. If the margin of a vote by Division is narrow, the moderator may also move to a ballot vote.

- Five voters may request a recount of a written ballot vote, "providing that the vote margin is not more than 10 percent of the total vote cast." In this case, "the recount shall take place immediately following the public announcement" of that vote (40:4-a).

- If there is something you wish to accomplish here but you are uncertain how to proceed, please ask. You can do that at any time during the meeting at one of the microphones, or you can approach any of us during a recess.

Jack Hutchinson presides as moderator of the Deerfield town meeting, flanked by town officials.

- Similarly, if during the meeting, something is not clear to you, please rise to a point of inquiry, then ask for an explanation.
- Finally, the role of the moderator is to fairly organize and regulate the meeting according to rules agreeable to the members. Rulings of the moderator are subject to appeal by any member. An appeal must be made immediately following the ruling. A second is required. The ruling and the appeal will be explained to the meeting. Then the members will vote either to sustain or to reverse the ruling.

Town Officers

Originally, town officers, from selectmen to cemetery trustees, were elected at the start of town meeting, a lengthy process since winners had to receive a majority of votes from those present. If voters on the first ballot wrote the names of eight different candidates, nobody would have a majority. The vote would be taken again and again, until the field narrowed and somebody got fifty percent plus.

Nowadays, we vote at the polls for a board of selectmen, school board, municipal budget committee, planning board, board of adjustment, and sometimes a police commission. We also elect a town clerk, tax collector, treasurer, cemetery trustees, supervisors of the checklist, and trustees of trust funds. Some towns elect their road agent and police chief. In other towns, these positions (which require specialized skills) are by appointment.

To run for elected office, a citizen submits his name to the town or school clerk by a certain date well in advance of town meeting, and, typically, pays a small filing fee. This can create some drama, as potential candidates may lurk at the town clerk's office on the filing date to see who else might be jumping into the race at the last minute. The lurkers want to assess the field before they commit to running. They file (or don't) as the clock ticks down.

In olden days some of the offices were the same as now—selectmen and town clerk, for example—but many were specific to the needs of those times. You'll see references to these antiquated offices in other chapters, but they are grouped here to show what needed doing in the 1600s, 1700s, and 1800s that no longer needs doing—how times have changed.

- *Deerkeeper*—Like a game warden; made sure the local herd was not overhunted.

- *Field Driver*—Rounded up domesticated animals wandering about in town. For a fee, the animals would be returned to the owners

- *Fence Viewer*—Not to be confused with a surveyor. His job was to look at the property line between neighbors, and decide who should take care of which parts of the fence. This is trickier than it sounds, since fencing a field is easier than fencing granite ledges, and since the fences must meet the standard of "horse high and hog tight."

- *Hog Reeve or Honard*—Charged with keeping swine under control and rounding up strays. A rooting 300 pound pig could do a lot of damage to crops. The hog reeve turned the errant hogs over to the Pound Keeper, who fed them until their owners turned up and paid a fine to reclaim them.

- *Orator*—Auditor.

- *Pound Keeper*—Watched over the granite enclosure where the wandering animals were deposited by the field driver or hog reeve.

- *Saxton*—Bell ringer.

- *Sealer of Hemp and Flax*—Charged with ensuring that all hemp and flax sales involved quality material at a fair price. The sealer was empowered to put his seal, or stamp, on all items he inspected and approved.

- *Sealer of Leather*—Regulated the sale and quality of leather.

- *Sealer of Weights and Measures*—Maintained standards of measurement for goods.

- *Surveyor*—Marked where the roads would go.

- *Surveyor of Lumber*—Gauged the value of fallen or standing timber for tax purposes.

- *Tythingman, Tithingman or Tidingman*—Ensured that people went to church and eschewed debauchery, profanity, night walking, idleness, or uncivil or rude practices. At church the tythingman collected "donations" and carried a rod with a knob on one end and a feather on the other. The feather gently tickled the women into paying attention. The knob was for the men. Tythingmen were also allowed to seize unlicensed liquors.

Let Us Proceed

With different rules imposed by different moderators at different meetings, it's a challenge to describe exactly what to expect. Much can be counted on to be the same, but always something new comes up, even if it's the new guy in town who asks a naive question that makes the natives smile (or pisses them off). The procedure for making, amending, and adopting motions is, however, standard. Some towns may use slightly different language, but the fundamentals are similar and have been in place since the beginning.

Here's an example of how an article becomes a motion: In 1925, Article 10 on the warrant for the town of Plymouth read, *To see what sum of money the town will vote to raise or appropriate for open air concerts during the summer of 1926.*

These days an article like that would likely include a money amount, so we'll update it: *To see if the town will vote to raise and appropriate $100 for open air concerts during the summer of 1926.*

The moderator reads the article and, in some towns, says, "I await your pleasure."

Someone in the crowd, often a selectman, says, "So moved." Someone else says, "Second." And the article is on the table or open for discussion. This is called making the **main motion**.

At this point discussion proceeds, perhaps leading to a **subsidiary motion**, that must be voted on before the main motion. A subsidiary motion alters, adapts, or eliminates a main motion. For example, someone says, "I make a motion to amend down from $100 to $50." The moderator may ask that this amendment be put in writing and presented to the clerk for the record. The moderator then reads the motion as amended. Discussion continues, then a vote is taken on the amendment. If the vote is yea, the amended motion becomes the main motion, *To see if the town will vote to raise and appropriate $50 for open air concerts during the summer of 1926.* If the vote is nay, we return to the original motion, *To see if the town will vote to raise and appropriate $100 for open air concerts during the summer of 1926.* Each person who speaks must be recognized by the moderator. In some towns, the moderator won't allow you to speak a second time until everybody has had a chance to speak once. This is a pretty good rule, because some people just don't know when to shut up.

Other amendments may be offered (e.g., up to $175 or down to $25). Each must be considered and voted on in turn. Finally, after all the changes have been made, there's a vote on the main motion, yea or nay. Either money is appropriated for the concerts or not. Either music will fill the air come summer or it won't—at least not if the town has to pay for it.

Simple enough. Except that other subsidiary motions besides amendments may come into play. For example, someone may call for the motion to be **indefinitely postponed**. If this gets a second, a vote must be taken. Instead of voting on whether *To see if the town will vote to raise and appropriate $100 for open air concerts during the summer of 1926,* voters decide yea or nay on a motion that essentially says, "We don't want to talk about it, ever." If the motion to indefinitely postpone passes, the moderator moves on to Article 11 and Article 10 is moot, squelched, dead as a doornail. If the motion to indefinitely postpone fails, then discussion returns to the main motion.

Another move that almost (but not quite) kills a main motion is a call to "Table it."

If a motion to **table** a main motion is called, that motion must be voted on before returning to the main motion. If the vote is yea to table, the moderator moves on to the next article. The difference between indefinitely postponing and tabling is that tabling puts the motion into limbo. Later in the meeting, someone may make a motion to return to the original motion—to untable it. I've never seen this happen. Once tabled, motions tend to remained tabled.

These are the primary four actions: The article turns into a motion with a "So moved" and a "Second." The main motion is amended. Or the main motion is indefinitely postponed (killed) or tabled (put in limbo). However, there are many more possible actions that may be taken.

- *Appeal*—If voters feel the rules aren't being followed properly, they may move for an appeal with which the group may vote to overturn the moderator's ruling.

- *Ballot Vote or Secret Ballot*—A vote taken by marking yes or no on a ballot. Most articles pass or fail on a voice vote. The ayes say "Aye"; the nays say "No." If the voice vote is too close to call, the moderator will ask for a show of hands. Any voter may request a ballot vote. In some towns, the moderator will call a ballot vote if five or more request it. Other towns hold a ballot vote if even one person requests it. Supervisors of the checklist pass out slips of paper. Voters mark the ballot and slide their vote into the ballot box. In some towns, the

The passing of the shoe box for a secret ballot vote in Deerfield.

ballot vote is very formal—with voters lining up, being checked off on the checklist, then casting their votes. Other towns opt for the less formal passing around of shoe boxes with slits cut in the covers. In Deerfield added security is provided by a rubber band around the shoe box further secured by a pencil twisted in the rubber band and piercing the box cover. The votes are counted by deputies chosen by the moderator and the results revealed right away.

- *Call to Limit Debate*—If discussion is dragging on, a voter may motion to curtail debate. The call to limit debate is not debatable, so a vote must be taken immediately.

- *Call for the Orders of the Day*—A voter who feels the agenda is not being properly followed or that there's good reason to vote on the articles in a different order than listed, may make this motion. Those present then vote, yea or nay, to deviate from the expected order of business. For example, if a controversial article is last on the warrant, voters may want to consider it earlier since not everyone has the stamina to stay through until the bitter end.

- *Call the Question*—When a voter calls the question or shouts "Move the question," this cuts off debate immediately—unless, the moderator feels the question has been called too early, before everyone has had a chance to speak or the matter has been thoroughly discussed. In that case, he may allow debate to continue a little longer.

- *Division of the House*—The yea voters move to the right of the moderator, and the nays move to the moderator's left. They are counted. This is what passes for action at a town meeting. Another incarnation of Division of the House is to ask voters to stand to vote yea or nay, or to raise their cards at the appropriate time.

- *Division of the Question*—A motion to break up a main motion or amendment into smaller parts that can be considered separately. Again, this is rarely used since it would complicate the voting and prolong the meeting.

- *Incidental Motion*—Has the same rank as the motion it rises under but never stands alone. It is always attached to another motion. For example, during the discussion of a main motion, the incidental motion may have to be considered first in order to decide how to vote (show of hands, yeas/nays, secret ballot). In other words, incidental motions are the procedural steps that must be taken before the main motion can be dealt with.

- *Point of Order*—A call for the moderator to follow the rules of the meeting or to explain them. This motion may legitimately interrupt a pending motion. When someone calls for a point of order, he or she has the floor. At town meeting the words "Point of Order" get everybody's attention right away.

- *Privileged Motion or Question of Privilege*—This motion relates to the physical conditions of the meeting, too noisy, no heat, too hot, microphone doesn't work, chickens in the hall, overcrowding. The moderator may try to solve the problem—by asking people to quiet down, suggesting another log be thrown on the fire, or the heat be adjusted, the chickens removed. The moderator may also choose to rule the motion out of order and continue with the business at hand. A privileged motion is voted on before a main or subsidiary motion. It is used to regulate adjournments, comfort, and safety.

- *Reconsideration*—Sometimes we vote one way at 9:15 a.m. but by 2:20 p.m., we've changed our minds and choose to reconsider the article. If the house votes to reconsider, an article may be voted on for a second time, possibly changing the outcome. This tactic has been used somewhat underhandedly when, say, a vote is taken in the morning to put $5000 into an account to fix a road behind the lake, then toward the end of the meeting, when all the lake dwellers have gone home, someone calls for reconsideration, a new vote is taken, and the $5000 is removed. To thwart such a move, voters may call for a vote to restrict reconsideration. This is allowed if the vote was in the affirmative and if a majority of those present say, "yea," we won't allow reconsideration. Sometimes, a voter will group articles and move to disallow reconsideration on, say, Articles, 4, 5, and 6 after they've been voted in the affirmative. Furthermore, a vote not to reconsider cannot be reconsidered. No reconsideration is allowed if a third-party contract is involved or if the vote involves the issuance of bonds over $100,000.

- *Suspend the Rules*—This motion, if it receives a majority vote, allows the assembly to contravene the established rules.

Municipal Budget Committee

Towns that vote to establish a municipal budget committee provide a layer of budget oversight in addition to the oversight of the selectmen and school board, and, of course, the voters. The budget committee comprises three, six, nine, or twelve members, one from the school board and one from the board of selectman. The majority of members must be property tax payers. Budget committee meetings are open to the public and must be posted at least seven days in advance.

Like the selectmen and the school board, the budget committee puts together a budget for town and school expenses. The committee develops its recommendations by consulting with town officers and departments regarding expenses, revenues, and what each department wishes to accomplish. The money amounts recommended by the selectmen and school board often differ from those recommended by the budget committee, though all are working from the same information. The selectmen might recommend an operating budget of $2 million and change, while the budget committee recommends $1.9 million and change. Bottom line, the town can *by law* vote no more than 10 percent over the budget committee's recommendation, giving this committee great power. No such limit is applied to the selectmen's or school board's budget.

Of course, voters may lower the budget by any amount they choose.

Glossary

These terms pop up in other chapters. Through context, you'll get the gist when you come across them. This glossary, however, is a chance to flesh out their meanings more thoroughly.

Australian Ballot—The system used for state and federal as well as town elections. Candidates are listed on a ballot, the polls are open a certain amount of time, and when that time has elapsed, the polls are closed and the votes counted. Zoning ordinances are voted on by Australian ballot. In SB 2 towns, all articles are voted on by Australian ballot.

Capital Reserve Fund—Most towns put a little money away each year in anticipation of big expenses down the road. For example, an article calling for $10,000 to be put into the Fire Department Capital Reserve Fund asks voters to look ahead to a time when the town might need to purchase a new fire truck at the cost of $100,000 or more. Instead of raising all the money in one year, the truck may be purchased—with voter approval—and money saved for that purpose over several years.

Contrary Minded—Those who don't go along with the crowd. As Seabrook's town moderator said when calling a vote: "Those in favor?" Pause. "Those who are contrary minded?"

Deliberative Session—A watered down annual meeting under SB 2.

Happiness Article—Not official business, but of interest. The moderator may set aside time for, say, the presentation of the Boston Post Cane to the oldest resident or to congratulate a retiring bookkeeper. (I once received a quart of maple syrup and some kind words from the moderator for my admittedly questionable service as unofficial town storyteller.) The happiness article helps us remember we have more in common than not, and that our political adversaries are also our neighbors. If your truck was stuck in a snow bank crosswise the road, just about any one of them would stop and shovel, push, or direct traffic.

Legislative Body—Collective term for the voters present at the town meeting.

Nonvoter—People who are not registered voters in town may attend town meeting but may not speak except with permission from the moderator. In turn, the moderator traditionally asks the voters if it's okay for nonvoters to speak. Traditionally, the house says, yes—but not always.

So who are these nonvoters who wish to speak? They might be the school principal or superintendent, a lawyer for the selectmen, or a representative from a special interest group with information relevant to the discussion.

Parsonage Lot—Acreage set aside for support of the churches, usually through money made from logging.

Proprietors—Englishmen who were granted large tracts of land called plantations by the King of England for commercial development. The first New Hampshire proprietor was John Mason, who did not set foot on New Hampshire soil himself but sent representatives. These representatives, according to Edwin David Sanborn, a nineteenth century historian, were by occupation "fishmongers, farmers and mechanics" sent in 1623 to fell trees, till the soil, fish, hunt, and mine. Sanborn submits that these earliest settlers were not that good at their jobs: illiterate, unchurched, unmotivated, and dishonest. Mason lost his shirt.

In 1642 (when New Hampshire was still part of Massachusetts) the General Court ordered that the inhabitants of Piscataquack (four seacoast plantations) "who were formerly free there, shall have the liberty of freemen in their several towns to manage all their town affairs, and each town send a deputy to the General Court." In this way the plantations divided into towns and towns began to govern themselves via town meeting.

Pure Democracy—This is the definition of town meeting according to *Knowing the Territory: A Survey of Municipal Law for New Hampshire Local Officials, 2011.*

> Unless specifically assigned by statute to a certain board or official, most of the policy-making authority resides in the voters at town meeting—the legislative body. Cities and towns with councils are representative democracies. Voters in these municipalities only have power to choose their representatives. However, a town meeting is a direct or "pure" form of democracy. Thus, when officials in traditional town meeting towns are in doubt about authority to take a particular action, the conservative approach is to put the question to a vote at town meeting.

SB 2 or Senate Bill 2 or Official Ballot—Since 1995, towns have had the option of adopting the SB 2 form of town meeting. A three-fifths supermajority is required to change from traditional town or school meeting to the SB 2 format. (Or to change back once SB 2 has been implemented.)

Under SB 2 a deliberative session is held some weeks prior to voting at the polls. At the deliberative session voters may discuss each warrant article. They may vote to amend the articles, but they may not actually vote to pass or fail the articles. That happens only at the polls. For example, the school board submits this article: *To see if the School District will vote to raise and appropriate the Budget Committee's recommended amount of Twelve million one hundred seventy-two thousand seventy-six dollars ($12,172,076) for the support of schools, for the payment of salaries for the school district officials and agents, and for the payment of statutory obligations of the district. The School Board recommends twelve million, seven hundred forty-nine thousand six hundred sixty-one dollars ($12,749,661).*

At a traditional town meeting, the voters present would hash out the numbers, come to a compromise, and vote for that amount. Under SB 2, the voters present hash out the numbers, come to a compromise, and leave. Two or three weeks later, voters go to the polls, see the compromise amount on the warrant and vote yea or nay. If they vote nay, this doesn't mean the school district has no budget. A nay vote sends the district into a default budget: the budget from the previous year (with exceptions for contractual obligations). Town officials, with approval from the superior court, may hold a special meeting and try again, but this is rarely done.

School District Meeting—Annual meeting to consider the school budget.

School Lot—Acreage set aside for support of schools, usually through money made from logging.

School Board—An odd number (usually three or five) of officials elected to oversee the affairs of the schools.

Select Board—An odd number (usually three or five) of officials elected to oversee the affairs of the town. Despite the feminist movement, the term selectman is still commonly used to refer to either male or female members of the select board. Among the selectmen's duties regarding town meeting is assisting the town clerk in counting votes (in effect since 1784). In 1816 selectmen were legally charged with announcing the time and place for town meeting at least fifteen days in advance. In 1855, selectmen were authorized to create and maintain the voter list, a duty later passed on to the supervisors of the checklist elected biennially.

Show of Hands—If a voice vote is questioned or unclear, the moderator may call for voters to raise their hands or voting cards, yes or no.

Special Meeting—In the event of an emergency or special circumstance, like a negotiated contract with teachers that needs to be funded, officials may request a special meeting at any time of year. The request must be approved by the court.

Standing Vote—In the event that a show of hands isn't decisive enough, the moderator may call for a standing vote. Yeas stand first and are counted, then the nays.

Supervisors of the Checklist—Elected officials who maintain the list of registered voters. At town meeting, the supervisors of the checklist check off the names of voters as they enter the hall. For ballot votes, they also check off names as voters drop their ballots in the box.

Town—We speak of the town as though it were a person, a living entity. And it kind of is. By law (1926) each New Hampshire town is "a body corporate and politic, and by its corporate name may sue and be sued, prosecute and defend, in any court or elsewhere." A town may buy property for public use and sell it. It may enter into contracts for the transaction of the public's business. A town can make bylaws and appoint officers to enforce those bylaws. Once a bylaw is in effect it stays in effect until revoked or altered by vote.

Town Clerk—According to *Town Government in New Hampshire*, proprietors of the early settlements chose clerks to keep records. When towns and parishes organized, the town or parish clerk "evolved naturally" from the proprietor's clerk. Some town clerks do double duty as tax collectors. It's not unusual for a clerk to serve for decades—why change horses midstream?—providing a valuable institutional memory.

Town clerks, as well as deputy town clerks, must be residents of the town. Among the clerk's duties: keeping town records, certifying the actions of selectmen and other officials, writing official reports, collecting fees, and serving as an election official. If you need to register your car, boat, or dog, see the town clerk. If you need to collect a death certificate for a loved one who has passed, see the town clerk. If you need a dump sticker or a beach pass, see the town clerk.

Unlike other town employees, the clerk is paid according to a vote at town meeting in the form of fees, salary, or a combination of the two.

Warning—Another word for warrant.

"Town Meeting may have developed from the Yankee frame of mind, or the Yankee may have developed from Town Meeting, but they go together like pork and beans and one explains the other."

JOHN GOULD, *NEW ENGLAND TOWN MEETING: SAFEGUARD OF DEMOCRACY*

2 ⚖

Character and Characters

Those of us who attend town meeting don't understand why so many don't. Too busy? We're all busy. We pick and choose what to be busy at. We set priorities. Surely for most jobs a person could request and receive time off for an activity high on a list of priorities—a family gathering, a hunting trip, a funeral, town meeting.

Maybe some don't feel the same civic responsibility. Maybe they're trusting souls content to let others set the tax rate and map out the future. Or maybe they're uncomfortable with conflict. Oh yes, town meeting hosts its share of conflict, mainly reasonable disagreements among reasonable people. Occasionally somebody goes off the rails—gets all red in the face, blames this one or that one, cites conspiracy. It's all part of the drama and, in retrospect, the fun.

Maybe the town meeting dodgers don't understand its significance, especially if they weren't raised in the tradition. Or feel they don't understand the proceedings and might look foolish if they spoke up at the wrong time. Maybe they don't feel welcome.

Heck, hardly any of us understand all the proceedings—moderator, town clerk, and perhaps a seasoned selectman or two excepted. And we all feel foolish at one time or another. At one of my first meetings, the matter being discussed was the closing of Lucas Pond beach to the public for swimming. The swimmers interfered with the fishing. And it cost money to keep a trash bin and Porta-potty on site, not to mention paying someone to oversee the beach and clean up the Porta-potty after rascals tipped it over in the night. Besides, we had two other beaches in town—one on Bow Lake, one on Northwood Lake.

Moderator Robert Johnson opened the floor for questions. I went to the mic: "I really like swimming at Lucas Pond beach. It's walking distance of my house and a lot of us like taking our children there on hot summer days," I said. Or something like it.

"Is this a question?" Moderator Johnson asked.

"Well . . . It's a really nice beach. Small and quiet. Good for kids."

"Is this a question?"

"Um . . . uh . . . "

"Do you have a question?"

I sat down.

Later, I thought, if only I'd said: "Isn't it true that a lot of young families really enjoy Lucas Pond beach?" or some such. But I didn't. I felt pretty foolish.

Nevertheless, somebody else said: "If we close Lucas Pond beach will some children be without a place to swim?"

And the vote went in favor of keeping the beach open after all.

Moral of the story: There are plenty of chances in life to feel foolish. Town meeting is just one of them.

As for the idea that newcomers might not be welcome, I have never seen any evidence of that. There's an old joke that a newcomer ought not speak at town meeting for at least twenty-five years, but it *is* a joke. All town residents are welcome. Welcome to speak. Welcome to vote their conscience. That's the whole point. One threat to the health and survival of town meeting is low attendance. Not that everybody needs to go, but the hall ought to be packed with a vigorous cross-section. For this grassroots democratic system to work, the town must be well and fairly represented. If the numbers get too low the representation becomes anemic, and then the doubters make their point.

Maybe some fail to see the value because they don't identify themselves as part of the town and the town as part of them. Many of us live in bedroom communities; we sleep here but that's about all. We work and play elsewhere. Our friend Christine lived in Candia for decades; she became active in town affairs, only after she retired from her job in the schools in Manchester. For her, community meant students and educators outside the place where she lived. For others, community might mean coworkers at a factory, or other artists, Model-T owners, cancer survivors, medical professionals, church members, Free Staters. Maybe they see themselves more as citizens of the world—a world that needs to work toward sustainable living or peace. Maybe the town just doesn't figure in to the list of things they really care about.

As different as are our opinions and ideas about taxes and how to spend money raised from taxes, one value that town meeting goers share is a sense that what goes on in town matters, and not just to our pocketbooks.

Ronald Jager's phrase "ambivalently cherished" from his essay "Pure

Democracy" (See Chapter 7) sums up the feelings of many. Some of us—selectmen, school board members, budget committee members, library trustees, fire chiefs, police chiefs, administrators, town clerks—spend much of January and February gearing up. We attend loads of meetings on cold winter nights when we'd rather be curled up on the couch with a remote or a book in hand and a cat on our lap. We do loads of reading, writing and 'rithmatic (might's well still be in school) to make sure those requests for appropriations make sense and the budget numbers add up. The legislative body has a sharp eye for inaccuracies and bull-feathers. It delights in discovering a $36 discrepancy in a ten thousand dollar budget line. If this one's off by $36, what other errors lurk in this jungle of numbers?

Exchange at one budget committee hearing on the school budget. (This is true; I was there.)

Budget committee member: "There's a mistake in the budget on page three."

School board representative: "Where's the mistake?"

Budget committee member: "Line 27, periodic tables. They should be listed under furniture."

Town officials must weather many challenges and much controversy (that's the exciting part). They must also plow through acres of just plain grunt work. Townsfolk are welcome to attend these preparatory meetings and put in their two-cents worth during public comment. A few of the faithful do. Nowadays if you can't make it to the pre-town-meeting meetings, you can catch them on cable. Slow, but oddly fascinating. One evening I found myself watching an hour of a budget committee meeting. I changed the channel after realizing it was a repeat. I mentioned to one of the selectmen how much I enjoyed watching selectmen's meetings on cable. Astonished, he said, "Why?" Then added, "Mostly we just pass papers around and sign them." Which is true. But you never know when something interesting might happen. It's the suspense that draws us in when, flipping through the channels, we spot the familiar table in the familiar hall with the familiar faces gathered around. We listen in as the business of our town gets done by our good neighbors.

Same with town meeting—it's the suspense. You never know when the pot will boil over or somebody's wicked sense of humor will produce a one-liner that evokes belly laughs.

Town meeting starts early and lasts long. Sure we could be doing something else on a Saturday in March or a Tuesday night 'til the wee hours, but no, we do our duty and attend town meeting. Visit with the folks. Get down to business. Some of which is boring, repetitive, and mundane. Some of which is, indeed, controversial. And some of which can turn downright ugly.

And yet, this is our tradition. Our opportunity to speak and be heard. Our opportunity to take a measure of control of our own destiny and that of our community. We recognize the privilege. We know how lucky we are. We accept the honor—even as our backs ache from sitting too long on the bleachers or in those cruel metal folding chairs. (The wise bring cushions.) Even as we sigh, "Oh no! Is she going to talk? Again? Shoot me now!" Even as we complain: "We have this same discussion every single stinkin' year." Even as we feel the despair of facing yet another hour-eating secret ballot. The relentlessly cheerful say: "Sure it takes time, but gives us a chance to stretch our legs. Visit. Go to the bathroom. Buy a cruller." Even as we debate, within our own minds, whether to go to the mic and explain the flippin' obvious or sit on our hands and fume.

A cousin of ours owns rat terriers. They are yappy little ankle biters, explosive with energy. Legs like springs. Smart. Demanding. A little bit crazy. Loving. Often naughty. They make her laugh. And they make her mad. Poppy says: "They're *awful!* But we love 'em." Ambivalently cherished. Like town meeting.

Choose Your Seat Carefully

Library people sit with library people. Conservationists sit with conservationists near the map of the new trail through the town forest. Relatives seek out relatives; you'll find a gang of Smiths or Colbys or Taskers gathered on the bleachers (if the meeting is held at the school gym) in the same spot each year. Spouses sometimes sit together; sometimes make a point of not sitting together.

"Have you seen my wife?"

"Yup, she's sitting over by the supervisors of the checklist."

"Good. I'll sit here, then."

Those of us with bad backs prefer the top row of the bleachers so we can rest against the cement block wall. Also, the view from the top is unparalleled. Folks new to town meeting will try different spots—different perspectives—the first few years. Then they'll settle into the place that best fits their political affiliations, philosophies, familial ties, or physical needs. There they stay—barring significant changes in affiliation, philosophy, ties or needs (like divorce or a broken leg).

A New Hampshire Character with Character

Deborah Arnie Arnesen is a well known figure on New Hampshire's political stage. She served as a state representative, ran for governor, ran for Congress, and for many years has hosted political talk shows on television and radio. She believes political candidates have a choice: To say what people want to hear in order to get votes or to speak the truth, lead the way, and accept the consequences. Arnesen always spoke the truth; which is, of course, why she didn't win the governorship or a seat in the U.S. House. She won, instead, a legion of fans like me.

Her political career got its jump start at—you guessed it—town meeting. In *Women at the Table,* Michaeline Della Fera profiles forty powerful political women in the Northeast. In 1982, Della Fera writes, Arnesen was living in Orford, long dominated by three-term Governor "Ax the Tax" Meldrim Thomson and his family. At the time his sons were serving as town moderator and selectman. Some, including Arnesen, thought the town could use a professional administrator to provide citizens better access to town hall business. Evidently the Thomsons disagreed.

She petitioned an article for the warrant and was prepared to speak to it, but "Guess what?" she said, the moderator "never called on me." She sat through the discussion with her hand in the air, but "to no avail."

"Finally," Della Fera writes, a woman sitting next to Arnesen raised her hand and immediately the governor's son recognized her. She said, 'It's obvious, Mr. Moderator, you can't notice the young woman sitting next to me. And she's been patient for over an hour and a half. I'm giving my time on the floor to her.'"

Arnensen got her chance to speak. And sure enough, the article passed; her first taste of political success and a fitting launch to her career.

Cast of Characters

"Somebody has to represent continuity," Ronald Jager writes in "Pure Democracy." Such are the folks who turn up at town meeting every year. Often they're the same folks who serve as town officers. Folks who stick around and tend to town affairs—as did their parents and grandparents before them. Maybe they stay to run the family hardware store or farm. Maybe the farm gets subdivided and each child inherits a plot of land to build a house and raise a family. Some go away, then come back soon-as-they-can to the old home place where they know their position in society: Ned Ford's son; Mildred Dino's first cousin; sister to George McNally.

Town meeting itself represents continuity. Its records constitute our institutional memory. But personal memory—however unreliable—comes into play as well. I was reminded of this by Joey Holmes of Grantham, who said how pleased she was to discover a story about her husband, Alfred Holmes, in my book *Could Have Been Worse: True Stories, Embellishments and Outright Lies.* I hadn't named Alfred in the story, but it was his story all right.

"Where do you suppose I got that story?" I said to Joey, because I couldn't remember.

"I must have told it to you last time you were in Grantham about ten years ago," Joey said. "The only thing is," she added, "you got it wrong."

Alfred Holmes had been dead seventeen years when Joey discovered the story in the book. And the storied event took place years, perhaps decades, before. Yet Joey remembered *exactly* what happened. As, no doubt, do many citizens of Grantham. Here's the story as it appeared in *Could Have Been Worse*, followed by the correction according to Joey's sharp memory.

> At Town Meeting a newcomer challenged the road agent's budget, saying, "You overspent last year and I'd like to know why."
>
> The road agent, leaning into the wall at the back of the hall, sighed. He took the long slow walk down the center aisle to the microphone at the front, all eyes upon him. Sighed again. Sniffed. Adjusted his suspenders. Adjusted the microphone. The newcomer repeated his request. "We all have to learn to live within our means; what caused you to exceed your budget last winter?"
>
> The road agent had just one word of explanation: "Snow."
>
> Then he sighed, sniffed, adjusted his suspenders, and took the long slow walk back to his spot on the wall.

Joey said, "Alfred didn't say 'Snow.' He said, 'It snowed.'"

I said, "Joey, that correction will be made in the next edition, should there be one."

In Grantham, Joey Holmes represents continuity.

People keep track. They note who attends and who doesn't. I missed some meetings over the years due to a conflict with the New Hampshire Young Writers Conference; I served on the steering committee and taught workshops at the conference. One year, knowing I'd have to miss town meeting, I made a special effort to put in my two cents at school meeting. Didn't help. "Didn't see *you* at town meeting," a friend said pointedly when we met at the post office.

Not everybody goes to town meeting, but those who do better go every year or eyebrows will be raised.

My friend Ginny told me she'd missed town meeting.

"That's too bad," I said.

She said, "I was in the hospital."

Being hospitalized or dead are about the only two excuses that will do.

So who are these faithful characters? We begin with Gary Patton's description of his town's deliberative session. Shakespeare wrote, "The play's the thing, wherein I'll catch the conscience of the king." From Patton's perspective, the deliberative session's the thing, wherein characters reveal themselves, ad-sometimes-nauseam. Gary Patton lives in Hampton, but these same folks play out their parts each March live and in person in every town we know.

Annual Town Drama Festival
Gary Patton

I am proud to announce that my town offers free repertory theater during its annual deliberative session. We have the form of town government where warrant articles are offered for possible amendment at a deliberative session, and then voted upon some weeks later during the municipal election. It is at the deliberative session that the talents of our local troupe of actors are put on display.

These amateur thespians simply cannot resist the allure of performing both before a live audience, and for those watching on the local community television. They stride to the microphone like Cicero or Demosthenes to amaze us with their oratorical skills and the profundity of their thought processes. Unfortunately, the rules of the meeting set no limit on the length of time or number of times our actors can speak. Thus, as the audience faints from hunger and keels over from fatigue, the deliberative session drags on through the day.

The cast remains largely intact from one year to the next. Let me take this opportunity to introduce some of the leading players to you.

- First and foremost, we have the **Ancient and Hoary Town Historian.** He apparently arrived with the earliest settlers, and ever since has been saving in his garage local newspapers that chronicle town events. Woe unto town newbies who get up to speak because the photographic memory of The Historian allows him to cite a warrant, rule, or ordinance from a generation or two ago that contradicts what the new arrival is saying. When not making his annual appearance at the deliberative session, The Historian can be seen in local supermarkets wearing his baggy pants at such low tide that it's an even bet that they will fall to the floor before he reaches the checkout line.

- Then, there is the bright, self-assured, and quick-tempered **Schoolmarm**, possessor of the sharpest tongue east of the Mississippi. When an unwary soul disagrees with her, I half expect the Schoolmarm to charge that person; rap their knuckles; and send the dissenter to detention.

- **The General**, a retired military officer, has an infallible way of knowing the truth. If the General hears himself saying something, it must be true. I have a terrifying fantasy where I have been assigned to his military unit. The General orders us to charge straight ahead over a cliff, telling us not to worry because he has repealed the law of gravity.

- Of course, we should not omit the apparently modest and self-effacing **Uriah Heep**. He simultaneously diminishes his own importance, flatters everyone within a three-mile radius, and persistently and smoothly advances those town special interests that use him as their undercover agent at the meeting.

- Not to mention **Mrs. Allsides.** To advance her personal agenda, she has a constantly damp forefinger which she consistently holds in the air to see which way the wind is blowing. Somehow, Mrs. Allsides is able simultaneously to be both for you and against you. Her favorite relative is Mom; her favorite dessert apple pie; and her favorite car is a Chevrolet.

- **Mr. Brevity** steps to the microphone and assures us that he will be brief. However, the sound of his own voice hypnotizes him. He drones on interminably until members of the audience can be seen attempting desperate means of escape (e.g., diving out windows, crawling out the door) to end their agony.

I have neglected the bit players in our town drama. They are the local candidates who are running in the upcoming town election. The chance to get some face time before the television cameras prior to the election proves irresistible, so they drum up some flimsy excuse to speak, in the process wrapping themselves in the flag and pledging undying fealty to the town.

Fred Courser

Fred Courser is a legend. We've heard many stories of the man—who owned a lot of land, collected old tools, and who knew the power of brevity and timing and used it. Fred kept Warner town meetings lively for decades, we're told. He was a Yankee farmer—frugal, conservative, and quick witted—with a gift for interjecting just the right comment at just the right moment with dramatic effect. A few words from Fred could turn the crowd one way or another in an instant. Town meeting in Warner used to be standing-room only, though, I'm told, after Fred died attendance dropped. A lot of people went, a local told us, just to hear what Fred would come out with next. Truth is, many towns are blessed with a Fred—the voice of deeply rooted, old-fashioned, no-nonsense practicality leavened with dry Yankee wit.

Dave Anderson—journalist, wildlife expert, and quite a character himself—told this story of Fred's antics at a meeting, probably not town meeting but one of the preliminaries. The story may be apocryphal but I don't think so—and even if it is, I've been told by some who knew Fred Courser that it sounds just like him. In any case, it's a classic example of Yankee humor cutting through the bull-feathers and hitting the nail on the head.

An official from the DES, that's Department of Environmental Services, was explaining a new septage filtration system, top of the line. "When the septage goes through the first filter," said the official, "it'll look like this." And he held up a water glass full of brown liquid. "When it goes through the second filter, it'll look like this." He raised a glass filled with tan liquid. "When it goes through the third filter, it'll look like this." He put the glass of clear liquid to his lips and drank. "Any questions?"

Fred raised his hand. "Yes, sir," he said. "I have a question. How many filters does it take to turn a turd into a cookie?"

You may very well have encountered some of these actors in your own town meetings. Perhaps, unbeknownst to me, ours have taken their act on the road, or, more likely, many towns have their own repertory groups who largely play the same parts.

Lest I be too harsh, let me close by being forgiving of human frailty, which we all share in abundance. More than a few of the participants in the deliberative session can be fairly accused of unabashed exhibitionism; nevertheless, they also have the best interests of the town at heart, and in many cases work very hard for free or on a volunteer basis. Like all humans, we Granite Staters are imperfect; but despite our imperfections, town government in New Hampshire is generally responsive, efficient, and honest.

So, my hat is off to our florid cast of town actors. And, to be honest, I secretly look forward to their wild and crazy antics at the next deliberative session.

Gary Patton gets us off to a good start on our list of town meeting characters with his **Ancient and Hoary Historian**, **Schoolmarm**, **General**, **Uriah Heep**, **Mrs. Allsides**, and **Mr. Brevity**. I'll add a few more perennials to the mix. You'll recognize them. Maybe you even are them. (I certainly am.)

- **The Loud**: Hard of hearing (or as grandma would have said, "deaf as a haddock"), but refuses to wear a hearing aid, sits in the back row, and compensates by bellowing. Frustrated by the inability to hear what is being said, the Loud bellows for the speaker to speak up, talk into the mic, and "say again." No one sits near the Loud, unless they're married to him, and sometimes not even then.

- **The Budget Guru**: Goes through the town budget with a calculator, a pencil, a magnifying glass, a fine-toothed comb, and a bloodhound. The Guru is miraculously able to find creative ways to save the town or school district hundreds, if not thousands, heck, millions of dollars. The Guru can spot fat a mile away and knows how to cut it. She is beloved or reviled, depending on whether or not it's your pet project, job, service, or kid's education on the receiving end of the slashing. Often the Guru gets so carried away with calculations that even the mathematically astute get lost in the wash of numbers, and the Guru's proposed amendment is voted down (confused voters tend to vote No), but not before the **Ancient and Hoary Historian** points out that "You can't cut individual lines from the floor! You can only cut the bottom line!" It's true. You may *suggest* that the selectmen close the dump on Friday and the assistant dumpmaster be fired, but in the end how they spend the money in the operating budget is entirely up to them. So the Guru's thirty-seven suggestions about exactly where to cut don't amount to a hill of beans.

- **The Across-the-Board Cutter** is the antithesis of the **Budget Guru.** He knows darned well the selectmen will spend the money where they see fit, so he doesn't bother suggesting specific cuts. The budget itself is, to him, irrelevant. He simply says, "This is too much money. We can't afford it. How are the old people supposed to live? I propose cutting the bottom line by 5% (or 10% or 25%)." Asked, "Where did you come up with that number?" the Cutter shrugs. Asked, "Where do you propose the selectmen (or school board) make the cut?" the Cutter replies, "That's their problem." Sometimes the cut passes. Sometimes not. Depends on the mood of the town and the state of the economy.

- **The Banty**: He struts, he crows, and he is always *this close* to unleashing his temper. If the moderator looks at him cross-eyed, he's mad. If he doesn't get a second or third or fourth turn at the mic, he's mad. If his road didn't get plowed in a timely fashion last winter, he's mad. If he has to pay a dollar for a dump sticker, he's mad. He already pays taxes; why should he have to pay for a dump sticker, too? Taxes infuriate him. He hates paying taxes, therefore he hates the town and school budgets that cause the taxes he must pay, and he's none-too-fond of those town and school officials who set the budgets that cause the taxes he must pay. He don't trust 'em as far as he could throw 'em. When the Banty takes the floor, the legislative body waits . . . for him to lose it. He seldom disappoints. Sometimes he starts off talking kind of reasonable: "We all are feeling the pinch of these hard economic times." But give him a minute or two and he'll wind himself up into a Banty rant. "We can't take it!" he'll say. "You people are spending our money like it was water. Well it ain't water. It's our money and we need it for stuff! These taxes are killing me! They're killing all of us. For god's sake. And you sit up there smirking like you're better than me. You think you're better than me? You think so!" Then he talks some more, and, in the end throws up his arms, sighs loudly in disgust, and struts back to his seat. The Banty is highly entertaining.

- **Mr. or Madame I've Changed My Tune**: When the **Budge Guru**, the **Across the Board Cutter** and such like, who've been openly and vehemently critical of the school board or the select board, get elected to those boards, sometimes they change their tunes. They'll say things like, "I didn't think we needed a fourth police officer either, until . . ." Or, "Yuh, that special education line seems like a lot, but 95% of it's mandated by the state. I don't like it but that's the way it is." This is how rebels turn into the Old Guard—by learning stuff. **Bantys** don't. Learn that is. They get elected, say, selectman, but they don't really want the job. They continue to strut and crow, get voted down two to one on every item, which makes them feel persecuted and misunderstood. Sometimes their heads start to spin like Linda Blair's character in *The Exorcist*. After a few months, exhausted, and with huge chiropractic bills, the Banty quits. It's much more fun ranting about how poorly the town is run than actually running it. He'll lay low for a few weeks or months, but given time, he'll get his spunk back, rediscover his strut, get real mad about something, and by golly, he may even run for reelection. And by golly, our memories are awful short, sometimes he wins.

- **The Outcast**: This is a person who has been consistently obnoxious over the years, and not just at town meeting but in general. We'll say he's a him called Smith. (But he could just as easily be a her called Jones.) His neighbors hate him. His kids avoid him. His wife moved to Florida, but didn't tell him. He is so despised and distrusted that even if he came up with the most brilliant suggestion *ever* for the town, it would be voted down, just because *he* presented it. This person's last name may go on to be used as a verb by locals: "Joe had a great suggestion at town meeting, but it was Smithed," i.e., voted down on account of negative associations.

A Relative Newcomer's Impressions

Long long ago—when I was using a typewriter instead of a computer and my husband and I had lived in town just a few years—I wrote this summary of my impressions of Northwood's town meeting and its characters. I was a young mother, and since my baby is now in her thirties, this essay dates back a ways.

After the piece was published, I received a note from a man named Arthur in the western part of the state saying he didn't realize I was in the hall at *his* town meeting taking notes. He wondered how I knew his name.

Of course, I wasn't there. I was in Northwood. Which goes to show that (1) Arthurs are the same wherever you find them; and (2) so, pretty much, are town meetings. Here's my time capsule:

THE COMMUNITY GATHERS.

Issues get hashed: Is the sign ordinance too restrictive? Should we put a road through to the back of the lake? Should the police commission be abolished for foolhardiness?

Grace works needlepoint, a sampler in greens and browns. Allies huddle: Who will speak for us? Not me, not me, don't look at me.

High school boosters sell doughnuts and coffee.

Enemies exchange glares. See how her cheeks are as pink as her turtle-neck? When her cheeks get pink like that, she's up to no good.

Diana nurses her baby.

Experts cite statistics (real and imagined). An official drones on with flip chart, flannel board and (oh no!) an overhead projector. We discuss the $400 dry hydrant for an hour; we discuss the $40,000 renovation to the Community Center for five minutes: length and intensity of discussion are inversely proportional to cost.

Toddlers climb the bleachers.

Arthur scribbles madly in his town report.

The moderator, dropping his r's and drawing his a's out long and Yankee, warns that high stakes and tensions are no excuse for inappropriate behavior, admonishes us to stick to the issues, and *please* leave the personalities out of it.

We try.

All eyes follow the dance teacher, late and in search of a seat, graceful and trim in her spandex. The microphone gets passed among reluctant selectmen. No, that information is not available at this time. No, this was not recommended by the Budget Committee. Why not? Ask them.

The moderator says: "You will all have an opportunity to be heard." When we groan or clap or raise our voices, he says, "House be in order," with an authoritative crack of the gavel.

Joann quilts and bides her time.

The moderator says: "What's your question? Is this a question? Are you going to get to your question soon?"

Children beg: "Daddy take us home."

Feelings erupt. Men puff their chests at one another, hands clenched, voices raised: "Do you want to step outside?" like actors in a Western movie.

The Newly Elected make promises. Incumbents make excuses. Mary—eight and a half months pregnant—speaks briefly, passionately; she makes sense. Jon speaks at length and makes no sense at all. The moderator says sharply: "Now you've said your piece; give someone else a chance." The moderator says, impatient: "We've had a *thorough* discussion . . ." He says, "I'll ask for a show of hands."

Someone demands a secret ballot. The house complains: that'll waste half an hour. The moderator calls for a show of hands on whether to hold a secret ballot.

Donald eats another steamed hot dog.

The police chief paces by the door. Money from the microwave raffle will go into the playground fund. Attend the status of the vote. Close under Article Sixteen. Open under Article Seventeen. Move to indefinitely postpone. Second. And the article is killed without discussion. What happened? What just happened?

People complain about being cut off, being confused, about the vote being called too soon or too late, about breach of parliamentary procedure. They complain about the moderator, about the selectmen, about the wording of the articles, about those who spoke and those who failed to speak, but mostly they complain about taxes, because taxes are what town meeting is all about. Put your hands in your pockets, citizens, and dig deep: the more we commit, the more it'll cost us come July.

The tax collector, administrative assistant, fire chief, and health officer herald doom: Overdue taxes! Overworked/under compensated town employees! Fire! Crime! Pestilence! And, worst of all, liability!

The moderator says, "I await your pleasure . . ." which, to me, is one of the most graceful phrases in the English language. My pleasure, Mr. Moderator, is the well-intended presentation of alternatives, seasoned with undercurrents of history, both civic and personal, that inform us beyond the words of the moment. My pleasure, Mr. Moderator, is exactly what is happening here at this town meeting.

Joe shares his box of Girl Scout cookies.

Sarah knits.

Dave yells from the back in a deep, insistent monotone—"*Move the question.*"

And the work of democracy gets done.

And there you have it—a cross-section of some of the personalities that populate town meeting. (Thanks to Susan Bruce for noticing several of them.) Of course, there are many others. The tut-tutters, the sweethearts who see the good in everything and everybody, the dedicated public servants, the philosophers, the jolly-jokers, the scout leaders, the peacemakers, the sincere, the sarcastic, the *Robert's Rules of Order* aficionados, firefighters with beepers, conspiracy theorists, conspirators, the Good Old Boys and Girls, the natives, the imports, the retirees who used to be summer people (who may love this town best of all), those who love to hear themselves talk, those who rise above the fray to speak unadulterated truth, and those who simply enjoy the spectacle of it all.

We're all there—present and accounted for—getting along and moving forward best we know how. That's the essence and the character of town meeting.

"But, Becky, how dear town meeting is."

JOANN BAILEY

The lines are drawn in Barrington, 2011. The Marxist won.

"I go to see, each time, if democracy works. The discussions are sometimes heated and sometimes lethargic, good decisions and bad get made, but it all seems entirely natural. This is the way government should be: you get together with your neighbors, discuss and vote."

HOWARD MANSFIELD, *IN THE MEMORY HOUSE*

3 ⚖️

Bake Sale

The best community gatherings feature bake sales. The best of the bake sales feature homemade delicacies—cookies, brownies, banana bread, and so forth. Also, coffee, tea, soda, sandwiches, and sometimes steamed hot dogs, beans, even soup or chili. At one of my first town meetings, I noticed the array of tempting foods artfully arranged at a back table, manned by members of the women's club. As I contemplated my selection, a native leaned in and whispered in my ear—regarding the whoopee pies: "I wouldn't bother with those; they're store bought."

Homemade *is* the standard. No homemade chocolate chip cookie is exactly like any other. We appreciate the personal touch, and evidence that somebody put serious effort into that cookie, even if it is a little dark on the bottom. So before wading into deep waters of history or scrutinizing the town meeting traditions of selected towns, or tracing how traditions and practices have changed through the centuries, I offer these short alphabetized nibbles—a bake sale, if you will, featuring the flavors of town and school district meetings across the state and over the years.

About As Scientific as It Gets in **Ashland**

Ken Forbes said the school board had the figures all laid out about how many students would be in each grade six years into the future. They'd even figured in the offspring of women known, at the time of the calculations, to be pregnant. (In a small town, it's not difficult.)

What about seven years out, frugal voters wanted to know.

Truth was, officials said, it depended on how many green apples the women ate.

Green apples?

Oh yes. Green apples lead to swollen bellies.

Campton Rocks As Told by Paul Yelle

Town meeting in our small town is well attended and has had its fair share of tension and drama. There are definite pods of people who sit together.

The running joke is how the big ticket items pass no problem—quick as a wink. And the smaller ticket items are often contested endlessly, with all sorts of pointed questions sometimes followed by grumbles from the crowd. My wife and I sit toward the back left near some other idealist friends, including our neighbors in the row ahead. This year their daughter, "Kyla," is there as well. She just moved back to town with her husband and newborn.

As people start to take their places and make nervous small talk, the moderator asks everyone to get settled in as the meeting is going to start. He introduces the reverend to say a few words. We all bow our heads—you can hear a pin drop. He starts with something like, "Dear Heavenly Father, let us be civil," etc. And then it happens. Kyla's phone goes off—full blast. And the song is AC/DC "Back in Black," a fine heavy metal anthem if there ever was one.

True story (we're told) out of **Canterbury**

This was when town meeting was held at the Old Town Hall. Like most other old town halls, granite steps led up to double doors. The hall was full. Joe Carboneau stood at the back, leaning against the double doors. They opened quick and Joe tumbled backwards out the door and down the steps. Moderator Ollie Fifield asked for a motion to recess, "So we can go see if Joe is all right."

Motion made, seconded, and passed on a voice vote. Joe was all right.

Chester's Voting Scandal of 1890

In *Chester Revisited: A History in Honor of the Town's 275th Anniversary*, author Richard Holmes airs some (allegedly) dirty linen. In the 1890 diary of Mary B. Noyes, he discovered her "distress" with the town fathers. Mary claimed the "supervisors have been at the town hall all afternoon with the check list and are there tonight acting dreadfully, taking off Republicans' names and putting on Democrats who have no right to vote here." One intuits that Mary was of the Republican persuasion. That year, according to Holmes, twenty-two people had their votes challenged because their names were missing from the checklist. All but one took the oath (that in fact they were residents of the town and entitled to vote) and were allowed to vote.

Furthermore, we learn, the last challenge to a would-be voter in Chester came in 1981. Selectman Janet E. Larkin stopped a man from participating in a town meeting vote. When he protested, "the floor voted against him and he left the hall." In a huff.

Deerfield's Opening Pledge

Moderator Jack Hutchinson opened the meeting with a pledge written by Joe Brown, a longtime, much admired former town moderator. The pledge, he told the voters, will be included "henceforth to honor our ties with Joe and his generation." So, as Joe Brown always used to say and as Jack Hutchinson will say for as long as he's moderator:

> *I suggest that we open this meeting by standing in silent meditation—asking guidance in our conduct of this Deerfield Town Meeting that may prove an effective self government for us all. Guide us in our voting by a sense of purpose and human understanding. In our hands today lie the business affairs of the town for the future. Grant us the sense of fairness to allow all citizens to participate regardless of experience. Help us to express ourselves with restraint and dignity that we may work together harmoniously for the well being of our town in the coming year.*
> *So let it be.*

No Wonder Deerfield's Pledge Implores Restraint

The headline of the *New Hampshire Sunday News* for March 15, 1959 read: "Deerfield in a Hub-Bub: Police Sent for by Hectic Town Meeting." It seems Moderator Preston Wares called Mrs. Charles P. Smith "out of order" and ordered her out of the hall. Mrs. Smith was not pleased, but by all accounts went peaceably. The moderator said this was the first time in his twenty years in the position that he'd thrown anyone out of town meeting.

The brouhaha resulted from hard feelings when six articles proposed by Admiral P. E. Pendleton were defeated by the electorate. Mrs. Smith was not pleased. She accused the powers-that-be of being a "dictatorial clique." When a resolution to have the selecmen appoint a committee to study zoning for Deerfield, Mrs. Smith proposed indefinite postponement. The moderator, unsure that this was a proper motion, "wanted to look it up." Mrs. Smith said he needn't, that it was a common tactic used by "the ruling clique."

That's when Moderator Wares invited her to leave the premises. Perhaps he didn't like her tone. The meeting recessed until Mrs. Smith could be escorted out by the police. She was creating a disturbance, the moderator said. She had to go.

Others claimed she'd "conducted herself like a lady" and hadn't disturbed anything at all.

Later, when the article was taken up again, the moderator explained that there was already an amendment on the main motion. You can't indefinitely postpone an article when an amendment has been proposed. First, you have to vote on the amendment. Mrs. Smith and her motion to indefinitely postpone were *definitely* out of order.

Deering Bides Its Time

The minutes of 1843 reveal that an article to raise money to fix up the town house was defeated. Best put off those renovations until next year when, maybe, times would be better. As it turns out, the renovation of the town house was put off not for one year, but for 159 years.

Who's Worried? Not **Effingham**

I'm told a police chief from away was brought in to explain why Effingham needed a second police officer. The chief pointed out that neighboring towns had much larger police forces. One had five officers, another had fifteen.

The local pointed out that Effingham had no such need. "Here in Effingham," he said, "we're better armed."

Enfield Builds a Bridge

This supposedly happened in Enfield. If it didn't, it certainly could have. Seems a bridge needed to be replaced and the proposal on the table was to match state money with town money to ease the burden. "What kind of a bridge were we talking about," a citizen wanted to know.

"Well," the road agent explained, "it would be a culvert under wood planking."

The citizen said, "Mr. Martel, wooden bridges aren't practical in New England."

The citizen may have been an engineer, but our guess is he wasn't from around here, and perhaps didn't know of our proud history of long standing wooden bridges, including covered ones.

Perhaps, too, he'd never heard the story of the lost tourist, who asked the local if he should go over the covered bridge to get to his destination. "If I was you," the local said, "I'd go through it."

Gilford Goes to the Dogs

Arthur Nighswander, an attorney, was known for his calm demeanor. One year the debate over imposing a leash law on Gilford's canine population got intense, loud, and long. When his turn came, Nighswander simply read a series of state laws pertaining to dogs, until it was obvious that state law covered every bad behavior in which a pooch might indulge.

He never said whether he was for or against the proposed leash law. When he was finished, though, the article was swiftly defeated.

Goffstown 1864—The Town Faces Its Own Civil War

In her book *Goffstown Reborn* , Elizabeth Dubrulle recounts a contentious meeting of March 8, 1864. Both Democrats and Republicans, she explains, were convinced that the other party was out to deprive them of their constitutional rights. In her research, she unearthed several versions of what happened, one of which is probably right, or close to it. Partisan politics, partisan reportage—so what else is new? She writes:

> The details of what actually happened are unknown, but initial newspaper accounts circulated shortly after election night suggested a mighty battle in Goffstown between members of the two parties that had left at least a hundred people dead and many more wounded. In the days that followed, these reports were proven grossly exaggerated, but because the newspapers themselves openly supported one party or the other, it is difficult to piece together a plausible picture of what really happened.
>
> The Republican Manchester newspaper The Daily Mirror & American reported the day after the election that the town meeting in Goffstown had been disrupted when a group of Copperhead Democrats had tried to take over using pistols and knives, although the Republicans had been able to elect a moderator before the meeting disintegrated into a fracas. Two days later, the same paper provided a fuller report, stating that the Copperheads had unjustly complained that their rights had been violated and seized the moment to surround the ballot box and take control of the meeting. When a Republican constable had tried to push through the crowd to intervene, he had been knocked over the head. The crowd continued to argue for the

rest of the day, and finally the selectmen adjourned the town meeting until the next morning. By that time, the Republicans had contacted the state militia in Manchester, which turned out to maintain order during the following day's balloting, resulting in a clear and resounding Republican victory in the town.

The Democratic Concord newspaper The New Hampshire Patriot and Gazette *painted a slightly different picture under the headline* "War in Goffstown" *when it published an account on March 16, more than a week after the election. That paper contended that the Goffstown Republicans had overreacted to a legitimate concern about the townsmen's voting privileges and had tried to intimidate the Democrats with threats of violence and retribution, while the noble Democrats stood firmly in defense of their rights.*

Both newspapers cite a third paper called the Union, *of which apparently no copies survive. It was a Democratic paper from Manchester that painted an even more damaging portrayal of the Republicans' attempt to subvert American democracy, blaming it all on the "Abolitionist Selectmen." But the paper also admitted that no one resorted to violence; rather the town meeting had become a stand-off, with "two hundred good Democrats . . . [standing] before the ballot-box and [demanding] their rights." The state militia, the paper contended, had already been prepared to turn out against the honest citizenry in Manchester if the Democrats caused any trouble there; thus they appeared on the scene at the Goffstown meeting house the next day ready to shoot some Copperheads. Alas, Goffstown Democrats were so disgusted by the whole chain of events they stayed home on the second day, thus allowing the Republicans to claim victory in the election by default.*

The truth is probably some mixture of all these accounts, but all the sources seem to agree on a few points. First, despite the rumors of violence, very little fighting actually occurred, although certainly the situation was tense and had the potential to erupt into violence at any moment. The state militia was posted to town on the second day of voting to maintain order. Second, each side claimed that the dispute in Goffstown was proof of a larger conspiracy to deprive the members of the other party of their constitutional rights. And third, the stories about the disruption of the Goffstown town meeting traveled far and wide in New Hampshire, substantiating the idea that New Hampshire politics were very divisive indeed in 1864.

Hart's Location Gets a Town Hall As Told by Susan Bruce

Hart's Location is the smallest incorporated town in New Hampshire, with a current population of forty-one hardy souls. For years, there was no town hall, which meant that town meeting was held either at the Notchland Inn or in Town Clerk Marion Varney's basement. The meeting bounced back and forth for years. Mrs. Varney even had a private voting booth rigged up in the corner, behind a shower curtain—not that anyone ever used it. Cats came and went throughout the meeting, and the recliners caused more than one snooze casualty over the years. The town reports were kept at the Notchland Inn, but some had disappeared over the years, because they were a popular item for scavenger hunts. Then the state rules about floor space at town meeting changed, and Hart's Location had to think seriously about a town hall.

Notchland Inn owners Ed Butler and Les Schoof donated a piece of land to the town. The Appalachian Mountain Club (AMC) was building what is now the Highland Center in Crawford Notch. Some of the old outbuildings were not needed for the new center, including bunkhouses that had been used by staff and hikers for years. The AMC offered them up to the public, rather than just demolish them. In this way, two of the bunkhouses moved to Hart's Location, and were joined together to form the new town hall. Unfortunately, the new town hall then had to undergo immediate fumigation to eliminate a bedbug infestation.

Come Hell or Cold Water in Hebron

Albert Fogg showed up at town meeting one March, we're told, much to the surprise of townsfolk. Albert lived clear on the other side of the lake, had no car, and even if he had the road was pretty much impassible on account of mud season. "Albert," they said, when he made his appearance, "How'd you get here?"

"Walked across the ice."

"But Albert, that ice is awful thin and punky. How'd you dare?"

Albert said: "I made myself as light as I could and walked right along fast."

Just Walk Single File in Henniker, a True Story from Bruce Tribolini

When Bruce and his wife Marilyn moved to New Hampshire from Chicago, they were excited to attend their first town meeting, but somewhat abashed by their first encounter. The topic was widening the sidewalks and the voter preceding them into the meeting had brought a ten foot length of pipe—to demonstrate how wide ten feet was, and to "beat this resolution down."

In Chicago, Bruce said, carrying around a pipe had an entirely different connotation.

Hill Votes to Build Character

In a *Concord Monitor* account of the 2009 town meeting, reporter Annmarie Timmins witnessed this exchange: "As she has for 40 years, Judi Pescinski asked the selectmen to save her from the dust and ruts that are a constant obstacle on her stretch of Currier Road. Plenty of others joined her. But they got the same answer they always get." Selectman John Lynch quoted radio commentator Paul Harvey: "Dirt roads build character." Nope, the town can't afford the paving this year, but, Lynch suggested, "Maybe in 40 years." Then added, "Just think of the character you're gaining."

Dare to Eat Pie in Monroe

Sue Robertson grew up in Monroe, a small (population under 800) town in Grafton County on the Connecticut River. Town meeting in Monroe, Sue said, was *the* event of the spring. A big dinner of beans, casseroles, and salads was always well attended. The older students, high school and junior high, got out of school for the meeting and to wait on tables at the dinner.

"I remember Mike Griffin eating a whole apple pie on a dare at one of those dinners," she said. "You could starve at town meeting now. At least there ought to be a well-stocked snack bar."

Her husband, Robbie Robertson, quipped: "Maybe we should set up a trough."

Newbury—Or Is It?

Susie Riley wrote this slightly chilling, but deadly accurate, impression of town meeting interaction for her blog.

> Town meeting—the closest hand of government an average person can touch. People say that up heah town meeting is a spectator sport. But wait: it's March. People are itching for an argument and anxious for hunting season.* Bad enough combination, but now they're all going to be herded into one room for three hours, to hear details on how their taxes are going up. Worse, they're being fed a ham and bean suppah right before. I'm afraid.

Most articles pass without bloodshed, but the last is about the town's plan to switch out the streetlights with halogen bulbs to save money. Suddenly the crowd perks up and people are queuing at the podium to have their say. The first speaker states that halogen bulbs emanate a hue that's not visually pleasing.

The second speaker firmly believes there are already too many streetlights on her road and we should rethink the number of them before we discuss the bulbs being used.

The last speaker claims that streetlights aren't even needed, since we all know where we're going.

At this point I hear, in the far corner of my brain, Paula Prentiss frantically screaming, "I don't know about you, but I'm getting the hell out of Stepford!"

*Deer hunting season starts in the fall, but hunters look forward to it year round. They start looking forward to hunting season, in fact, as soon as it's over. The spouses of hunters, who are not hunters themselves, look forward to it, because it gets the hunters out of the house.

Bourbon and **New Castle** Water

Some years back, the building of a sewer system in the island community proved a contentious issue. It was going to be darned expensive, for one thing. But not building it was going to be even more expensive: The state threatened a fine of $1000 a week until a good set of plans had been developed and the project set in motion.

The legislative body realized this project must be undertaken, but wasn't happy about it. George Pitts summed up the frustrations of many when he said: "I told you it was a mistake to put in town water!"

His neighbor said, "George, don't you drink your bourbon with water?"

George said, "You know darned well I drink it neat."

Family Dynamics in **Northwood**

Joann Bailey recalled the vote of 1955. She'd served three years on the school board and was running for a second term. She remembered the date because it was the year her daughter, Robbie, was born. "My husband didn't vote for me," she recalls, more than fifty years later. "I wanted a second term. He didn't vote for me and I lost to George Rogers. It would have been a tie if Bob voted."

She added, "The senior third-year person on the school board had to keep the books. I didn't know anything about bookkeeping at that time,

Becky, but I learned. The total school budget that year was $48,000. Can you believe it?"

Nottingham: A Good Preacher is Hard to Find

In *Nottingham-250*, a short history commemorating the 250th anniversary of the town, a summary of town records suggests a rift between town and church—or at least between town and the Reverend Mr. Butler. In June of 1769 the Reverend Mr. Butler requested a raise in salary as well as twenty cords of wood annually. Instead of honoring his request, the town voted to dismiss him. Good-bye, Reverend Mr. Butler.

Five months later, the town voted to revoke the previous vote. A committee of three were given the task of talking the situation over with the reinstated minister. In the end, it was agreed that those "dissatisfied" with the Reverend Mr. Butler no longer had to pay any "church rate or tax in the future."

The stitching didn't hold for long. In 1770, the Reverend Mr. Butler was once again dismissed. This time he took the hint and left for good.

The Uncertainty of Winter in Seabrook

Peter Randall served on the Seabrook budget committee. He recalls that one night the road agent came in with his proposed budget, written on the back of an envelope: "Summer maintenance: $10,500. Winter maintenance: you do not know and I do not know."

The Center of Sharon

In Sharon, population approximately 300 at the time, discussion focused on where exactly the town center was located. Vi Newton, the oldest resident present, was tapped to resolve the controversy. "Well," she said, "our one streetlight is right out front of this meeting hall, so I guess this is it."

Is Nothing Sacred in Temple?

Police Chief Russ shows up at town meeting. He gives his report, saying the department was moving ahead and had bought some new equipment, including a new fingerprint machine.

"How's that new fingerprint machine working out?" someone asked during the follow-up Q & A. Chief Russ allowed as how he couldn't really say.

"Why's that?"

"Somebody stole it."

Unity Takes Its Time

Sarah moved from California to retire in Unity. She was excited to attend her first town meeting, but surprised to see tables laden with food and drink at the back of the hall, at 9:00 a.m. She expected the meeting would last maybe an hour.

Six hours later, she says, she had consumed quite a lot of that food—grateful for it—and the tables were nearly empty.

Town meeting is a marathon, not a sprint. Food for thought and food for the body ought to be in plentiful supply.

A scan of the *Highlights in the History of Unity, N.H.*, published in 1964 by the Historical Committee for the Bicentennial, provides several other tasty Bake Sale items.

1776—the town voted that all ox sleds should be four foot wide from the inside to the other inside of the runners "in order to brake open the snow in the highways to accommodate ourselves and the neighboring towns for transportation."

Oh, and that same year, Unity resolved to support the revolution (not then called revolution) and "to the utmost of our power at the Risque of our lives and Fortune with ARMS, oppose the Hostile Proceedings of the British Fleets and Armies, against the United American Colonies. "

This is followed by the signatures of twenty-five townsmen, and a shorter list "of those (four) persons who Refused to sign the within Declaration." The lines were drawn.

1785—The town voted to award $5 to any of its residents who killed a wolf within town boundaries.

1788—Four school districts were laid out with a school house to be built in each.

1805—Unity chose the letter U to be the symbol for the town seal.

1806—Residents would be paid seventeen cents each for crows' heads.

1807—The going-rate for crows' heads was raised to twenty-five cents.

1817—Unity showed its appreciation for its soldiers on Muster Day when it "Voted to refresh the officers and soldiers belonging to Unity to be provided with a dinner of good Beef and Mutton well cooked and good wheat flower bread to eat with it . . . and cider to drink while eating and an apple pie to every four men and each man is to have a pint of good West India Rum delivered to him in the morning of said day. . . ."

1877—Town Auditor Harvey Sanborn declared the town free of debt—adding, "and it may be well said to afford good reason for a day of Thanksgiving and rejoicing."

Weare For Art Thou, Justice

In 2006 in the town of Weare, wisdom prevailed. Somebody (probably from away) got a petition going for an article to seize Supreme Court Justice David Souter's family farmhouse and turn it into the Lost Liberty Hotel. While it's true that Weare has no hotels, it doesn't really need any—being a town of under 8000 souls. Some folks were mad at Justice Souter because of a ruling in a case out of New London, Connecticut, where a neighborhood was seized by eminent domain for the building of an office complex. The Supreme Court ruled that it was up to the states, not the federal government, to control such matters.

When push came to shove, Weare supported its most famous resident. In an article in the *Concord Monitor*, moderator Neal Kurk said: "The people of Weare are sensible folks. And we don't punish judges for making decisions that we don't agree with."

When Souter retired from the court a few years later, Weare was prepared to welcome him home with open arms. But he bought a house in Hopkinton and moved there, lock, stock, and extensive library.

Wilmot Gets Religion

From *Home to the Mountain: A Bicentennial History of Wilmot, New Hampshire* by Thomas S. Curren and Kathy Neustadt: At the first town meeting in 1808, Wilmot voted to appropriate money to support "four days of preaching at $2 per day." "One Mr. Evans" was the town's first preacher. Later on, Elder Robert Dickey preached "on the common." According to an old story, when Lydia Hastings was being baptized by the elder, the ceremony was "interrupted at the moment of immersion when her horrified brother cried out, 'Help! Help! Old Dickey is Drowning Lyd!'"

On the Hot Seat in **Woodford**

Sometimes selectmen don't listen to the body of electors as carefully as they might. In a town we'll call Woodford (this is a true story; but the teller didn't want his town named), a warrant article passed to put in a bathroom at the town house. Folks were tired of the outhouse. It was time to move into the 20th century.

A year passed. Town meeting came again, and though the money had been appropriated for the new bathroom, no new bathroom had been built. The selectmen, as is their legal right (if not their moral obligation), had shifted the money from the new bathroom line to cover expenses in other areas of the town budget.

People were not happy. The selectmen got lambasted. We want our bathroom, the people said.

Next thing you know, an electric toilet was installed in a closet. If you've ever owned or used an electric toilet, you know how it works. Deposits fall into an insulated chamber, the heating coils kick in, and the materials are incinerated. If you avail yourself of the facility during the incineration process, you can actually see the glowing coils at work just inches from your . . . self. Townspeople were afraid to use it.

Whether those selectmen fared well in subsequent elections or found themselves on the hot seat, the teller did not say.

"Town meetings are to liberty what primary schools are to science; they bring it within the people's reach."

ALEXIS DE TOQUEVILLE

The Exeter Combination

4 ⚖

In Context

We had town meeting before we had a State of New Hampshire, not to mention a United States of America. In the Exeter Combination, 1639, colonials formed a rough-and-ready government complete with taxes. That first meeting, held for the purpose of coming up with the tax plan, is counted as the first town meeting in New Hampshire. No doubt following that first town meeting and the setting of that first tax rate, folks grumbled: These taxes are too damned high; I earned that money (or grew that corn); how are the old people supposed to live?

In the early days, land ownership was designated and towns incorporated under charters issued by royal governors from England. The towns governed themselves for the most part, though the cutting of designated mast pines was forbidden. These were saved for the king's navy. Typically, the charter named an individual to call the first town meeting and get the ball rolling. In those days, voting privileges belonged only to English Protestant men who were "settled inhabitants," at least 24 years old, "not vicious in life but of honest and good conversation" and worth a minimum of twenty pounds—in other words, mature men of property, substance, and the correct faith. A few years later, the voting age was lowered to 21. It took another couple centuries for the rest of us (women, non-Protestants, minorities) to get the vote.

Town meeting gained even more official status with the passage of the New Hampshire Town Laws of 1692: It shall "bee lawfull for the Select men . . . to Convene the free holders of there towne to geather, to Consider debate & Conclude of Such things as are Necessary for the prudentiall affairs of their towne . . ." Besides attending to the "prudentiall affairs," voters elected the selectmen, town clerk, tax collector, and road agent (then called "surveyor of highways"). They also chose overseers of the poor, firewards, constables, tythingmen, fence viewers, sealers of leather, sealers of weights and measures, hog reeves, cullers of staves, and measurers of wood and bark. A new position of building inspector popped up in the 1890s. Clearly, town officials have always had considerable business

May 4, 1639

The Exeter Combination

Whereas it hath pleased the Lord to move the heart of our dread Sovereign Charles by the grace of God, King of England, Scotland, France & Ireland, to grant license & liberty to sundry of his subjects to grant themselves in the western parts of America—We his loyal subjects, brethren of the church in Exeter, situate and lying upon the river Pascataquacke with other inhabitants there, considering with ourselves the holy will of God and our own necessity, that we should not live without wholesome laws and government among us, of which we are altogether destitute, do in the name of Christ and in the sight of God combine ourselves together to erect and set up amongst us such government as shall be to our best discerning agreeable to the will of God professing ourselves subjects to our Sovereign Lord King Charles, according to the liberties of our English colony of the Massachusetts, and binding ourselves solemnly by the grace and help of Christ, and in his name and fear, to submit ourselves to such godly and christian laws as are established in the realm of England to our best knowledge, and to all other such laws which shall upon good grounds be made and enacted amongst us according to God, that we may live quietly & peaceably together in all godliness and honesty.

John Wheelwright	Darby Field	Richard Morris
Augustine Storer	Robert Read	Nicholas Needham
Thomas Wright	Edward Rishworth	Thomas Wilson
William Wentworth	Francis Matthews	George Rawbone
Henry Elkins	Godfrey Dearborne	William Cole
George Walton	William Wardhall	James Wall
Samuel Walker	Robert Smith	Thomas Leavitt
Thomas Petit	Ralph Hall	Edmund Littlefield
Henry Roby	Robert Seward	John Cramme
William Winborne	Richard Bulger	Philemon Purmot
Thomas Crawley	Christopher Lawson	Thomas Wardhall
Christopher Helme	George Barlow	

From: *Town Papers—Documents and Records Relating to Towns in New Hampshire, Volume IX*, published in 1875 by Charles C. Pearson.

to conduct. What we think of as simpler times weren't all that simple. As schools and libraries were established, the scope of town business expanded even further.

New England town meeting didn't start out as democracy, but theocracy. In a theocracy, God is recognized as the head of state, with locals—usually ministers—interpreting God's expectations to keep the community on a divine track while attending to the earthly needs of the citizens. Instead of church and state being separate, they were one, despite the oft-quoted fisherman's protest: "We came for cod, not for God." Early meeting houses were used for worship as well as politics—a practical choice, since meeting houses were usually the only places in town big enough for folks to gather in larage numbers. Clarence M. Webster, in his 1945 book *Town Meeting Country*, writes: "The church did not rule the town; neither did it stand aloof in holy and theological state; it was, instead an agent of the people as well as of the Lord." Preachers worked with elected officials; they supported each other. Had to. The job of carving settlements from the wilderness required constant attention. Figuring out how to get along wasn't easy either. Points of contention were put to a vote. And the vote settled the dispute. As it does today.

In *All Those in Favor: Rediscovering the Secrets of Town Meeting and Community*, Susan Clark and Frank Bryan note that by the time the founders met in Philadelphia in 1787 to craft the Constitution, "New Englanders had already invented democracy. More accurately they had *reinvented* it in New England, where it had been in full operation for more than a century." Clark and Bryan trace town meeting back more than 2000 years to ancient Greece. Though there may be no direct line between the Greek customs and those of New England (i.e., the first did not spawn the second) there certainly are similarities. In Ancient Greece and in New England, people gathered to make "binding decisions as the legislature of a political union— *a government*." And, Clark and Bryan add proudly, "We still do."

It's no wonder historians have trouble agreeing on town meeting's direct ancestry. Wherever and whenever well-intentioned folks gathered to make decisions for the good of their community, wherever and whenever the notion of one-person-one-vote was put into effect, these were the origins of town meeting. The idea caught on in New England and stuck.

Before town meeting settled into a pattern of one annual meeting held each March, folks met to seek consensus on what to do about problems that arose seemingly as they arose. During those early years of settling a strange new continent, just about everything presented a challenge: how to preserve and divide food, how to fend off an Indian threat, whether to welcome a newcomer or eject him as undesirable, how and where to build a meeting house or school or road.

In *Town Government in New Hampshire: The New Hampshire Historical Records Survey Project*, published in 1940, town meeting is described as "one of the best examples of unspoiled democracy. Possibly the Swiss cantons [small independent governed 'states' comprising Switzerland] are the only political units in which the voice of the people finds an expression as clear and direct as it finds in the annual March meetings in New England towns." Town meeting is also compared to the German "tun"—meetings originally held in the fields for farmers to discuss crops and the logistics of the harvest.

"My hay's about ready to cut; how 'bout we get together Saturday and take care of my field, do yours next week?"

"Gute idee."

Early town meetings went far beyond discussion of crops. An article compiled by the Nottingham Historical Society on the occasion of Nottingham's 250th anniversary in 1972 describes the range and power of town meeting:

> Town Meetings of the period noted, 1766 to 1795, set the tax rate of the town for the ensuing year, and "gave in" or abated (the amount to be paid in taxes) in part or in whole, particularly when a family was burned out of their home. They also settled such actions as school districts and the wages and expenses of ministers. Sometimes they took action against delinquent tax collectors, and as often against private individuals in certain matters. In fact they were as sovereign and complete a ruling body as ever existed. They had to be as the lack of transportation and their very isolation naturally led to a small number of families holding the majority of offices for years.

The article notes that only about 50 percent of tax payers voted, "perhaps due to a belief that one had to be a person of that substance to be accorded that privilege." It further notes that the members of the "leading" families took turns holding offices. This is still true is many towns. Public service runs in families. In Nottingham the names Cilley, Simpson, Neally, Davis, Tuttle, Dame, McCrillis, Leathers, Hodgdon, Butler, Bartlett, Harvey, and Garland turn up again and again in the old records. Though "occasionally a new name and face did slip into the assembly."

Thomas Jefferson was a fan. Town meetings, he wrote, "have proved themselves the wisest invention ever devised by the wit of man for the perfect exercise of self-government and for its preservation."

However, another founding father, James Madison, was not enthusiastic. He wrote: "In all very numerous assemblies, of whatever character, passion never fails to wrest the scepter from reason. Had every Athenian citizen been a Socrates, every Athenian assembly would still have been a mob." Luckily, we have moderators to help us keep our passions and scepters in place. Luckily, few of us are Socrates. Or are we? Truth is, when we're on the winning side of a vote (whether it's for replacing the old bulbs with halogens or electing a president), we tend to agree with Jefferson: together we are so smart! The losing side favors Madison: majority rule sometimes stinks. *What is wrong with you people? Use your heads.*

The position of moderator dates to the time of the charters. The man named to call those first town meetings served as a kind of moderator, then called the Ruler. By 1847 laws had been adopted specifying the role of the moderator—appointed by selectmen, or, if no selectmen showed up, elected by the people. Later, the position of moderator became an unequivocally elected position. Then as now, moderators set the rules, ran the meetings, kept order, and announced the votes. Then as now a good sense of humor served a moderator well. Then as now, as the old saying goes, "The moderator rules but does not reign." He or she is kind of the boss of us, but not really—if we put up a big enough stink. It's our meeting after all. And we can vote to overrule any ruling made by the moderator.

We are, and always have been, a feisty bunch. Note the spirit of this vote, recorded by Roxanna Richardson in her *History of Northwood, N.H. 1878–1946*. At the town meeting of March 1879, Northwoodians "voted to instruct the Selectmen to ascertain if the town is liable for the bill presented by John Bennett, if so, pay it, if not, fight it!"

Of the following year, 1880, she wrote, "The voters seemed to be in a stingy mood, for they voted to indefinitely postpone raising money for the maintenance of the poor, for school houses, for public libraries, and for preparing and publishing the early history of the town." Wonder how that discussion went?

"It's our duty to help the poor!"

"Why don't they get jobs like the rest of us?"

"The school house needs repair to the roof."

"It'll last another winter."

"Money don't grow on trees, you know."

"The library is the heart of the town."

"A library is a frill we can't afford."

"Town history? What the heck do we need a town history for? Especially if we don't have a library to keep it in."

Wonder what the moderator did to keep the lid on that debate.

New Hampshire and Vermont Have a Few Things in Common

Susan Clark and Frank Bryan make a compelling case for preserving town meeting in *All Those In Favor*. Their research was done in Vermont, but, let's face it, New Hampshire and Vermont have a few things in common. Clark and Bryan describe the reaction of an Afghan woman who visited Vermont to learn about our system of government. When she saw how town meeting worked, she was full of wonder.

The authors warned her, "Serious conflict often breaks out at town meetings. People get angry, feelings are hurt. Besides, it takes a certain amount of preparation to understand how direct democracy works."

The woman was undaunted. "Feelings are hurt? Well, at least no one is carrying an AK-47!"

What Afghans need is proof that democracy exists somewhere, she told them. "You must understand what it would mean for an Afghan woman to see another woman stand openly in public and engage in a political debate . . . It's hope we are after here. And there is no better place to look for democratic hope than in your state."

Or in New Hampshire, perhaps.

New England is one of the few places on earth where town government thrives. In other places, county, state or federal government provide an area's identity, and pretty much run the show. Here, the center of the political universe is the town. Blame it on the hills and valleys and rivers and lakes; the New England terrain naturally divides itself into small geographic bites. The Merrimack River divides Canterbury and Boscawen. You can look across the river from one farm to another, but it would be some difficult for those farmers to get together for a confab, short of a big, expensive bridge. I remember when a bridge did connect Boscawen and Canterbury. We drove over it to buy milk from the Jordan Farm. But when the bridge fell into disrepair, each town called upon the other to pay to fix it. Neither would vote to do so. So the bridge didn't get fixed. End of bridge. That's democracy.

Some say the people of New Hampshire are among the most politically aware in the country. Our dynamic town politics undoubtedly contributes to our interest in and knowledge of state and national politics. Oh yes, we get excited about electing governors and senators and representatives. With our first-in-the-nation primary, every four years we work ourselves into a frenzy over presidential politics. But for true grassroots campaigning and intense political engagement, just watch the fur fly when two candidates for selectmen go at it, or when some whippersnapper tries to take over the job of road agent that's been held for the last twenty years by Judd Merrill's youngest boy Hoppy.

Up Close and Personal

We prefer our presidential candidates up close and personal. How you gonna know who to vote for if you haven't met him or her? Without undue effort, the people of New Hampshire can meet every one of them in person—shake their hands, too, if we want. In an election year, candidates are thick as fleas on my cat Dusty. When Dennis Kucinich, on short notice, decided to make a campaign stop at Susty's Vegetarian Cafe at the top of the hill, word spread quickly. Dennis and Viggo Mortensen were coming to town.

"Who's Viggo Mortensen?" some asked.

"Why he's a big movie star."

"What's he been in?"

"Movies."

Susty's filled to bursting. We'd never been so physically close to some of our neighbors before, and weren't sure we liked it all that much. Kucinich's campaign staff had to stand outside in the cold so the locals could squeeze into the room. A couple of young people, not from around here, played and sang folk songs while we waited for the candidate and the movie star to arrive. They were late. Each gave an impassioned speech. Both were smaller than they looked on screen. Consensus seemed to be we might or might not vote for Kucinich, but we certainly appreciated his stopping by.

Selectmen, school board members, town clerks, tax collectors, and road agents don't get paid much, but their jobs matter. To us. In our daily lives. Vote in the wrong person and we're messed up. And it'll take a year or more to get un-messed-up. It happens in every town, every so often. Somebody gets elected on promises of this or that, but we soon learn he can't even figure out when a warrant needs to be posted, doesn't know the first thing about budgets, and can't read a contract to save his life. He makes the staff at town hall so mad they quit en masse, so anybody who could have helped run the business of the town properly is out the door. Oh, dear.

Town is not just home, town is who we are. Town officials are us, and in the twenty-first century our towns are big business, so a level of competence is needed to keep the paychecks going out to the town workers, to apply for that grant to help renovate the gazebo, to make sure there's enough sand at the town shed to keep the roads safe in the next snow storm. Our officials need to *know* what it takes to keep the town running and how to get it. It's incumbent upon the voters to *know* enough to elect leaders who can do the job.

In those earliest days, according to William R. Bliss in *Colonial Times on Buzzard's Bay*, written in 1894, the whole idea was to *know* the town's Mind, with a capital M. Those first voters put their trust in the democratic process. Through it, they believed, the town could unite as one Mind, a collective wisdom, and make wise decisions to everyone's benefit. He writes:

> The object of all town meetings was "to know the Town's Mind;" whether it was for doing this, or for doing that, or for doing something else. In warrants it was written with capital letters, and was alluded to as if it were a distinguished person, slow to act, and to be consulted on every matter, small or great.

That trust in the Mind steadies town meeting. And that collective wisdom still exists. I've seen it.

At the 2010 Northwood town meeting, the legislative body couldn't seem to wrap its collective Mind around Article 20 *To see if the Town is in favor of the adoption of an Ordinance relative to the regulation and use of the Northwood Athletic Fields.*

Evidently the selectmen had been advised that without an official ordinance setting out rules for use of the fields, the town would be inviting lawsuits. So before the kids could be set loose on the fields in the spring, the town would have to set some rules. Otherwise, baseball and other outdoor sports would be seriously curtailed. Nobody wanted that. We like our youth engaged in sports. Sports give the little buggers something to do.

The Mind didn't seem to mind the general idea of rules and regulations, but the list of rules and regulations the selectmen proposed proved controversial. These included banning off-road vehicles. Snowmobiles would be allowed only on marked trails. No fires. No glass containers. No firearms, fireworks, or throwing stones. No alcohol. And no unleashed dogs.

Everybody seemed to have a different idea about the sense and fairness of the regulations. Many objections were raised. Some dogs, for example, didn't need to be leashed to be under control. And some dogs liked to run on those fields when they were empty. What was wrong with that?

Also, what if somebody wanted to have a picnic? Maybe bring a charcoal grill and cook hamburgers? Would that be allowed?

And what about special events?

And what about this and that and the other?

Debate dragged on.

The moderator was adamant. He would not allow the legislative body to rewrite the rules at town meeting. We were to vote yes or no on the article. Then somebody made the mistake of saying: "But under *Robert's Rules* . . ."

Our moderator, Robbie Robertson, countered "We are not under *Robert's Rules*. We are under the moderator's rules. We are under Robbie's Rules."

That didn't set well with some factions of the Mind.

Moderator Robbie added, "I am the moderator but the people have the right to overrule me."

Someone shouted, "We are the people!" and got gaveled.

The Mind couldn't make itself up. We were in a political pickle. Until, Arlene Johnson, retired town clerk, went to the mic and said, softly and calmly, "I think I have a solution."

The Mind waited. Hopeful.

Arlene said, "Maybe it comes from being old. And maybe it comes from being an English teacher." Then she explained that a careful reading of Article 20 revealed that we were voting for "an" ordinance, not this ordinance in particular. Perhaps we could approve "an" ordinance at this meeting, and ask the selectmen to look further into what that ordinance might actually be between now and baseball season. Perhaps hearings could be held to discuss the shape those ordinances might take and public input could guide the selectmen in their task.

Relieved, the Mind agreed to support the adoption of "an ordinance yet to be determined."

The meeting moved on to Article 21, *To see if the Town is in favor of the adoption of an Ordinance to provide for the control of dogs, cats, small pets and undomesticated animals that may become a problem within the Town of Northwood.* After the heat of the preceding discussion, the moderator suggested that he, himself, might fall into the category of "undomesticated critter."

Once again, the selectmen provided two pages of rules and regulations, including fees and fines.

Would the selectmen hold hearings on these rules and regulations?

Sure they would.

So without much discussion, Article 21 passed. We could agree to have *an* ordinance. And interested parties would, at future hearings, be allowed to express their opinions on what that ordinance might look like.

The Mind figured it out. With help from our dear Arlene Johnson.

While some of us may lose our individual minds in the heat of town meeting, never (knock wood) do we completely lose our collective Mind. The decisions we make may not be perfect, and sometimes may be just plain wrong, but come another year we will make up our Mind to do better.

Who Can Claim to Be a Native?

When someone from away asks where we hail from, we don't say New England. We *might* say New Hampshire. We would never say, Cheshire County. Or, god forbid, The Lakes Region. We say, Wilmot. Or more specifically, Wilmot Flat (as opposed to Wilmot Center or North Wilmot).

Because of our strong town identity, the status of native takes on special significance. A ninety-year-old who's lived all her life (so far) in the town of Bath earns respect not just for longevity but for staying put. If her parents and grandparents and great-grandparents also hailed from Bath, her native status is even more secure. Who can claim to be a native? Well, it helps to have seven generations in the ground. (Five, in a pinch.) In Bristol, a local was asked if she were a native. "Oh, no," she said, "I was born in Hill. I married a Bristol man—forty-eight years ago."

Some say you become a native when the last person in town who remembers you moving in dies.

In 1945 Zephine Humphrey published a valentine to our region, *A Book of New England*, including a tribute to the origins of town meeting. Early on, there was much to decide, but no set policies or procedures to rely on. Settlers were shaping the way towns functioned—and the way democracy in New England still functions. The earliest meetings of the Mind were, Humphrey writes, "vastly important. . . . The questions were sometimes trivial then as they are now, yet (some were) important with a life-or-death value. It is no wonder that, even in the twentieth century, there is a special manner about the way a New Englander mounts the steps of his Town Hall on Town Meeting day. Unconsciously he remembers that he once went thus to help shape the life of a nation; dignity crowns his head."

Of course the early practice of getting the gang together every day or once a week or once a month to discuss town issues turned out to be impractical in the long run. People had forests to clear, homes to erect, crops to sow, hoe, and harvest. So they elected selectmen to represent them through the year, and, over time, added helpers for the selectmen, including the aforementioned town clerks, tax collectors, hog reeves, and fence viewers.

Anybody who didn't work out could get unelected next time around—so every term of office served as a probation period. Any decisions made at one meeting could be unmade at the next. Humphrey observes that town meeting built a strong community that was "flexible enough to grow." *Flexible enough to grow.* No wonder some of us cringe when the phrase "because this is the way it's always been done," gets invoked to support an argument for the status quo. Town meeting is not about preserving "the way it's always been done" in vinegar; it's about maintaining what works and changing what doesn't. We like our cukes fresh as well as pickled.

Early town meetings began at daybreak and lasted all day. Both women and men came in from the hinterlands, having done the farm chores extra early. Women weren't allowed to vote, or even participate in the discussion, far as we know. Their role was to cook a big dinnah for noontime (Yankees call the midday meal dinnah, not lunch; the evening meal is suppah) so the afternoon's voting could be done on full stomachs. When women finally demanded and got the vote, well, according to Zephine Humphrey, the change was not entirely for the better. She writes: "Whatever may be said in favor of woman's suffrage . . . there can be no doubt that it has impaired the character of Town Meeting. For now, in order to do two things at once, the women run in and out of the meeting, voting for the measures which they have most at heart, then scurrying back to go on with the dinner. This introduces a restlessness and distraction which are regrettable." She adds that though men might not admit it, they are forced to behave a little better in the presence of women—restrain themselves, so to speak—and this they must find "irksome."

Over time the Australian ballot (voting at the polls on paper, at a time separate from town meeting) replaced voting by voice or the raising of hands for election of town officials. Naturally, this change diminished the drama. No more surprise nominations and on-the-spot coups. Over time, town meeting started later in the day, at 9 or 10 a.m., and ran shorter. Over time, the work of the church and the work of the town separated and concerns at town meeting turned to how much taxpayers could afford balanced against the needs and wants of the community. Over time, everybody in town—over age eighteen—earned the right to vote.

Yes, town meeting has evolved. At its core, however, it remains the same Mindful institution it has always been.

[Town meeting is] "one of the best examples of unspoiled democracy.
Possibly the Swiss cantons are the only political units in which the
voice of the people finds an expression as clear and direct as it
finds in the annual March meetings in New England towns."

TOWN GOVERNMENT IN NEW HAMPSHIRE: THE NEW HAMPSHIRE
HISTORICAL RECORDS SURVEY PROJECT, 1940

5

Town Meeting:
Symbol for a Nation

by Jere Daniell

How does the world perceive town meeting: good, bad, indifferent? In the mid-1980s, Dartmouth Professor Jere Daniell addressed this question from a historian's perspective in an article for a regional magazine. In the end, editors at the magazine deemed the article too academic for their readers. Maybe so, but Daniell knew it was not academic enough for a scholarly journal. Besides, he liked the article as it stood and was, therefore, not inclined to rewrite it. So he moved on to his next project and the article was never published—though colleagues over the years consulted it for their own research and writings.

Professor Daniell knows more than anyone in the world (no exaggeration) about New Hampshire towns and their history; he's been giving talks about them for decades, often at local historical societies and libraries sponsored by the New Hampshire Humanities Council. He lectures on Colonial New Hampshire, our state during the Revolutionary and Civil Wars, and the New England town itself. He may not have spoken in and researched every town in New Hampshire, but pretty close. (Why isn't he writing this book then, since it's right up his alley? I asked him. He said he'd rather talk and leave the writing to me.)

I spent an afternoon with Jere Daniell talking about town meeting. During the interview, he unearthed the retired article. I took a gander and felt like Goldilocks. The article may have been considered too academic for the regional magazine and not academic enough for history journals, but it was just right for this book. In the article, Daniell takes a broad view of the history and tradition of the New England town meeting.

So in the spirit of celebrating the treasures that fall into our hands, and resisting the temptation to reinvent the wheel, here's Jere Daniell's take on what has made town meeting so central to community life in New England for more than 200 years, and the changing ways in which the rest of the country, and the world, have viewed our unique institution.

Town Meeting: Symbol for a Nation

As for the New England town meeting, every UN delegate from the Near
East is sentimental about it, and Americans from Davenport, Iowa sigh
with nostalgic fondness: "Ah, if the Russians could only attend a town
meeting in Massachusetts."

Robert Cendella, "A Lesson in Civics"
American Heritage, December 1960

Hereabouts the action begins in mid-February. Local officials draw up
the warrant, polish reports, set time aside for interviews, and, in some
cases, arrange for public "Pre-Town Meetings" to lessen the burden on the
real thing. Aspiring officials test the waters of candidacy for school board,
planning board, and selectman. In smaller communities where the meeting dinner is an established ritual, women prepare bean dishes, salads and
pies for what someone described as "the biggest church supper of the year."
The regional press gets ready. Reporters receive their assignments—no
town is too small to escape coverage. The production staff decides whether
to use the gavel or a white church in this year's logo. And the letters editor
preps for a deluge of correspondence. My local newspaper has solemnly
requested that its readers "keep letters as short as possible" and "write
no more often than once every two weeks." A "Roads Are In; Acid Rain
is Out" headline makes the front page the second day of March. It's town
meeting season.

The first New England town meeting convened somewhere in
Massachusetts (Dorchester has the best claim) soon after John Winthrop
and his associates settled in the Bay area. By the 1650s the meeting had
become a well established institution of local governance.

The town proved such an effective unit of communal organization that
it spread wherever émigrés from Massachusetts settled. Within towns the
regular meeting of legal voters grew increasingly important as a forum
for discussion, as the setting in which local officials were elected, and as
a legislature for local affairs. By the early part of the nineteenth century
there were over a thousand communities holding such meetings in the
six-state region of New England.

Town meeting, however, never became a national institution. For a
variety of reasons having to do with geography, religion, practicality and
patterns of migration, the county became the dominant form of local governance outside New England. Only in the midwest, where the Yankee

exodus of the nineteenth century carried many New Englanders, did anything like town government develop. There it competed with county government and witnessed a gradual erosion of authority. By the 1930s few
decisions of importance could be made by what remained of town meetings outside New England.

But that's only part of the story. At the symbolic level, town meeting
became, and still remains, very much a national institution. The process
began with the American Revolution and gained momentum as the nation
refined its political beliefs. European travelers in the United States published descriptions of towns and town meetings which would please the
most romantic fan of New England localism. Town meetings came under
close scrutiny by the national press in the early part of this [the twenti-
eth] century—some writers condemned them, some praised them, but all
shared the assumption that town meetings reflected the weaknesses and
strengths of America as a whole. The last fifty years has witnessed even
more intensive national fascination with New England's "peculiar institution." Three of the past ten years the meeting in Thetford, Vermont, has
been covered by major television networks. Neighboring Strafford made
60 Minutes in 1982. Ask any adult anywhere in the United States about the
New England town meeting. They'll know what you're talking about.

Town Meeting and Nation Building

Independence created lots of problems for the revolutionists. In their mind
the most important of these was the establishment of a political system
which would not be subject to the corruption and decay they identified
with England in particular and European monarchies in general. Their
attempts to create such a system were shaped by their commitment to
republicanism, an abstract concept based on the central idea that ultimate
political authority lay with the people. The people ruled through elected
representatives who, if they failed to satisfy their constituents, could be
removed from office. Regular elections, the accountability of elected officials to the public, and the opportunity for voters to express their opinions
about proposed legislation thus were essential to the proper functioning
of republican government. The logic of republicanism led to the writing
of state constitutions and, soon after the war ended, to the adoption of a
federal constitution.

The commitment to republicanism also began to put town meeting on the national map. Spokesmen for the new nation saw in these New England town assemblies the purest form of popular government. John Adams, for example, cited town meetings as one of the four cornerstones of the republic. Sam Adams, a consummate politician whose manipulation of the Boston town meeting had played an important role in the coming of revolution, made similar statements. Towns were discussed at length when the members of the Continental Congress debated how best to organize western lands acquired in the revolution. Thomas Jefferson, who participated in those debates, became a vocal advocate of the New England township system . . .

Jefferson's admiration was tested when dozens of New England town meetings passed resolutions condemning the Embargo Act adopted during his presidency, but his response to these resolutions made clear the depth of his support. "How powerfully did we feel the energy of this system in the case of the embargo," he wrote in 1816. "I felt the foundations of the government shaken under my feet by the New England township . . . the organization of this little selfish minority enabled it to overrule the union. What could the unwieldy counties of the Middle, the South, and the West do? Call a town meeting." Jefferson concluded by recommending the system of towns and town meetings be adopted throughout the United States.

Developments in what historians call the Jacksonian Era made the town meeting even more visible nationally. In the broadest sense this visibility grew out of the shift from a republican to a democratic political ethic. Republicanism had aristocratic components and did not include the belief that the majority of voters should determine public policy. Democracy, by contrast, emphasized the moral obligation of elected representatives to heed the dictates of majority opinion. It also emphasized voter participation in decision making and direct rule whenever possible. The New England town meeting fit even better with the new idiom. Where else could one find a purer example of direct democracy?

A number of New England's emerging literary giants were quick to point out the linkage. Timothy Dwight, whose *Travels in New England and New York (1821–1822)* had a national audience, glorified the town and its governmental traditions. Henry David Thoreau commented on the town meeting in several writings. In one essay, entitled "Slavery in Massachusetts," he implied that the institution might be used to articulate the growing regional opposition to chattel servitude. "When in some obscure country town the farmers came together to a special town meeting, to express their opinion on some subject which is vexing the land," Thoreau wrote, "that, I think, is the true Congress, and the most respectable one that's ever assembled in the United States." Sara Josepha Hale's *Northwood*, a romantic novel contrasting life in a New England town to life in the south, expressed similar sentiments.

It was Ralph Waldo Emerson, however, who produced the most elaborate town meeting eulogy. Emerson had been asked by the citizens of Concord, Massachusetts, to deliver an address at the 200th anniversary of the town's founding. He prepared by doing extensive research in town records. The climax of the address—which took nearly two hours to deliver and, in its printed version runs over sixty pages—stated boldly that "In a town meeting the great secret of political science was uncovered, and the problem solved, how to give every individual his fair weight in government. . . . Here the rich gave council, but the poor also; and, moreover, the just and the unjust. . . . In this open democracy," Emerson concluded, "every opinion had utterance; every objection, every fact, every acre of land, every bushel of rye, its entire weight." The message could not have been clearer. The New England town meeting was the nation's most powerful expression of democracy.

Soon thereafter—Emerson spoke in 1836—the town meeting hit center stage. Emerson and Thoreau might be ignored as biased regionalists, but Alexis de Toqueville was a figure of international renown when his *Democracy in America*, based on travels throughout the United States, began to circulate in America. The French nobleman was not the first or only European visitor to praise town governance, but he became by far the most widely read: In the nineteenth century alone there were over fifty separate editions and printings, in English, of *Democracy in America*. Virtually every academic and journalist who has written about town meeting since the 1830s quotes from the work. One example of his enduring impact: an article on town meetings in the March 14, 1977 issue of *Time* ended "De Toqueville would have been pleased."

The substance of de Tocqueville's commentary was that local institutions potentially put liberty in reach of the people and that in New England the local institutions fulfilled this potential much better than elsewhere in the United States. He described, with reasonable accuracy, the functions of selectmen and other town officials, but emphasized "the body of electors" which "gives them directions in everything beyond the simple, ordinary execution of the laws of the state."

For example, de Tocqueville wrote, should officials "want to start a school, the selectmen summon all the voters to a meeting on a fixed day and place; they there explain the need felt; they state the means available for the purpose, how much it will cost, and the site suggested. The meeting, consulted on all these points, accepts the principle, decides the site, votes the tax, and leaves the selectmen to carry out its orders." Moreover, citizens could require the selectmen to call a meeting by getting as few as ten signatures on a petition. The entire arrangement, de Toqueville concluded, explained why, "in general, New England townships" led "a happy life."

The words of Emerson and de Tocqueville caught on for several interrelated reasons. One was the domination by New England writers of American intellectual life and literary publications. Hawthorne, Whittier, Lowell, Longfellow, Emerson, Thoreau, and many others all helped keep New England and its institutions, including the town meeting, in the national limelight. As early as 1866 an article recommending "Town Meetings for Great Cities" appeared in the *Nation*. John Fiske, the historian, published an article on town meeting in *Harper's Monthly Magazine*; Edward Everett Hale wrote one which appeared in *Cosmopolitan*, and recommended, among other things, that novelists and playwrights should use town meeting scenes to enliven their work.

Several writers participated in endless debate over the origins of the town meeting. Altogether close to twenty articles explicitly on New England town meetings appeared in the handful of national magazines published in the late nineteenth century.

A second reason was the reinforcement by other European travelers of the praise de Tocqueville had provided. By far the most visible and widely noted of these was the English aristocrat, Lord James Bryce, whose *American Commonwealth* appeared in 1895. Bryce concluded after a lengthy analysis of American types of local government that "the town . . . with its popular primary assembly, is admittedly the best. It is the cheapest and most efficient; it is the most educative to the citizens who bear a part in it. The town meeting," Bryce added with a flourish, "has been not only the source, but the school of democracy."

A third reason was the spate of American Revolution centennial celebrations which gave orators and writers ample opportunity to link town meeting with developments of national significance. The meeting received credit for causing the revolution, for contributing to the military victory, and in general for training individuals in the exercise of self government.

Several men connected the New England town meeting to the origins of the Federal Constitution and its eventual adoption. Whatever anyone liked about American political institutions somehow led back to town meetings. President James Garfield, a midwesterner, reportedly said at one of these celebrations: "The germ of our political institutions, the primary cell from which they were evolved, was the New England town, and the vital force, the informing soul of the town was the Town Meeting . . ."

Garfield's statement epitomized a century of good press for the New England town meeting. The meeting, indeed, had become one central political symbol for American democracy as a whole.

Corruption in Paradise: Town Meeting under Attack

In 1897 an article entitled "The Decay of Town Government" appeared in the *Nation*. The author, A. G. Sedgwick, began by noting that until recently "to question the excellence of New England town government would have seemed like questioning democracy itself . . . " But he felt obliged, based on his personal observations, to engage in just such questioning. Towns throughout New England had fallen victim to corruption. Town meetings no longer expressed the will of the people. Instead they were dominated by "Village Tweeds"—a reference to Boss William Tweed of New York City—who used a variety of devices to fix elections and to adopt public policies with the sole aim of lining their own pockets. And Sedgwick was not alone. In the two decades before the start of World War I, dozens of similar articles appeared in newspapers and national press.

The attack on patterns of governance in New England towns had dual origins. In one sense it was simply an extension of the logic of self-labeled "progressive" reformers intent on making the United States live up to its professed standards of political purity. The attack also reflected a general belief, articulated by journalists and academics throughout the nation, that rural New England was experiencing a rapid decay of morals, religion, population, and self respect. What one observer labeled the "rural degeneracy cry" inevitably affected attitudes toward the town meeting.

Some writers were content simply to describe what went on in town meeting. The *Atlantic Monthly* published an article which contained the following passage: "One is not surprised to find a dearth of public spirit. The civic sense of Dickerman (a hypothetical community) manifests itself once a year only, at town meeting, chiefly in reducing its regular and necessary appropriations to the lowest possible limit, in protest against innovations . . . and in quarreling over trifles. . . . Civil honesty, naturally enough, is at the same low ebb as civic spirit. The buying and selling of votes has been in vogue for years." One can almost hear Emerson turning in his grave.

Others offered explanations for the depressing state of affairs. Several blamed immigrants who, as one historian put it, lacked "the tradition of the town meeting." A contributor to the *Unitarian Review* put the matter more bluntly when he wrote that Irishmen, Germans and French Canadians lacked "Yankee thrift" and were happy to sell votes. C. N. Hall in the *New England Magazine* cited civic ambition as the source of corruption. Local politicians catered to the public craze for expensive buildings and improvements. These necessitated hiring town laborers, whose votes could be manipulated "to perpetuate the reign of the ruling party." Hall and others specifically pointed to the town highway departments as strongholds of purchased town meeting votes.

The public savaging of New England town politics reached its climax in an article published in 1914 by Lincoln Steffans, America's most outspoken muckraker. For some time reformers had been attacking the system of legislative representation in Connecticut, and to a lesser extent Vermont and Rhode Island, for giving too much power to the small towns—some labeled them "rotten boroughs"—in those states. Steffans took on all of New England. He called it "the darkest part of the country"; a region made up of "exploited Massachusetts; drunken, prohibitionist Maine; rich, little, old, purchasable Rhode Island; beautiful, dying Vermont and New Hampshire; and meanest, crookedest Connecticut." The source of the corruption? "The good old American stock out in the country and in the small towns" was "regularly for sale" and had been so for some time.

And town meetings played a key role in the pattern. It was there elections for the state legislatures were fixed by local ring leaders in cahoots with the state bosses. Steffans' article gained wide circulation through republication in the *Literary Digest*. The editors of the *Digest* reported later that response to the accusations was surprisingly subdued.

The town meeting, of course, had its defenders who refuted Steffans and other critics. But the net effect of all this negative publicity was unmistakable. By the second decade of the twentieth century the New England town meeting no longer served as a much admired symbol of democracy. As one journalist put it: "Always known as an institution peculiar to New

England, we place it today among the other curiosities of the Pilgrims, and consider it as having as much practical bearing upon our needs as the ducking stool, pillory, and whipping post." Then, for more than a generation, the nation forgot about town meeting.

Town Meeting Rediscovered

The New England town meeting has made a remarkable come back in the last fifty years. Developments both national and regional have restored its reputation. People still differ on its merits. Nobody, however, compares it to the whipping post and pillory.

The process of rediscovery began in the mid 1930s. The first indication of public interest was an *Atlantic Monthly* article reporting how conflicting interests of farmers, gentlemen of leisure, college professors, and people of diverse ethnic backgrounds had been accommodated and problems resolved in a town meeting. In 1935 a restless young New Hampshireman, Robb Sagendorph, founded a new magazine called *Yankee*. Within a year it had published a short story entitled "Town Meetin'" [see Chapter 14] and an article on New England town reports. But what really put the meetings back in the national limelight was the extraordinary success of the radio program, "Town Meeting of the Air," which began broadcasting the same year *Yankee* got started. The opening words of the program—"Town Meetin' Tonight! Town Meetin' Tonight! Which Way America—Fascism, Communism, Socialism or Democracy?"—cemented in the minds of Americans from coast to coast the symbolic ties between the central political institution of New England towns and the fate of the nation. Throughout the country thousands of voluntary discussion groups met to talk about issues framed by participants in the program. "Town Meeting of the Air" did for twentieth century America what de Tocqueville had for the nineteenth.

Other factors fed into the process. Popular regional novelists like Joseph C. Lincoln and Dorothy Canfield (Fisher) began including town meeting scenes in their fiction. The climatic scene in Canfield's best selling *Seasoned Timber*, for example, was a town meeting in which the citizens of Clifford, Vermont, rejected a huge gift to the local academy because the potential donor wanted to exclude Jews from future enrollment. John Gould eulogized the town meetings of coastal Maine first in a *Yankee* article, next in the *New York Times Magazine*, and finally in a book with the boldly political title *New England Town Meeting, Safeguard for Democracy*. *Scribners*, *Life*, and the weekly magazine of the *Christian Science Monitor* all published town meeting articles before Pearl Harbor.

Participation in World War II provided additional momentum. "Town Meeting of the Air" dropped its discussions of competing political philosophies, cooperated fully with the war effort, and became an even more effective advertisement for its model. As one journalist put it in 1942, the program became a "nationwide adoption of the New England town meeting." Norman Rockwell, America's most famous illustrator, used a town meeting scene to portray the "Freedom of Speech" theme in his nationally distributed "Four Freedoms" series of posters. *Time* magazine covered town meeting for the first time in 1945. By the end of the war the imagery had become so deeply rooted in the American psyche that the governor of California, of all places, could state solemnly, "It is neither necessary nor desirable for the national government to depart from the spirit of the old town meeting of New England."

The prime consequence of this decade of national exposure was to reestablish town meeting as a symbol of pure democracy. But the exposure served an additional purpose. It helped to reshape images of those who attended town meetings. Turn of the century Americans had been bothered by descriptions of politely passive townsfolk indifferent to the education of their children, lacking in civic pride, and eager to sell their votes. The new image was far more attractive.

One frequently voiced theme emphasized the education provided by town meeting. Several writers noted with approval the mock meetings run by students in local schools as training for the real thing. *Life* printed a photograph with the caption "Watching democracy work, children from the neighboring school perch quietly in a rear pew" (no mention of the spit balls and pinched bottoms I recollect). Maine's Rufus Jones recalled in a personal memoir published in 1941, "It is easy to see what a school of life, what a training place of education this free democratic Town Meeting was for a wide-awake boy. I never missed a word, or lost a point. . . . It was out of these meetings of the people," he added, linking his boyhood experiences to the history of the nation, "that the Constitution was born and government of the people, for the people and by the people, came into being." Gould noted with pride that "At twenty-one, the new voter is well skilled in Democracy."

The literature also emphasized both local and national civic pride.

The former was evident in the care exercised in raising and allocating tax monies for the betterment of community life. The latter shone in the very rituals of town meeting—the Pledge of Allegiance to the flag especially. "When it was all over," *Life's* writer noted, "they brought in the flag, locked their hall and headed home, glowingly conscious of their role as heirs and servants of a glorious democratic tradition."

No commentator mentioned corruption. Quite the opposite, in fact. "The self rule which they provide allows no room for graft, red tape, or abuse of public office," wrote *Colliers* of a meeting in Cornish, New Hampshire. The reason: New Englanders were "individualists." Gould insisted that "absolute independence characterizes Town Meeting (capitalization of the term had by now become commonplace). No one tells a Yankee how to vote, no one dictates; and only another Yankee persuades."

"The final authority in town meeting, when you get to the bottom of it, is God and a man's conscience," one Cornish resident said to the *Collier's* reporter. What if the two were in conflict? "God hisself done some things I'd hate to have on my own conscience."

Practicality and thrift topped off the newly emerging portrait. The terms applied both to expenditures and language. Stories about the unwillingness of New Englanders to spend money have been around for a long time, but what earlier had often been associated with civic indifference and cheapness now had positive connotations. "Making do" had national appeal in a time of shortage. At the level of language the phenomena was new. The pithy, pointed, understated retort which today serves as the basis for much regional humor was in part a product of the town meeting revival. My favorite example comes from *Colliers*. When asked why he voted against paying the selectmen any salary, a native reportedly answered, "Politics comes high enough anyhow, without having to pay extry for the politicians."

John Gould understood the implications of all this as well as anyone. "Town Meeting," he wrote, "may have developed from the Yankee frame of mind, or the Yankee may have developed from Town Meeting, but they go together like pork and beans and one explains the other." Clarence Webster acknowledged the same connection when he gave his study of Yankee culture, published in 1945 as part of the American Folkways series, the title *Town Meeting Country.* Both Yankees and Town Meeting had been the beneficiaries of a dramatic shift in national sentiment.

Predictably, the heady romanticism generated by international conflict could not be sustained once the war ended. "Town Meeting of the Air" stopped broadcasting. Academics, their curiosity piqued by all the hoopla of the forties, began serious study of town governance. Some decided that the actuality bore little resemblance to prevailing image. Two Columbia professors reported that to their surprise the praise of town meeting by Gould and others was "mainly folklore, a sentimental devotion to a past misunderstood and a present vastly exaggerated." The failure of most citizens to attend town meeting, several emphasized, made mockery of the "pure democracy" theory. One critic quoted a newspaper report from Athol, Massachusetts: "Despite a dramatic effort by the Fire Department last night's second town meeting session failed to attract a quorum. . . . The Department staged a fake fire at Town Hall, complete with a general alarm sounded on the warning system, screaming sirens, roaring engines and flashing lights in an attempt to attract townspeople to the building."

In the mid-sixties the editors of the *National Civic Review*, a professional journal that had published dozens of articles on local governance, applauded what they considered "the inevitable drift away from this precious but outdated and outgrown memory of the past."

Myth shattering, of course, is a well established academic tradition, and it is not surprising that political scientists should find town meeting less than perfect. What does surprise is the number of academics who came to the defense of the institution. Most visible among these was Joseph Zimmerman whose *The Massachusetts Town Meeting* appeared in 1967. His conclusion—"the open Town Meeting has proved a lithe and tenacious institution which demonstrates that government by mass meeting of interested citizens is still possible." Andrew Nuquist had come to an identical conclusion in a study of Vermont town government.

The national media, meanwhile, kept town meeting in the public eye. The *Saturday Evening Post*, *Harper's*, *American Heritage*, and regional magazines with a national audience—*Yankee* and *Vermont Life* especially—all provided coverage. *Newsweek* couldn't make up its mind how to treat the subject. In 1962 it ran an article headlined "Farce Down East" which poked fun at "local historians and starry-eyed artists like Norman Rockwell" who sanctified town meeting. Four years later it wrote about "this venerable and distinctly American institution" which was "still a spry and vital form of government." One wonders whether the editors were consciously trying to make up for past sins.

National television contributed to this visibility. The initial exposure grew out of the first-in-the-nation New Hampshire presidential primary which is still held on town meeting day.

As early as 1964 *Yankee* writers noted, with obvious pleasure, "the eyes of the nation—the lens of television—and the voice of the press all focused on New Hampshire's Big Town Meeting Day." Town resolutions protesting involvement in Vietnam were dutifully reported, packaged with observations about "the people" exercising their right of free speech and "participatory democracy." A friend of mine even recalls hearing de Tocqueville quoted on one nightly newscast.

By the early 1970s the critics were in full flight. Retirees, yuppies, and refugees from the "establishment" all began flocking to rural New England, in part because they wanted to participate in town meeting government.

President Carter spoke at an elaborately staged special town meeting in Clinton, Massachusetts, to demonstrate a campaign pledge to stay close to the American people. Antinuclear and acid rain protesters, with full cooperation of the media, used town meetings to gain national attention. Citizens from Mississippi to Oregon organized public sessions modeled on what they read about or saw happening in New England. Town meeting, as it had been in the century following independence and World War II, was back in the limelight.

As an enduring symbol of popular government, town meeting can't be beat. Yesterday United Press International called—they wanted an interview about New England Town Meeting. Tomorrow is meeting day in Hanover. I just might attend.

[Town meetings] "have proved themselves the wisest invention ever devised by the wit of man for the perfect exercise of self-government and for its preservation."

THOMAS JEFFERSON

Checking in at the Northwood Town Meeting 2010.

Members of the Harvey Lake Women's Club— Helen Sherman, Peggy Montgomery, Mary Billings— serve lunch 1962.

Big smiles around the stove pipe warm the Northwood Meeting House 1966.

6

One Town Representative of Many: Northwood through the Years

Why Northwood?

New Hampshire native Sara Josepha Hale set her 1827 novel *Northwood* in the small town of the same name. Traveling east to west, from Portsmouth to Concord on the First New Hampshire Turnpike, Northwood is the last town in Rockingham County. It's considered a seacoast town, though the closest it comes to the Atlantic is the view on a clear day from the top of Saddleback Mountain or from Upper Bow Street on the Ridge. In the novel, an eldest child gets plucked from his large, hardscrabble family in Northwood and relocated to the home of his wealthy but childless aunt and uncle in the Deep South. There he bumps up hard against cultural differences between the North and South. He's particularly conflicted about the dependence of the Southern economy on slaves. When he returns to Northwood as a young man, the differences between Northern and Southern lifestyles and values reveal themselves dramatically. It's a fascinating social study disguised as a romance by an author best remembered for a children's poem, "Mary Had a Little Lamb."

But this literary claim to fame is not the reason I chose Northwood for my focus on town meeting over the early decades. I could have chosen any town. The records are there: in libraries, town historical societies, the state historical society, and the state archives. I chose Northwood for two reasons. I've lived here for thirty-three years, so far. I'm not a native, but the citizenry doesn't seem to hold that against me. Over those thirty-three years my husband, daughter, and I have grown familiar with and fond of this place and its people. We don't know everybody in town (there are more than 3000 of us), but we know a good many. Naturally I was interested in researching my home place.

That was one factor. The determining factor, however, was Marion Knox. Marion is not a native of Northwood either, but her husband's family traces its roots to the shore of Pleasant Lake back several generations. Marion and Joe Knox have lived in Northwood since 1967. Both have served the town in a number of capacities. Joe's been town treasurer for more than twenty years. Marion worked as administrative assistant in the town offices. After retiring from that job, she ran for selectman as a write-in candidate against an incumbent. "I had also put myself on the ballot for the budget committee," she said. "Here I was running for budget committee and write-in for selectman. I got 400 votes for both, which was unheard of. Then I had to decide. I took selectman. If people wrote my name in 400 times, they can find somebody else for budget committee."

Asked what drew her to town government and public service, she said: "I guess it was just meant to be." After high school she worked for an insurance company and an advertising agency. When she and Joe married and had children, she immersed herself in volunteering for the church. "I'm just the type of person that liked to be involved in doing things. Maybe I got it from my father's father who was an alderman in Lawrence, Massachusetts. Maybe it's in my genes."

Always up for a project, several years ago she embarked on a massive one—to organize by topic (schools, roads, cemeteries) the selectmen's minutes and town meeting minutes all the way back to incorporation in 1773. The early minutes were handwritten, with ye olde hit-or-miss speling of the tymes. Some town clerks had good penmanship. Others scribbled and took a good deal of deciphering. "Edith Schawb's minutes were always exact," Marion said. "You could read every single thing that she wrote. It was a pleasure to copy hers, really."

Some minute keepers stuck to the dry facts; some commented on the proceedings. Arlene Johnson, who served as town clerk for twenty years and retired just a few years back, "put a little bit of something in once in a while. She had quite a nice way of doing it."

Generously, Marion entrusted me with three thick notebooks on early town meetings (the first hundred years, give or take). Her labor of love and civic interest details the development of town meeting in Northwood. Much of what went on in those gatherings was boiler plate and repetitious, same as today. But every once in a while an item pops up that indicates a shift, seems historically important, or suggests a good story. The bulk of this chapter comprises highlights gleaned from her research.

Also included: information from two town histories: *The History of Northwood, N.H., 1878–1946* by Roxanna Spiller Richardson and *A Guide*

to the History and Old Dwelling Places of Northwood by Joann Bailey, pub-
lished in 1973, then revised and republished in 1992. I also consulted *Town
Government in New Hampshire: The New Hampshire Historical Records Survey
Project, 1940* to see how state laws influenced town government.

In the Beginning

Town meeting arose out of need—the need to band together in the wilderness. Town meeting arose out of the need for these settlers to look out for
one another—their physical needs, their political needs, and their souls.

As needs changed, so did the meetings and, eventually, those changes
were codified as law. Just as selectmen must by law perambulate town lines
every seven years to make sure the town still sits where it's supposed to, you
are invited to perambulate some highlights and lowlights of Northwood's
early town meetings. Hopefully, this perambulation will provide a sense
of the lay of the land for town meetings in many towns during those times
beyond the memory of anyone still living.

The authors of *Town Government in New Hampshire* call it "amoeba-
like"—the way states and towns were formed in early New England. In
1680, New Hampshire separated from Massachusetts. In 1773, Northwood,
home to twenty-six families, separated from Nottingham. By all accounts
these separations were amicable, the natural division of the large tracts of
land awarded by the English crown to the original proprietors: "Mother
towns gave birth to daughter political units." In fact, town government
came before either state or county government. New Hampshire had
towns before it was New Hampshire; heck, it had towns before it was
Massachusetts. Our earliest settlements, Portsmouth, Dover, and Exeter,
"existed for several years as virtually independent republics under a town
form of government prior to the early sixteen-forties at which time they
came under the jurisdiction of Massachusetts."

Northwood, not more than twenty miles northwest of Exeter as the
crow flies, came much later to the game—130 years or so. But it got straight
to work. At the first town meeting held on March 23, 1773, residents voted
in "a Comitey to setel with the town of Nottingham" along with "Four
shilinges loful money for scoling." Translation: Four shillings of lawful
money for schooling. From the beginning, the education of our young
people took priority.

Town officers were elected the following year when the call came for:

All freeholders and inhabitants of the parish of Northwood qwalified by law to act in parish affairs to meet at the house of John Harvies in said parish of Northwood on Tuesday the twenty-second day of this instant March current at ten of the clock in the forenoon and when met first to choose a moderator. 2ly to choose a parish clerk. 3ly to choose the select- men. 4ly a constable and all the officers as the law directs. 5ly to see if the parish will raise any money to supply the parish with preaching for the present year or any other votes that the parish should see fit to pass.

Benjamin Hill
Samuel Johnson Selectmen

Church and town are one entity, the parish. The John Harvies house, the site of the first meeting, was the first of several Harvey Houses belong- ing to John and his relations built near the body of water that came to be called Harvey Lake. Some of these dwellings still stand, including one built in 1782 that, according to Joann Bailey's *Guide to the History and Old Dwelling Places of Northwood*, caused "'general comment' at the time of its erection, for it is a big building with several uncommon features" includ- ing "the arched drip caps over each of the first floor windows." That Harvey House, like so many old dwelling places, passed through many incarnations, most often as a tavern and an inn.

Bailey's book also provides information on Samuel Johnson, one of the men who called that second meeting, earning the title Town Father. In fact, according to Bailey, "Few of the first settlers of Northwood are as well remembered as Samuel Johnson." A plaque marks the ledges, known as "Sam's Rock," where he spent his first night in town, then wilderness. Sam made the exploratory expedition. He deemed Northwood an accept- able place to homestead. He and his wife, Lydia, settled here in 1765. Many Johnson descendants still reside in Northwood. A well-known landmark, Johnson's Dairy Bar, though no longer run by the family, serves ice cream and food to travelers along the First New Hampshire Turnpike, also known as Route 4.

At that second town meeting, selectmen were empowered to "chang rangways for highways for were they are wonting." Folks traveling the roads found them "wonting." (We still find some of them wonting, particularly in frost heave season.) Residents depended on good roads, and complained when they didn't get them.

At that meeting voters also formed a "comity to fit a place for to set a meting house on." If you're going to have town meetings, you need a space big enough to accommodate the crowd. As the town grows—and these early settlers seemed optimistic about growth—you can't always depend on holding meetings in somebody's front room. Today, Northwood town and school meetings attract more than a hundred voters, sometimes closer to two hundred. Having outgrown the town hall, they are held in the gymnasium of the elementary school or high school.

Joann Bailey paints a stark picture of what life must have been like for those earliest settlers:

> Both men and women worked ceaselessly on the business of providing enough food to keep their families from starving and to give them some kind of shelter, however primitive, as a protection against the severe winter weather. The first settlers came on foot, bringing with them only those possessions they were able to carry. Thereafter nearly everything they used had to be made or grown here. The early settlers came from Lee, Hampton, Salisbury and other towns where sawmills, gristmills and tanneries had long been established and where there were fields and roads. Blacksmiths, coopers, shoemakers, tinsmiths and tailors worked in these towns to provide the necessities. The Northwood settlers had been accustomed to living in houses offering relative comfort and protection against the weather. They had livestock to supply meat and milk and eggs and wool. In coming here they began all over again, learning to wrench a living from the land in the same way their great-grandparents had done a hundred years or more earlier.
>
> The new town of Northwood was barely started when the colonies began their fight for independence from the British; Northwood men and women assumed their full share of the sufferings and sacrifices of those trying years.

The Beginnings of State Government

In the same year that Northwood was taking its first wobbly steps as a town, our state government also began to take shape. As with town government, all it took was a few men, an idea and a declaration to get the ball rolling. In this case, Robert Hill, Joshua Furber, and Samuel Shirborn called for a "Convention at Concord in said state on the tenth day of June next for the sole purpose of forming and laying a permanent plan or system of government for the future happiness and well being of the people of this state, and to pass any vote or votes relative thereto that may be deemed expedient. All persons concerned are desired to attend."

Taking Up Matters Large and Small

Scanning the minutes of the early meetings, one held in 1778 catches the eye. That meeting was called specifically to address whether "Maray Grant should have her things from Nathaniel Moril's and live where she youst to live." Seems the town involved itself in matters great (the creation of a state government) and small (where Maray Grant would live). Oh, the story that simmers behind the question of Maray Grant's things and place of residence. Who was she to Nathaniel Moril? And Nathaniel Moril to her? Did they have a falling out? Did he hold on to her stuff in hopes of holding on to her? Or was it spite? Where did she live before? And with whom? And doesn't it seem grossly unfair to our enlightened, modern eyes that the men of the town got to determine the fate of Maray Grant and her things, since only male residents of means were allowed to vote in those days?

To our disappointment, the minutes of this meeting were all too brief: "Jerel Hodgdon chosen and voted moderator. This meeting desolved." So which way did the vote go? Or was a vote taken? The minute taker left out the best part! Maybe everybody in town knew all about Maray Grant and her business, so he didn't feel it necessary or appropriate to record that business in the official record. Or maybe he just forgot.

A year later, 1779, the Revolutionary War officially touches Northwood when Nathaniel Chandler, William Walles, and Levi Dearborn were "chosen a commite to hire three men to serve in the Contenental Service durend the war." The names of the three men "hired" to go to war do not appear.

That same year fourteen citizens voted for and three voted "agin" the plan for state government formed at the convention in Concord, electing Asahel Blake to attend. In 1780 another six men were sent to serve in the Continental Army for three years. Men were paid to serve. And men could pay *not* to serve. In addition, the selectmen were tasked to "collect our proportion of beef for the Continental Army."

But the consuming issue at that town meeting was not war but roads. The roads must be "open and paisable: in the event of "blocking snows." Each man must work "upon the rodes, two days on a single head." And those slackers who "wont work or refuse to work on the rodes when legally warned shall pay a bushel of corn per day or the prise of a bushel."

Yes, war was being waged elsewhere, but close to home the roads must be clear so people and goods could get where they needed to go. And those who benefited most from the roads were asked to pay for them: Isrel Hodgdon must pay for the land his "rode" goes over on the way to the Caswels. And Calup Clough must pay for the "rode" through his land.

Do We Really Need Those Streetlights?

Two hundred and thirty years later, at the 2010 town meeting, Northwood decided to let one of those paths through the woods—the upper end of Old Mountain Road—go back to nature. We voted to reclassify part of it as a Class A Municipal Trail. Nobody drives on it anymore—too rough. And nobody lives out there. Let it be preserved as a place for cross-country skiers, hikers, and bird watchers.

As for the roads we maintain for travel by automobiles, trucks, motorcycles, and so forth, instead of asking each able-bodied person in town to put in a couple days labor or ante up a bushel of corn, we appropriated $639,400 that we'll raise in property taxes. That's about $180,000 for help and equipment, $250,000 for paving and reconstruction, $50,000 for highway cleaning and maintenance, $150,000 for snow and ice control, and, while we're right there, $325 for street lights.

The frugal Yankee asks: Do we really need those streetlights?

Rules is Rules

After the annual meeting of March 18, 1794, petitioners called for a fresh meeting in April to revoke the votes of the March meeting, which were not "insearted in the warrant of said day." So on April 28, voters gathered and a motion was made for a poll. "The moderator ordered all of them that was for confirming the votes as if they had ben insearted in the warrant to stand on the righthand and all those that was for reconsidering to votes to stand on the lefthand and ther was thirty-three for reconsidering the votes and ther was fifty-six for confirming the votes. The moderator declaered the votes to be confirmed and not reconsidered."

So a meeting was held and nothing changed. But the rules were followed and, no doubt, the sticklers satisfied. Over time the rules have multiplied. Timelines for posting announcements of meetings and warrants have been established and are strictly adhered to. The wording on those warrant articles has been refined and legally vetted. Right to know laws have been established to make the workings of town government transparent. No back room politics allowed. Great care is taken to do everything properly—making the jobs of selectmen and school boards more complicated and creating the need for layers of administration: managers, secretaries, bookkeepers, administrative assistants, technology gurus. The business of preparing for and implementing the decisions made at town meeting goes on year round. And the public is always watching.

Dry No More

In 1799 Josiah Bartlett gained the selectmen's blessing to "retail distilled spirittown liquors." Meanwhile, crime rears its homely head and perpetrators shall be punished when it is voted "that the SelectMen shall prosecute those who have trespassed on the Town's Land," in particular the parsonage lot. Were the culprits cutting wood? Squatting? Hunting? Whatever their offense, the selectmen would handle it. Meanwhile, the issues of roads and taxes were reconciled, at least for those living in the section of Northwood called Griffin Town. Those "what live in Griffin Town" would be permitted to "work out their Town, State and County taxes" on their road.

A special meeting in August of 1802 took up the question of dividing the parsonage lot—one half for the Congregational Society and the other to the Baptists. Negative on that one; the lot would remain intact. But yes on the question of falling fifty acres of trees there. Most towns established both school and parsonage lots with the idea that any profits gleaned from logging or other uses would help support those institutions.

At that same meeting the decision was made "that SelectMen cause Peter Blasdel's wife to be removed out of Town forthwith."

The mix of church affairs, affairs of domestic life, perhaps morality (one surmises some moral judgment with the eviction of Peter Blasdel's wife), and the harvesting of trees seems a strange one, but in those days town meeting was a catchall for problems in need of solutions.

Stray Mare Colt

Come into the inclosure of the subscriber on the tenth day of Feby inst. A stray mare colt three years old dark bay, about 13-1/2 hands high trots all & is now impounded in Northwood Pound. The owner may have said colt by paying cost & damages.

Daniel Hoit
Northwood, Feby 26th 1803

Of Stones and Bones

A time to reap and and a time to sow, a time to live and a time, in 1804, "to see if the Town will vote to appropriate a part of their land at the Upper Meeting house for the use of a burying yard." Thomas Knowlton, Joshua Hoit, and Samuel Johnson would determine the setting and dimensions of the burying yard on the Parade for the first of Northwood's five public cemeteries. L. Sherman Elliott, Jr.—cemetery caretaker and supervisor since 1970—counts at least sixty-four small, family cemeteries in addition to the public ones. He writes, in the town history:

> The custom of burying one's family members on family land nearly stopped with the creation of public cemeteries in each of the town's districts. Many of the deceased were moved to these newly-purchased lots and given new headstones. Following Yankee tradition, the old stones marking these graves, some only a few years old, found new use as porch and foundation supports, steps, workbench tops, or as shelves in a cool cellar.

That same year, 1804, was also a time to kill crows: Voted that every person in town who "shall kill a crow between now and our next annual meeting shall be entitled to 12 cents per head half that sum for young ones, provided they deliver the same to the selectmen."

And that was back when 12 cents was real money!

To raise money needed to paint the Congregational meeting house, Johnathan Clark, Samuel Johnson, and Solomon Bickford were instructed to plan, build and sell four pews in said meeting house. The practice of selling pews to raise money for construction or renovation was a common one. The pews provided reserved seating for families and showed community spirit, similar to the modern practice of engraving stepping stones or bricks with donors' names when they contribute to, say, an addition to the library or the new gazebo in the park.

A special meeting in August of 1804 authorized the building of one hundred rods of stone wall on the school lot to be inspected by the selectmen. Evidently the building of that stone wall couldn't wait until the regular meeting in March.

The report on the November meeting shows just how detailed warrant articles could be. Voters wanted to know they'd get their money's worth when they approved the building of a house on the school lot and hired the job out as follows:

Article ———. To see what assistance the town will give Joseph York toward building a house.

Voted to build a house on the School Lot for the use of Joseph York & family. The frame to be 30 feet by 16. The out side to be borded with good board and fethered and well shingled, four 12 squared window frames, one outside door, a brick chimney with two fireplaces, iron mantle pieces and two crain eyes, one flue oven, one room to be 14 ft by 16, the other 10 by 14 one heart work, one inside door, one closet door, and double flore throughout the house well jointed. The chamber flores jointed and abeted. The posts to be seven feet between joins and underpines with rocks from the pond. The doors all to be hung with iron hinges, the foundation for the chimney to be dug down two feet. Said house to be set where and as high from the surface as the Selectmen shall determine, all of the work to be done workman like or to the Selectmen's acceptance—any person who shall have said house struck off to him and not comply as above shall pay town two dallors and the same set up again.

Struck off to Stephen Emerson for 112 dollars.

Stephen Emerson won the job, and he'd better do a good job: the town watches and measures.

Sometimes, as we saw with Peter Blasdel's wife, the town rids itself of those whose presence is no longer desired. Sometimes, though, the town shoulders social responsibility by caring for the poor, the infirm, those unable to care for themselves. In the case of this next article, it appears that the the town instructed the selectmen to pressure Benjamin Rawlings to do his duty. Meanwhile, the town stepped in to support Hannah Hall and her child:

Article———. To see what the Town will do respecting the action commenced against Benjamin Rawlings on account of Hannah Hall's Bastard she now being a Town Charge.

Voted that the action against Benjamin Rawlings respecting Hannah Halls bastard child shall be supported & that the Selectmen carry it on.

Sometimes a Little Music is Just What We Need

In Northwood, 1808 was a banner year. The town voted to purchase one drum and two fifes for use of the Cadet Company. One imagines a parade on the Fourth of July with a band of local musicians leading the procession.

Where are they now, we wonder—that drum and those two town fifes? What a treasure they'd be for the historical society.

The saga of the house on the school lot continues. Joseph York, per vote of the town, may *have one half of the house he now lives in & one acre of land round the building for improvement.* Joseph York was slowly paying off what the town had put up for the building of that house, probably with work rather than money. In 1814, the town voted that *Joseph York occupy the house and land that he did last year.* Whatever work Joseph York was doing, the town seemed pleased with it.

Another topic taken up at the 1814 meeting was that of the U.S. Constitution, evidence that national as well as local matters were deemed appropriate to come before the legislative body. The town acted on an article "to take the sense of the qulaified voters on the subject of a revision of the Constitution." Results: 98 opposed revision and 1—Mr. J. B. Virgin—supported it.

The War of 1812 made political waves that year as well. Concerned citizens minced no words in their petition to selectmen:

> *At the present allarming situation of our National affairs our Country being invaded & the Capitol of our State threatned. We the undersigned with the impression that we ought to be prepared for defense request you to call a meeting of the inhabitants of said Town to consult on measures to be adopted & the means of defense such as arms ammunition.*
>
> *Northwood Sept. 26 1814*
> *Mason Norton, Valentine Mathes, Daniel French, Joseph Harvey, Stephen Hoitt, Richard Hoitt, Shurburn Blake, Joshua Hoit, John Nealey, Simon Batchelder, John Shurburne, Samuel Rand & twenty others.*

The selectmen called a special meeting at which voters approved several purchases and assigned Ebenezer Coe to make them: ten guns for the use of the town, fifty pounds of powder, 100 pounds of lead, 400 flints.

The British didn't invade Northwood. But if they had, we'd have been ready for them. How strange in this time of relative safety—terrorist threats to our cities and infrastructure notwithstanding—to think that small towns in a small New England state felt compelled to defend themselves against a threat of invasion.

The next year the town supported troops by voting to pay "those men who are detached as soldiers . . . to stand in defense of their Country" an additional ten dollars per month over what was "allowed the militia by Government." Yankees may be frugal, but we're also patriotic.

On July 4, 1819 this article was put before voters: "To see if the Town will take any measures & if any what measures to express their sentiments respecting the present alarming situation of our National affairs—& the war which has lately been declared against Great Britain & pass any votes or resolve relating these to which shall then be thought fit—then to pass any vote or votes that may be thought proper."

Disposition goes unrecorded, but the article itself sends a message—we stand united against a national threat. Don't tread on us.

Domestic Affairs

In 1827 the town auctioned off the care of the poor to David Davis, who would be paid $290 to "support all that are now or may be liable for support" through the year.

In 1838, perhaps hoping to ward off trouble, or in response to trouble that had already occurred, the town voted that "no spiritous liquors be sold on the Parade or near the meeting house on annual meeting or adjourned meeting days next year." Alcohol and politics do not mix. Never have.

In a housekeeping effort, the selectmen were authorized to "destroy certain papers and notes that are now in the Town Chest that they think good for nothing." Oh dear, the historian laments, what was lost with that vote? On the other hand, some culling in any household—municipal or personal—seems prudent.

As the human population grew, so evidently did the domesticated animal population, prompting a vote in 1830 to fine the owners of wandering horses, cattle, or swine a hefty $4 per infraction.

Town Officers

The creation of town officers reflects changes in town life. Legislation at the state (or colony) level opened the door for towns to fill the positions as needed. The positions and dates enacted show the activities that were central to public life and, in turn, how the towns developed. Town charters typically named the man who was charged with calling and running or moderating the first town meeting. That man might become one of three elected selectmen, the managers of the town. Many towns still have just three selectmen, Northwood included, although some boards have expanded to five. School boards, too, typically have three members, with some towns—Northwood included—expanding to five.

Town Officers (Continued):

From the beginning each town kept records of civic proceedings. This position, say the authors of *Town Government in New Hampshire*, "evolved naturally from the proprietor's clerk." The proprietors—recipients of the original land grants—were businessmen and their clerks kept track of business. Our town clerks still keep our records in order, from the minutes of meetings to births, marriages, deaths, car registrations, and dog licenses.

As early as 1680, the New Hampshire provincial government declared "That the freemen of every Town shal have power to chuse their own particular officers." No doubt moderator, selectmen, and clerk came first, with other offices added as needed. Three named in a law enacted in that year were constable, grand and petit juries, and surveyor of highways

In 1791 the broadening economy—more lumbering, farming, building, making of leather, and trade in general—is reflected in the following offices named by law: treasurer, fireward, collector of taxes, surveyor of highways, fence viewer, clerk of the market, sealer of leather, sealer of weights and measures, corder of wood, surveyor of lumber, culler of staves, hay ward and field driver.

At this time, too, the needs of the less fortunate are addressed with the creation of an office for overseers of the poor. At some point the position of pound keeper—the person responsible for putting wandering livestock in the town pound—came into being.

In 1849 it became legal for towns to appropriate money for libraries, which were also allowed to receive gifts or bequests. With libraries came library trustees.

Towns were given the right to appoint measurers of wood and bark in 1879. Four years later they were required to do so.

In 1893, the law made way for building inspectors.

With cemeteries came cemetery trustees. With trust funds came trustees of trust funds. Eventually towns would establish boards to oversee parks, playgrounds, and recreation. Planning boards and boards of adjustment were established to control building, land use, and growth. Municipal water systems required water commissioners. As voter checklists became standardized, towns needed supervisors of the checklists to keep them updated. Expanding police departments led, in some towns, to elected or appointed police commissions. Some towns, even now, elect their chiefs of police. Some, including Northwood, elect their road agents.

And to keep everybody and all the numbers in line, every town and school district retains an official auditor.

We Are the World

This note from the minutes of March 2, 1842, illustrates a broadening world view: "Voted that the Selectmen purchase a small globe for each school district in town."

In 1843 an attempt was made to lease land and part of the town hall to the "Academy Corporation hereinafter to be established." It would take nearly twenty-five years for the Academy, now called Coe-Brown, to be built at a cost of $1000, paid for by the issue of 100 shares at $10 each. Coe-Brown is one of just two remaining public-private academies in the state (Pinkerton Academy in Derry is the other). Public-private academies are run by a board of directors but may accept tuition money from the town. They used to be fairly common.

But Northwood wasn't quite ready for an academy in 1843, so the article was "dispensed." Later the town voted not to pay the "Superintendent School Committee" for their services. Even then, it appears, there was tension between school and town, the value of education pitted against the value of good roads, caring for the poor, and the building of "a suitable desk in the town house for the convenient transaction of town business." One pot of tax money, many uses.

On the other hand, the town was ready to "send Dolly Piper to the Insane Hospital six months and longer if the Selectmen think it best." Here we see the selectmen living up to the name Town Fathers. We still call them Town Fathers, even though many of them are women.

Trouble and More Trouble

Seems the Town Fathers and others suspected their neighbors of modesty (that's the polite word for it) in reporting their holdings for tax purposes: "Voted that the Selectmen put every man under oath in giving his inventory."

A mite of trouble in 1844 required a vote at town meeting "that the Selectmen be instructed to have the windows brought back which belong to the town house." Do we detect a whiff of misappropriation? Somebody helping themselves to something that didn't belong to them? Where did those windows go? And what did the town house do for windows in their absence?

Another faux pas (or as I like to say "fox pox") comes to light with a vote directing the selectmen to "refund to Capt. John Sherburn, an Error, if any, on his tax by taxing the Bickford farm to him after it was sold and his house after it was distroyed by fire."

Momentous on the Mountain

One line from the town meeting of March 9, 1847 rings with historic significance: "Voted that the slaves on the mountain be liberated immediately." Were these the only slaves in Northwood, we wonder. Who owned them? What was the impetus to free them at this time? Once liberated, did they stick around?

That year the round number of $1000 was slated to be raised "for town purposes." Eleven men bid for the job of caring for town paupers at the town farm. Bids ranged from $295 to $1500, with final disposition left to the selectmen. The winning bidder would be responsible for the "poor now on the Town Farm together with Dolly Piper for the present year."

The building of a town pound was approved with the selectmen given the job of locating a suitable spot.

The highway surveyors received the go-ahead to "lay out what they think proper in cleaning out the South Ditch so as to make the Turn Pike passable in the winter."

And, fair's fair, the parsonage lot rent would be equally divided between the three religious societies in town.

Town House at Last

A second 1847 March meeting, held on the 27th at the School House in District No. 4, took up the question of building a new town house, after the old town house burned earlier that same month. Here's what happened:

> Voted that a committee of five be appointed to report to this meeting what kind of a Town House shall be built.
>
> Voted and chose for said Committee the following persons—Jonathan Hill Jr, Ezra Tasker, J. R. Hoitt, H. J. Clark, Philip E. Bartlett.
>
> Voted that the Town House be erected on the Parade.
>
> Voted that the New Town House shall cover 1600 sq. feet of ground.
>
> Voted that a committee of three be appointed to superintend the building of the new Town House.
>
> Voted and chose the following persons for said committee—G. C. Buzzell, H. J. Clark, Ezra Tasker.
>
> Voted that the above committee locate the New Town House on the parade where they think proper.
>
> Voted to raise $500 for the building of a Town House in addition to $1000 raised at an annual meeting for Town purposes the present year.
>
> Voted to build the Town House and pay for the same the present year.

At the 1854 town meeting, voters agreed to let the bells ring out at the Free Will Baptist Meeting House twice a day, if the Selectmen could find "some person to do the job for 25 dollars for the year ensuing." We wonder, after all these years, why that bell needed ringing. And why the town saw fit to pay for it. The article illustrates that church and town remained closely tied. References to using money raised from the parsonage lot come up at many town meetings during the 1800s, as do references to using money from the school lot and the Literary Fund for schools. In 1855, the schools received $50 from the Literary Fund.

The tradition of voting on some of the smallest details of civic life continued. Also in 1855 Northwood voted to "instruct the Selectmen to build an avenue in front of the desk in the Town House 2 ft. wide." This year, too, James Griffin "commenced an action against Dudley Hill overseer of the poor for refusing to give up a bundle of cloths claimed to be his." After some discussion—oh, if only that discussion had been recorded—the town voted "that the whole affair be left with the Selectmen to manage as they think will be for the interest of the town." Another sensible decision by the Mind.

And yet, suspicion between neighbors continued with a vote that the selectmen "put under oath every man & woman to see how much money he or she may have." Thank goodness we now have the IRS to keep us honest.

Liquor Means Money

State run liquor stores featuring low prices remain a fixture in New Hampshire. Those just off the interstate do a whopping business with tourists. This system traces its roots to 1855 and an act by the legislature that was then put to a vote town by town. Here's how the act was addressed in Northwood. The language, no doubt boilerplate, shows a concern for quality control. Spirits were to be "pure and unadulterated." The resolution also spells out how liquor sales were to be handled and the benefit to the town coffers. Though couched as legislation "for the suppression of intemperance," clearly the more liquor sold, the better for the town coffers. When it comes to intemperance, the town gets a healthy cut.

> *Resolved that the following be adopted as the rules and regulations for the government of the town. Agents appointed in conformity with provisions of an act passed by the Legislature of New Hampshire June session A.D. 1855 entitled An Act for the Suppression of Intemperance.*
>
> *Art. 1st You shall keep for sale and shall sell only the following liquors*

Viz—Alcohol Brandy—Gin—Rum and Wines which shall be pure and unadulterated.

Art. Sd A distinct account shall be kept by you of the purchases and sales made by you in the Agency.

Art. Third You shall report to the board of Selectmen all your dealings as such agents once in three months and shall pay into the town treasury the nett proceeds of sales made by you during the time for which your report is made up.

Art. Fourth Liquors shall be sold by you at an average profit of twenty-five per cent combine until otherwise ordered.

Art Fifth You shall at every annual meeting of the town make a report verified by oath or affirmation of all your purchases and the cost thereof and of all your sales and the proceeds thereof specified the number of sales, the respective quantities and kinds sold for cash of the purposes of which he is authorized to sell and the quantity kind and cost of all liquors remaining on hand at the time of such meeting and no other particulars.

Art Sixth When any agent shall cease to act as such he shall deliver over to any other agent or to such as may be appointed agent all liquors papers receipts and other property in his hands as such agent and shall pay the proceeds of sales made by him and remaining in his hands to his successor.

> *Given under our hands this twenty-fifth day of August 1855—*
>
> *Richard Hoitt, Jr.   N. D. Caswell   A. J. Fogg Selectmen*

And Then . . . Civil War

Town Meeting 1862: "Voted that the sum of fourteen thousand dollars be raised and appropriated to encourage voluntary enlistments in the present war." Northwood, like its neighbors, did its part to support the Union cause in the war that shaped and scarred our country and cost so many lives.

Full Circle

In Northwood's centennial year, 1873, the town appropriated $500 "to aid in the Centennial Celebration to be held on the sixth day of Sept. next." Oh, and while we're at it, the town votes to pay "Lyman W. Smith fifty dollars for injury done to his horse on the road near Mr. Pillsburys."

From New Hampshire Laws of 1874

as recorded in *Town Government in New Hampshire:*

Towns are hereby authorized to appropriate money for any of the following purposes:

- Support schools
- Maintain the poor
- Lay out, build, and repair highways
- Light streets
- Repair town-owned meeting houses
- Aid hospitals
- Obtain a free hospital bed for the use of inhabitants receiving town assistance
- Aid dispensaries established for tubercular patients; or aid visiting or district nursing associations or the American Red Cross
- Encourage voluntary enlistments in case of war or rebellion
- Establish memorials
- Defray expenses incurred in decorating graves of service men on Memorial Day
- Provide and maintain armories
- Provide means for the extinguishing of fires
- Establish and maintain public libraries
- Establish and maintain parks, commons, cemeteries
- Acquire, set out and maintain shade and ornamental trees in public places
- Establish and maintain playgrounds
- Aid free public band concerts
- Distribute town advertising material
- Prepare and publish town histories
- Defray expenses of observance of old home week or celebration of anniversaries
- Maintain and record weather observations
- Support a resident physician
- Procure the detection and apprehension of criminals
- Exterminate insect pests
- Employ a town counsel
- Defray all necessary charges arising within the town

This chapter, up to this point, is just a sampling of the growth of one town through its first hundred years as told in its records. Perusal of those records over the next few decades show the development of industry—shoe factories in particular—through the tax exemptions given to get them started. We see school expenses rising as the population grows. A seminary is established—later to be taken over and used as an elementary school. In 1891 the town resolved without opposition that "a railroad to this town would be of great benefit to our industries and our people." And, in 1893, we witness the righting of an old wrong:

> Article to see if the town will vote to deed the John Grifin lot so called to Benjamin F. Kelley in full of all claims for volunteer services rendered in the War of the Rebellion. Voted that if in the judgment of the Selectmen Benjamin F. Kelley has a legal claim against the town for services rendered in the War of the Rebellion, then the said Selectmen shall deed to him the John Griffin Lot so called, the same being in full payment of all such claims against the town.

In 1894 road surveyors started being called road agents, and the name still in use for the town employee who oversees our highways, makes sure they're passable and plowed. That same year the town appropriated $25 for the library "in addition to the amount required by law." The school board received authorization to "loan books to the Academy and Seminary, as far as they use the same books that are in use in the town school."

The fire department may trace its beginnings to the vote to "purchase two or more Hand Fire Engines" as well as "one thousand feet or more of Hose suitable to be used with said Engines." The following year five fire companies were formed.

The meeting of 1895 also turned its attention to roads, and turned a corner on their maintenance, establishing the pay rate for road agents at 20 cents per hour. Voters set a schedule, deciding that "two thirds of the amount raised for repairing highways and bridges be expended in the summer and one third of the whole amount reserved for winter use. To assist with those repairs the town voted to purchase two Road Machines."

And, here comes the future: In 1897 the selectmen granted permission to the Northwood Telephone Company to erect and maintain a telephone line through town. Fourteen years later, the town voted to have a telephone installed in the Town House.

Later Years: Within Living Memory

Just as the minutes, so painstakingly organized by Marion Knox, allowed us to see the evolution of Northwood's town meeting over the first hundred years, give or take, so did interviews with longtime residents allow a look back over the last few decades.

For living memories of Northwood's meeting, I begin with, you guessed it, Marion Knox. She and her husband Joe participated in their first town meeting in 1967. Just prior to that meeting, Marion said, "We were told by a Northwood resident who Joe knew quite well that we shouldn't try to change the way we do things here! We took it to mean that whatever we did in our old state should stay there, and we should not disrupt the status quo of Northwood."

In 1967, the town was still in the practice of holding both the election of officials and town meeting on the same day. The election started in the morning and the business session started at 1:30 in the afternoon. "People would come in and vote, get some homemade baked beans from the kettle on the wood stove (the only heat in the building—and an outhouse outside), and would stay for the business at hand, sitting on the wooden benches."

Those benches still line the walls of the town hall. And they are both firm and narrow!

Within a couple years of her moving to Northwood, Marion said, "There were enough people who could not attend the daytime meeting that felt they were being left out of important decisions, so a petition was presented to change the time of the business meeting to either evening hours or a Saturday. The evening hour meetings did not last long as it made for a very long day for the town clerk and other officials, so finally the business session was changed to the Saturday after the Tuesday election—first at town hall, then, because of the number of people attending, at Coe-Brown Northwood Academy."

She recalled with amusement a lively meeting from the late sixties. A poultry inspector arrived at the evening meeting after his day's work. During a discussion, he lost his temper, caused a bit of a scene, and was subsequently asked to leave. Which he did—returning a few minutes later with several chickens fetched from his vehicle. He turned the chickens loose in the hall, then walked out for good.

Marion didn't elaborate on what happened next, but one imagines the moderator crying fowl, as well as a good deal of scrambling and squawking from both chickens and voters.

1962. Earl Linnell, Clinton D. Carlisle, and Walter Gerrish on the Bench at the Northwood Town House.

COURTESY OF NORTHWOOD HISTORICAL SOCIETY

"Town meetings became more organized as the years went by," Marion said. "However, there were certain things that stayed the same. People always sat in the same place, with the same people, and usually raised their hands to vote at the same time." *All those in favor raise your hands on the first call*, the moderator chants. *In favor?* The hands go up. *Down hands. Opposed?* The hands go up. *Down hands. The vote being manifestly in the positive, the article passes.* Or fails. Depending on the hands. Marion said: "There would always be the hecklers present, and Moderator Robert Johnson knew how to handle them."

Over the years, she recalled just a few times when outside events influenced the timing of the meeting. "Twice I can remember the meeting being recessed so people could travel to Plymouth for the boys basketball championship game. And the year that our Sunshine McVicar died tragically the meeting was recessed at lunch time for an extra hour so people could attend her service."

One other strong memory for Marion was when she decided to wear a skirt instead of her usual trousers. She sat at the head table facing the crowd, and, she recalled, "Seems like there was more of my legs showing than one man liked. During a break he informed me than I should always wear slacks when sitting at the head table, or a curtain should be placed along the front of the table! I always wore slacks after that!"

I asked Joann and Bob Bailey how Northwood's town meeting had changed over the years. Bob is a native and has served on many boards and committees in town, including the board of selectmen. Joann's been trustee of trust funds for more than twenty years, as well as serving on the Conservation Commission and the school board. She's also the town historian.

Here's how that conversation went.

JB: Of course the biggest change has been in the venue—when town meeting left town hall and went to Coe-Brown. It was so different. At town hall everybody would be jammed into that room, which isn't really very big. It would be compressed. There would be some people in the back of the room yakking away, like Rocky Magoon. Then something would get their attention and there'd be a big thing. People sitting on the long benches, the settees, would be trying to hear and would shut up the ones in the back.

The stove pipe ran the whole length of the room. Then, of course, in that same corner where all those men would be standing was the food counter. People would be serving meals.

RR: I like to sit in the back so I can see everybody.

JB: I like to sit right up front so I can be seen. I try not to talk as much as I used to. You get sick of hearing the same people. Some people, you know what they're going to say. You know what side they're on.

But, Becky, how dear town meeting is. Every year I'm so afraid that somebody is going to come up and try to push through SB 2.

BB: All I remember is (Selectman) True Chesley used to pile wood on the floor at the town hall so he could build a fire. When I got on the board, we stopped doing that. I said, "We've got a woodshed out in back. We'll put the wood out there and I'll bring it in. Piled it right in the corner, they would. Piled all the fire wood right there in the corner where they serve the food now. That was the wood pile.

The stove was up on that platform and the stove pipe ran all the way around. That's what heated the building. Hung by wires.

JB: Did you go to town meeting? You never went before we were married.

BB: Sure I did. We set on the wood pile in the corner. That's how I remember the wood pile. It's what we used to sit on as kids.

JB: Where was the food then?

BB: They didn't serve any food. The meeting never lasted long.

JB: My first memory is of having to choose whether I would go to town meeting or school meeting. How many years did that go on?

BB: It went on for years. But town meeting didn't last but a couple of hours. What'd we have to talk about?

RR: What did you talk about?

BB: Town roads mostly. School meeting, nobody even went to it. Wasn't nobody there but you and a couple other people.

JB: I remember that first year I chose to go to school meeting, because that's what I was interested in.

BB: At the Legion Hall.

JB: Am I right in saying at the same time you were having town meeting people could come in and vote? So they'd come in, walk up, and vote.

BB: Polls never closed.

RR: On a Tuesday. People took a day off from work.

BB: Right. I think Strafford still does. They don't have any budget committee or anything. They're entirely different. They get their town and school over in one day, I think. There didn't used to be so many articles, so many warrant articles.

RR: The last few town meetings everything's a secret ballot.

JB: Let them do it. That's our effort to not go to SB 2, so they can't say they're not able to vote in private.

BB: Without town meeting, all those people couldn't get up and talk.

RR: You're not fans of SB 2?

JB: It's much more cumbersome. Sandy, Charlie's wife, works in Gilford, so we hear about Gilford nowadays. It goes on and on. Starts with the deliberative sessions in January and doesn't finish up until May.

BB: And no one goes to the meetings except the budget committee. And they're still fighting over the rules of it. They can't decide the way to interpret the rules. Everybody does it differently. Every town is different. It's just ridiculous. Regular people can't get up and talk with SB 2, cause there's nobody to talk to. Nobody to listen.

JB: We don't even vote at town hall anymore. We vote at the church. Safety issues. I was so against it and so sad about the change, until last year's November [2008] voting. That never ever could have gone on at town hall. When they came to vote for or against Obama, they just came in waves that day. Somewhere around 250 newly registered that day and then voted. I felt overwhelmed at the end of the day at having been a part of something really great.

RR: What do you love about town meeting?

JB: The repetition of it. Being a part of tradition. How long it's gone on. And how unique we are. I like to see the same people and am impressed with how many people you don't know, sadly.

One of my best memories from being around voting last year is this woman I know, she was at both town and school meeting. She's in a wheel bed. A thing comes around her head. If she can make her head go to the left, it moves it that way and so on. For a long time, she had a scooter. I was just so overwhelmed that she would go to the effort to be there. She and her husband were there—and she told me frankly they were there to vote against the budget. Her husband has had to give up his job to care for her. He said they just couldn't stand any more taxes. They didn't prevail. I thought, Such devotion. They weren't angry. They were needing for the taxes not to go up.

She was able almost without a voice to be able to voice it.

I had some fun little moments. You know Jean Lane always has her candies. I said (to the woman in the wheel bed), "Can you eat a candy?" She nodded her head. I said, "Do you need me to unwrap it?" She nodded her head. I said, "Do you need me to put it in your mouth?" She nodded her head and I did. She had her piece of chocolate.

RR: Jean Lane and her chocolates! She knows how to look after us.

JB: I want to remind you of Bob Lowe's little thing. When I was doing research for the town history, Bob Lowe said he thought town meeting was different way back, way back before my time, because the community was smaller and people gathered. There were lots of stores, all up and down Route 4, because some kid had to be able to walk to the store to get a loaf of bread. Bob Lowe said, all winter long, because the stores had stoves and were warm, people sat around and discussed everything and knew what was coming, so town meeting went quickly.

Of course, now they have tweeter and all that stuff.

RR: Has the tenor changed?

JB: I don't think so. People don't get quite as overwrought as they used to. They could get some upset. Although some still do a pretty good job of it.

I think there's more control than there used to be. We started having to register when you came in and get your card. There used to be none of that.

I think most of us who consider it all think anything is worth it to keep town meeting. Let them have secret ballots every other article if that will keep people from saying, We can't do this anymore because people will know how I vote.

RR: If we lost town meeting, what are we losing?

JB: Well, we're losing the elemental form of government. To me, that's what you're giving up. I know there are a few who have jobs and can't attend. Our neighbor down the street works in a place that produces power for a big company down in Massachusetts, and he has his shifts. Someone like that couldn't easily go. But there are so many who don't go to town meeting who could. Oh, they say, that's always the day I buy groceries, or that's always the day I go visit Grampa. That doesn't cut any ice with me.

I think town meeting is efficient. To me, from hearing people and reading about the SB 2 procedures, I think this is much more manageable.

I think for most of our lives as we live them today, we have less feeling of community. Town meeting is a way of staying connected. When you have kids in school you're connected to all that. Maybe it's a way of staying connected after your kids are grown.

I would like to add, I feel I can make a difference. I feel like I have made a difference over the years. I've always been so proud of when we voted the new school building, the first eight rooms. It was a week to the day after my fifth child was born and I was at that meeting. There were people all over town doing telephoning. It was a big effort.

RR: Was the baby with you?

JB: She must have been. Where else would she have been?

A Favorite Son

The Robert A. Johnson Highway in Northwood (previously Mountain Avenue, previously Route 43) is named for the man who, likely, holds the record for the longest stint as town moderator. First elected in 1938 at the age of twenty-two, Bob kept the lid on town meeting in Northwood with grace and good humor for sixty years. He served as School District Moderator for almost forty years. He also served in the New Hampshire House from 1941–50 and 1984–2007. Some say he controlled discussion at the town hall with the woodstove. He'd let the fire die down to cool things off; or instruct his assistants to pile on more wood to get people sweating.

Marion Knox said: "Bob could handle hecklers. He had a way of saying, Let's wait a minute. Let's think about what we're doing here. He'd either start on a little tale or else he had the right words to say that would quiet things down. He always had a little tale to tell."

When Bob died at the age of ninety-two in 2009, the town of Northwood lost a favorite son. In this picture from the Northwood Historical Society, Bob shows off his new baby boy at town meeting in 1966.

Robert Johnson, moderator, with his new son and a supervisor of the checklist, 1966.

COURTESY OF NORTHWOOD HISTORICAL SOCIETY

*Washington
circa 1978*

7

Pure Democracy: Town Meeting in Washington in the 1970s and 1990s

by Ronald Jager

Ronald Jager, one of the finest chroniclers of rural New England life and history, described at length the town meeting of 1976 in his history of Washington, Portrait of a Hill Town, which was co-written with his wife, Grace. Later he turned his firsthand account into a chapter of his book Last House on the Road: Excursions into a Rural Past. Much of that chapter is reprinted below, with a few omissions to avoid repeating what's been said in other parts of this book. The 1976 meeting expanded into a portrait of the way meetings ran throughout the 70s—the characters, the issues, the process and procedures, the dynamics. Then he painted a second portrait—Washington town meeting in the early 1990s, when Last House on the Road was published. What was the same? What had changed? What was lost? What was gained? Who among the old guard remained, and what did they think about the evolution of the town's oldest, continuous tradition?

Jager's thoughtful look at town meeting in Washington is, I think, a masterpiece on the topic. You know what they say about the gorgeous rolling lawns of English estates? Question: "How do you get the lawn so nice?" Answer: "Three hundred years of daily maintenance." Same with Jager's portrait of town meeting. Question: "How do you know so much about town meeting?" Answer: "Go to the same one for forty years in a row and pay attention."

Jager's longevity in Washington, his engagement with his neighbors, his keen powers of observation, and his insightful analysis make for an extraordinary look at one town's meeting across decades. His relaxed yet graceful writing style catches the undercurrents, crosscurrents, and vitality of the gathering.

Have town meeting's essential qualities changed much between the 1970s and 1990s? (Or between 1776 and 2011, for that matter.) I don't think so, but judge for yourself.

Is this pure democracy? Judge for yourself.

Pure Democracy

Act one: The 1970s

One institution is ambivalently cherished more than any other in Washington, and that is the annual town meeting. Here is the community in a nutshell—democracy still pure and proud and free.

Our town maintains its practice of devoting the entire day and as much of the evening as is necessary to the town meeting. (Roughly speaking: the smaller the town, the longer the town meeting and the larger the percentage of the town's business done there.) Each annual meeting has its own character, its own combination of contentious issues, filibustering, generosity, high spirits. In the blue of memory all the Washington town meetings of the early 1970s swirl and dissolve and gather into one sustained act. Let it be 1976, the year of the two hundredth anniversary of Washington:

Townspeople begin to gather and cluster in the Town Hall about nine-thirty. The room is cold and most leave their outdoor wraps on. Someone says he remembers "when this room was het by a wood stove." But no one now alive ever saw it in its original form, before this ceiling created a second floor above and closed off the galleries. The meeting room is now plainness itself. Only the remnants of the original panel, the old glass of the windows, the worn floors, the deacons' benches, and a few fine pillars suggest its actual eighteenth-century vintage.

Women are behind the counter at the south end of the hall making coffee, laying out homemade doughnuts, "town meeting cakes," and sandwiches. The three supervisors of the checklist have spread out the large handwritten sheet with the names of the town's registered voters: 184 in 1976. Winonah Babb, town clerk of Washington since 1953, has arrived with two ten-pound leather-bound Town Record books. Once in a while the moderator will call upon her to clarify what the town actually decided by asking her to read from The Book. No one ever questions The Book.

More townspeople jostle in as ten o'clock approaches. There will be up to one hundred voters throughout the day, two or three dozen of them will show up only to vote for town officers and to linger a while and leave. Donald Crane, moderator, is checking his watch. The three Selectmen, suitably suited and tied, have joined Winonah Babb in the raised box on the north side of the hall, where the pulpit used to be, and Crane now joins them. The atmosphere is brisk, chatty, informal. Only in the telling of it, or in the selective chapters of memory, is there any solemnity, for everything

Recipe for Town Meeting Cake

Bake at Your Own Risk

    Sometimes called Election Day Cake, this hearty cousin to the fruit cake is designed to stick to a voter's ribs, and tide him or her over the long day of hard-core civic exercise. Linda Stradley, on her web site *What's Cooking America*, offers several variations, including this one from *American Cookery*, a cookbook by Amelia Simmons published in 1796.

> 30 quarts flour
>
> 10 pound butter
>
> 14 pound sugar
>
> 12 pound raisins
>
> 3 dozen eggs
>
> One pint wine
>
> One quart brandy
>
> 4 ounces cinnamon
>
> 4 ounces fine coriander seed
>
> 3 ounces ground allspice

    Wet flour with milk to the consistency of bread over night, adding one quart yeast. Next morning work the butter and sugar together for half an hour, which will render the cake much lighter and whiter. When it has risen . . . work in every other ingredient except the plums,* which work in when going into the oven.

*The amount of plums is not specified, nor is the temperature for the oven or length of cooking time. With these details, you're on your own.

in this chamber is entirely relaxed, casual, familiar. Washington, a city-state perched in the hills, has assembled to express itself, to enjoy itself.

Yet, imagination needs to strain only a little to see this hall as a stage with a drama about to begin. The actors are checking the props, to see that the pieces are in order. Everyone is part of the cast: living theater, democracy-in-the-round, and there is no real audience, except the eye of tradition and precedent, and so no one is self-conscious. The neighborly disassembly begins to compose itself now that curtain time approaches.

There may be some expectancy in the air after all, for this enactment reaches back across the town's two hundred years to the first town meeting with more continuity than anything else that happens here. Then as now the agenda for the meeting, called the warrant, was posted by the Selectmen in February, and in March the people left off what they were doing—which was not very much—and came to this place. On this spot they struggled and quarreled, made friends, made laws, made history; here they debated and shouted, compromised, voted, spent and saved, learned to win and lose with dignity. From these walls, hundreds of times, the independence of the town and the importance of "the-will-of-the-people" was amplified. Here and now, and within twelve hours, the framework for the next twelve months will be constructed with slow and steady strokes. There are several dozen articles on the warrant, and on each one a motion will be discussed until no one wishes to say anything more; only then will there be a vote.

Donald Crane begins absentmindedly to finger the gavel, which is very familiar to his hand, like a pipe to a habitual smoker. He has fingered that gavel, twirling the head in his hand, for several hundred hours since he was first elected town moderator in 1964. Everyone in town simply assumes that he will be moderator for the foreseeable future. Now it is ten o'clock and he taps lightly with his gavel on the slab of polished granite at his elbow—the sound is a brittle click, lacking authority—and declares that the annual town meeting is in order. It isn't really in order, but that is because everyone knows what he will do next. He will proceed immediately to read the warrant, every word of it.

In 1976 there were twenty-six articles; in 1876, there were thirteen. Almost everyone has picked up a copy of the Town Report by this time; many are following the moderator's reading; others are trading quick bits of whispered talk with their neighbors ("Sugarin' yet?" "Thought I'd wait."); others are blowing on a cup of coffee, settling in. At least a dozen people are sitting in exactly the same place they sat last year, and the year before, and the year before that. There is a comfortable buzz; the orchestra tuning up while the conductor runs through the score . . .

After the reading of the warrant, the next order of business is ceremonial: the moderator takes the large wooden ballot box, opens it, shows the assembled voters that it is empty, locks it, hands it to the police chief, who delivers it to the ballot clerks, who will supervise the voting throughout the day. The voting process for town officers was changed during the 1970s. Until the recent past townspeople could expect to be met at the Town Hall door by aspiring candidates handing out small slips of paper with their

Reading the Full Warrant

In many towns the tradition of the reading of the full warrant at the start of town meeting is long gone. Instead the moderator entertains a motion to dispense with the reading of the warrant. Voters say "yea" and the moderator moves on to read just Article 1. Read, vote. Read, vote. Saves time. But sacrifices some of the poetry, some of the substance of tradition found in the protracted reading of the whole, the laying out of the whole right at the beginning so folks can see where they are and where they're headed, get a sense of how the articles stack up one to another. Those towns, like Washington, where time is allotted for the full reading, understand this.

The full warrant is always printed in the town report so folks could take time to read it silently—but where's the community in that?

names written on them—a clear signal that the person was running for some office or other, but only the grapevine knew which. Some candidates disdained the brazenness of doorway electioneering and depended on their constituency to write down the proper name at the proper time. One by one the town offices were then filled: the voters passed by the supervisors of the checklist and the police officer to the moderator, who put each ballot in the box as he called out the voter's name to the clerk. A majority of the votes cast was required for election, and this meant that second and third votes were not uncommon. It was a very time-consuming business, but it left room for alliances to form and shift with the winds. When the victor was finally identified, he or she was sought out and sworn in on the spot.

Such, or approximately such, was the practice in Washington for almost two hundred years, a method which dramatized democratic procedure. I think it might now be called "quaint." It certainly was monumentally inefficient: it took an entire morning, and often more, to complete the town elections. For a century and a half, or perhaps almost two centuries, this did not seem a major drawback: there was time enough; elections were important enough. What brought change to Washington had more to do with justice than efficiency: not everyone who wished to vote for town officers could take time off from a job to be on hand through the entire morning. A ballot system, adopted in 1972, which allowed voting for town officers at any time during the day until the polls were closed, at 9 or 10 p.m., permitted every citizen to vote

Now the meeting is in full gear. Discussions are lengthy, male voices predominate, written ballots are frequent. Time was, years and years ago, when the moderator's uncertainty how to call it on a voice vote was resolved by a show of hands. Not any more; uncertainty is now always resolved by a secret written ballot—just as we used to do with electing town officers. The principle of the secret ballot and the principle of uncurtailed debate are treated in this town with a piety reserved for few other things. Punctuating the long meeting with a frequent "paper ballot," as it is called here, relieves tedium, rearranges the seating, fosters sociability, extends the market for coffee and sandwiches. Other than this, the twelve-hour marathon is broken just once, with a recess of sixty minutes at noon. The meeting presents a neat paradox: the high pitch of political self-consciousness, and the low key of the process itself.

At eleven o'clock we receive a delegation from the village school, the children filing in and sitting for a time at respectful attention. This is a civics class, field trip, and glimpse of the local road show all rolled into one, a you-are-there slice of local history-in-the-making. They have been well coached. But they soon discover that it is not an epiphany: becoming restive, they are led away. Was not Democracy a more solemn and lofty thing than this? Aren't these just the old folks down the road talking about that old backhoe? Yet, the subtle mystique of the meeting will take on artful and cunning forms, working on the spirit of the populace and making it hard to imagine any other way of executing community affairs, forming a granite sense of local process.

The road agent, Robert Crane, gives an oral report, full of force and forthrightness. He knows "it's a tremendous lotta money I'm askin' you folks to spend," but he reports that "we've had pretty good luck on the equipment this year," the extra help "have been doin' a real good job." Like a road grader he plows full throttle into the uneven qualms and queries of the town, making rough places plain, gearing down to meet the toughest spots: "You people have been awful good to me; and I'm not going to stand here and say we can't get along another year without this new machine; we can." So perhaps we can postpone it? Not at all: "we don't get a chance like this often . . . wise investment for the town . . . if we had to hire this kind of work . . . my thought was, if I see a place where I can save the town a buck I ought to be churning up the sod to get to it." Some say he could sell ice in Lapland.

Steadily, patiently, slow as the early sap, the meeting marches on.

("Please be courteous to the speaker; you may not be interested in what he's saying but he is.")

Hours pass. By mid and late afternoon, few have any sense of the time, and there is still no sense of hurry. Obligations at home have been arranged for. Mothers go home, nap the children and return; informal rump sessions convene at the post office and the store. Whereas a hundred years ago sixty barns with cows waiting to be milked hurried the democratic process, now there are but two. (Frequently in the 1930s and 1940s the annual school meeting was held in the afternoon on town meeting day after town business was disposed of—years that seem gone forever now, gone without regret.) Time to decide, let the world wait. Talk, tobacco smoke, coffee, and adrenaline substitute for eating. Agreement seems easier; the world more remote; everything that matters is right here. Marathon negotiating and group therapy, those sophisticated urban pastimes, were surely born in the New England town meeting.

Discussion ambles crosswise through the warrant, sniffs and then nibbles gently at the edge of controversial tidbits and is briskly snapped to heel by the moderator. Always there is one formidable issue doggedly pursued, often two or three: the cemetery wall, a new addition to the garage, the town dump, land use regulations, a new road. They are issues that most people deplore—and wouldn't miss for anything. Sometimes we seem to celebrate the length of our meetings just as we celebrate the severity of our weather: we think both derive from natural causes, and both confer virtue.

In 1976 James Hofford took a tape recorder to the town meeting and asked veterans how the meetings of today compared with those of yesterday. Calmer, some said, not so exciting; people don't get so riled up like they did; people used to speak out more, shout even. "Oh, we used to have some warm ones," says Ernest Cram, who has been observing them since the beginning of the century. Others said people are more considerate now, they think more about the town than about themselves. And others that the meetings are just the same as always; they were always pretty good; still are. Some remember when men used to spit tobacco juice at the sawdust box beside the stove before they talked; some wish the women would talk more, "but they never have, much—except Elba Chase . . ." Nostalgia for an earlier, heartier race merges with a conviction that things are still fundamentally in place—and entirely unpredictable.

Ghosts of the recent past hover above the chamber: Wally Chamberlain shuffles to the front, removes his weather beaten hat (surely an heirloom), grins like a leprechaun, respectfully moves to dismiss the article. Then he replaces his hat. Formality mingles with informality; most stand to speak, and Oliver Chase has kept the "Mr. Moderator" tradition alive for years. An Otterson warns of a dangerous precedent about to be set, a Barker appeals to some civic virtue, a Hofford sums up the views of a dozen others and then joins the consensus he has just postulated, a Crane deplores some new state restriction, a Rolfe appeals to decency and detail, a Niven looks to the future, many voices cite the past. About once every twenty years John Tweedy speaks, cutting neatly through the issues with a quiet logic.

Someone asks why the insurance on the Town Hall is so low—would it not cost many times that much to replace it? Is this an oversight, or what? The meeting, suddenly hushed, sucks in its breath, waiting for explanation. And many might respond, but it happens that Ralph Otterson, fireman, puts matters into perspective with succinct eloquence: "The insurance is mainly to cover repairs in case of serious damage; you cannot really insure the building for what it is worth: insurance won't cover that. This building is priceless; it could be repaired, but it cannot be replaced." Silence. The words strike home. The meeting exhales. Today's lesson—"priceless." Then we return to business.

The moderator keeps order and keeps out. ("It's your meeting. I'm not here to sway it, just to run it.") He knows this audience, knows their views, knows whom to recognize first and last, knows from long experience how to elicit the drama and the consensus, and how to keep chaos at bay ("it seems to me there's an awful lotta noise here, not real loud, but an awful lot of it"); knows parliamentary procedure and how to use it; knows how to solicit a motion or frown and puzzle one to death; knows how to inject his fiscal counsel ("that's the policy of havin' it and spendin' it, instead of spendin' it and then trying' to get it"); knows and employs everything a good moderator needs to know. Knows especially how to sway a meeting by running it. They say he turns to granite if he is losing, but they don't often see him losing. . . .

A free people reared in the town-meeting tradition may have a political outlook slightly different from that of Americans of other traditions. Here people may have a sharper belief that things are and ought to be within their control: have a different understanding of the meaning of the ballot, for our ballot makes law, levies taxes, decides controversies, and does not merely elect others to do these things. Hence too the yearning to believe that all government ought to be like local government—and is creditable to the degree that it is. And from this derives the local wariness, shading into active distrust of far-off governments and of politicians not present for accounting; and thus the contrast, echoing through the town meeting, between "them and us."

How long will this style of governing endure? It is not fragile, for it is tough as the landscape to which it attaches, but it is a political culture exposed to wear and tear from within and without. Within—these hallowed forms of democracy contain little that has inclined the town, for example, to regional cooperation, or to broad viewpoints, or even to seeking out modern means to preserve the cherished ways of the past. And without—there are many prowling legalities, state and federal, administering life, wearing down the local initiative from the swift pace of life, shortening attention spans and fostering impatience with the familiar manner wherein, by drift of talk, prejudice, and instinct, the latent spirit of the community slowly finds itself. So the margins wherein the local mind can be brought to bear seem to be narrowing and the time available to detect that mind and apply it seems to be shortening. Both facts may breed resignation—and a dark awareness that the same American culture which still idealizes the small town may be quietly subverting it.

But nothing subverts the underlying sense of equality among citizens, which is the strength and the genius of the system. It is a sense of equality that is not so much a theory or an ideal but simply a fact—rooted in long community experience and perhaps even nourished by the natural environment. Here the very frame of life itself is composed, not by the systems and hierarchies of men, but by the earth and its seasons, its beauties and caprices, a system which is no respecter of persons and is a great equalizer: the sun shines and the storm beats on the wise and foolish alike.

During the 1974 town meeting, the plan to write the history of the town was being discussed, when a blunt voice from the back shouted: "What's the purpose of the history?" The challenge was aggressive, and the implication in the town was evident: it's likely to cost money, what's it for, what's the point of a book? The inquiry fell into a roomful of glum silence. How to respond in a few words? Moderator Donny Crane slowly scratched his ear, gazed without expression at the window, twisting the gavel in his hands, and then with an evenness in his words that might have gone for pride, he guessed that the purpose was "just to tell it like it was . . ."

Act Two: The 1990s

Now it is another town meeting in Washington, nearly twenty years later. March 8, 1994, nine o'clock, and we have assembled for our 218th annual gathering. Today we are nearly a hundred strong, with more drifting in— almost twice the number that gathered twenty years ago. As of old, we will be here for the next ten or twelve hours, and we will love every minute of it, even the parts we came to loathe.

Who are we? We are Swamp Yankees, Natives, Newcomers, and Flatlanders; we are the Knitters and the Needlers in the center, fingers working all day long; we are the Standees in the back, with caps on; we are those of the Folded Arms Club, and those of the Flannel Shirt Society. We are Everyman: carpenter, farmer, mason, electrician, housewife, teacher, writer, artist, factory worker, secretary, shopkeeper, computerman, radio-man, businessman, real estate agent. And we are retired folk: banker and businessman, clerk and bureaucrat, truck driver and factory worker, scientist and civil servant. We are far, far more varied in our professional lives then we have ever been.

How many of us here today were present for the two hundredth town meeting in 1976? A third of us at most. Two dozen, maybe, have an attendance record that goes back farther then that. Yet a few—Cranes and Ottersons, for examples—have been coming to this town meeting all their lives as did their parents and grandparents. Somebody has to represent continuity.

For today's meeting, as always, many citizens slip into their roles, and some slip into uniforms. At the head of the room is the moderator, Michael Otterson, who continues the town's long tradition, almost unbroken, of having a native son in that position. The moderator always wears a suit and tie on town meeting day, part of his ensemble, part of our tradition. This is a ceremonial occasion, after all, he is king for the day, and he should look the part. Beside him are three Selectmen, executive officers of the town, who are responsible for just about everything. It's sometimes called a thank-less job, but when they leave office we always thank them.

The police officer is in full regalia. Uniformed, badged, and probably armed, he adds a touch of color and authority to the air. He keeps a watchful eye on the ballot box until the polls are closed. And he usually presents the police budget for the ensuing year, pointing to the local crime statistics, assuring us that it could have been a lot worse, but for our assistance, et cetera, et cetera—just look at Massachusetts, for example. We think about Boston for a brief minute, gazing out the window at the clean snow, and remember why we live here, and pass the budget with a voice vote. Not every year, of course. Once we drastically cut a proposed budget for the police department, and the chief resigned before the town meeting began, so we cut the budget again. The position may exceed selectmanship in thanklessness, and we run through police chiefs at a pretty brisk pace in Washington, as do other small towns.

The fire chief is here, also fitted out for the occasion, uniform, badges, buttons, and a name tag that says "Robert Wright, Fire Chief." Not that we didn't know. He will present the budget items for the fire department, and he long ago discovered what the local police also have known, that when presented by uniformed officers proposals get more support, or at least respectful acquiescence. Anyway, under his chiefdom the fire department has become a well-equipped and highly professionalized organization.

The road agent is here, with a budget big enough "to read without bifocals," somebody said. In fact his budgets have been flat lately and the roads relatively smooth, so he will get what he asks for, which may be less than what he needs, without having to admit, as did his predecessor, Robert Crane, that he is asking for a "tremendous lotta money." Although he is.

The radios are here, too, dozens of them, resting like pistols on the hips of firemen and rescue squad members. Wherever these citizens go, they go radio-armed. Like the American cowboys of the mythical Wild West with a holstered six-gun, they can draw their radio and spring into action or form a posse to face an emergency. These are our Minutemen—except that they are not all men and they respond in seconds not minutes. That's one way the community takes care of itself: several dozen patrols always at large, radio-armed, alert for trouble and trained to fix it. Should we wonder that there are but muted votes against their budget proposals? Police, Fire Department, Rescue Squad—you want to vote against apple pie? Not I. I have had their trucks roar in to fight a chimney fire, and I have been carried out of the woods on a litter by these troops. The "ayes" have it.

In 1994 we are no longer meeting in the Town Hall at the center of town. Although we have one of the few surviving specimens of eighteenth century meeting house architecture in New Hampshire, it is now vacant on town meeting day after 204 years of unbroken service. On the village green, together with the school and Congregational Church, it forms a justly famous and historic composition. Over the years, the interior of the Town Hall has been altered many times, the outside hardly at all; it still houses the town offices, and at various times it has served as school and church and dozens of other things. But the space available for the growing annual town meeting became inadequate, and it is not handicapped accessible.

When erected in the summer of 1787 it was called the Meeting House; in the next century, when the Congregational Church moved out, it came to be called the Town House; the twentieth century knows it as the Town Hall. By whatever name, it housed our annual March town meetings more than two hundred times. . . .

In 1992 the meeting was moved from its historic setting into this larger space a mile away at Camp Morgan . . . I felt a personal sense of loss at the move. That's mainly a Flatlander's response, I found; few natives complained. Some suspected, however, that in a new and alien setting, without the brooding witness of the old familiar walls, a chamber alive with memories and echoes of memories, we might make unguided decisions. Moderator Michael Otterson has a different view: he believes we were so crowded in the dimly lit Town Hall, invading each other's private space as it were, that it may have made us edgy and cranky. The brighter light and larger space we now use puts us in a better humor, he feels. Others say our better humor is to be ascribed to the moderator's skills in that office. It's an argument the moderator can't lose.

I took a casual survey of opinions of town meeting veterans about how our meetings have changed. Among others, I talked to Phil Barker, Robert Crane, Bobby Crane, Julia Dunton, Jim Gaskell, Michael Otterson, Ralph Otterson, Bill Rhoades, Jim Russell, John Tweedy. I asked, What has changed significantly in our town meetings during the last couple of decades? For better? For worse?

Here's a sampling of what they said:

- "What's changed the most, I feel, is confidence in our leaders. You know, thirty years ago, some people—and usually one or more of them was a selectman—were simply above reproach. Now it ain't that way. We're suspicious."

- "Changed? I think it's the financial complexity of the issues; it makes us mentally withdraw from the process. There are fewer and fewer places to apply plain common sense."

- "Oh, I dunno, I think possibly *I've* changed at least as much as town meetings have. I'm not quite so romantic about it. I now sometimes feel: Do I have to listen to all that?'"

- "I think our meetings are more democratic than they used to be. When I came here a few families had almost total influence. There are now more voices, more kinds of voices, heard from today. I think Mike is probably more fair than Donny. Actually, I think the meeting is better than it ever was."

- "Like the general quality of life, I think it's probably going downhill. There's bureaucracy and number crunching now, and things are so much more complicated. Less of the Norman Rockwell, I guess—though it is still democratic as hell. I still love it."

- "We're more impatient, I think, than we used to be. Twenty years ago we could just worry a bad idea to death, or let it go away, now we think we've got to kill it."

- "There are too many people that come up here from the city, with their city agenda. They oughta listen a few years, and find out what's going on."

- "I don't think the meetings *have* changed that much—not that I can see. Wouldn't miss it for anything."

- "We've become security nuts: we're forever yakking about liability and safety. Our speechmaking is saturated with talk about litigation, insurance, liability, indemnity, state mandates, security. Where is our confidence? Our supposed self-reliance?"

- "Well, they're not as interesting as they used to be. We used to have some nice family-type fights. And I really miss Oliver Chase and Wally Chamberlain, guys like that. We used to have some real characters."

- "I notice that there are a number of people who don't come anymore, and I wonder about that; and this year the crowd was smaller than last year, even though the checklist is longer. Is that going to be a trend? People are less likely than they used to be to take off from work for town meeting."

As with most subjects, there is more than one viewpoint.

Several remarked on the clearer air in today's meetings. Air? I was reminded of how, less than twenty years ago, we did our business in a haze of thick-enough-to-slice-it tobacco smoke, such as would not be tolerated today. From the first, American democracy was nurtured in tobacco smoke, but those days have gone the way of town meeting spittoons.

Most of my neighbors alluded to the rapid growth of the town, and always with regret. The population census numbers for our town from the Office of State Planning are these: pop. 162 in 1960; 248 in 1970; 411 in 1980; and in 1990, 628. Only a small proportion of the newcomers make a living within the town. Many are retired folk, many are people who can retain their professional connections elsewhere and live here in the countryside, some have day jobs they can commute to from Washington, a few are back-to-the-landers. The town today has almost twice the population of 1976 (628 vs. 320), but three times the number of registered voters (554 vs. 184).(Many registered voters today are summer residents who aim to register cars and take out insurance from a New Hampshire address.) The numbers may be confusing, but the fact is that the town has grown more rapidly recently than at any time since the early years of the nineteenth century—and yet our population is nowhere near the 1140 it had reached in 1840.

Starting about 1850 our town slowly declined in numbers each year for over a hundred years, beginning to grow again only in 1960, going from 162 to 628 in thirty years, part of a trend echoed in dozens of New Hampshire towns. Reflecting on town meetings of the 1970s, I observed the many threats to the way in which, "by drift of talk, prejudice, and instinct, the latent spirit of the community slowly finds itself," drawing upon "unimaginable patience while consensus gathers." It seems an every-receding ideal.

Today, as usual, we cover dozens of topics, and we appropriate hundreds of thousands of dollars—a hundred and seventy-six in the first five minutes, an astonishing record. We take up highways, cemeteries and trust funds, 911 Emergency systems, and the fire station furnace; we discuss dogs, tax maps, and pagers; we vote on recycling, the library, on complying with the American Disabilities Act, on Class VI roads, the town forest plan, the Town Hall boiler, diesel fuel, tax deeds, and the summer program. We consider how to reconstruct Cram's corner, sponsor an Old Home Day, close the landfill, and buy a new computer. Are we knowledgeable about all these things? We will be before we vote—or we just might vote No. We go on to Welfare and recycling and tax deeds and Marlow trash removal, and move on to health insurance, retirement benefits, tipping fees, and block grants.

We spend nearly two hours on the matter of bringing the Town Hall into compliance with the ADA law, and decide to postpone it. Not much comes up that we can't handle.

All the money appropriated by us today is raised by our property taxes, so there is a direct and extremely well understood connection between one's vote and one's tax bill. I can easily calculate before I vote that the new grader will add about one hundred and twenty-four dollars to our tax bill. Since no other taxes are so directly related to our decision-making we tend to take it as a model: indeed, town meeting government panders to the idea that this method of taxation is the only legitimate form. Any wonder New Hampshire has a generally negative view of taxes?

And we like our meat raw. Please don't give us information cooked by committee. In fact, skip the committee step entirely, since any intervention between people and data is deeply suspect. We save our jeers for the idea of appointing a committee to study something. We'll all decide right here, thank you. The basic idea is that a proposal does not gain credibility but actually loses it by having a committee process it! Even departmental budgets that are winnowed by the Selectmen (or a Budget Committee—perish the thought!) interfere with pure democracy. Committees don't clarify proposals, they contaminate them. Give us the bare facts, and then "let the people decide"—that's the battle cry.

Does this make sense? No. But it makes our democracy purer. The visitor new to this process might be appalled at this attitude (some are), feeling that it would make sense only on the assumption that the folks at town meeting have perfect pitch in judging miscellaneous raw data, without advice, study, or investigation. Well, maybe we do; anyway, don't tell us we don't. But the visitor will find it rather touching, too, for its absolute faith that the process on the floor, in all its noise and showmanship, its bluster, confusion and occasional eloquence, could not possibly be improved upon. And the visitor can eventually see something more subtle: everybody has a chance to put in an opinion or ask a question. The merit of that is completely intangible but very real. Someone might not care to contradict a committee, but she'll tell us what she thinks of the raw idea and go home satisfied Democracy is a messy business; pure democracy is messier still.

All this works out in practice better than our visitor will think it deserves to. Long-winded discussion often eventually exposes the weak spots in a budget or an idea that needs more thought. This makes it safe to vote against it. Yes, with some committee processing we might have had a matured idea we could be for, instead of a half-baked idea we are against. So there is a built-in conservative drag in the process. Is that regarded as a criticism? Not here.

Last year we had a roaring raw meat debate on the school bell. The bell is old style, heavy cast metal, operated with a rope. We have built a new school, but the old school building still housed the bell in its tower. Should the bell be moved to the new school? Well, there were two schools of thought on this, both eager to pay tribute to local history—or something. One side led off with the assertion that respect for tradition and historical continuity required that the old bell be moved to the new school, to serve a new generation; the other side wanted to leave the bell in its tower in that original historic building, which was on the National Register, after all. During the long and eloquent debate many hands were in the air, as if everybody in town had an opinion on the bell's destiny. Eventually someone managed to squeeze in some simple questions. Would the bell be used at the new school? When had the bell last been rung? Nobody could remember. Somebody thought it may have rung on the Fourth of July in 1976! A teacher said schools, well, don't use those old bells any more. Alas, all the fun seemed to go out of the argument. "Hey, it was a good fight while it lasted," said John Tweedy.

Random advice from recent town meeting discussions: "If you are for it and everyone is speakin' against it, why are you sitting on your tongue?" On the fine points of the Land Use Ordinance, Hans Eccard, in a rich German accent: "It's insulting and un-American." Marty Harrison, perhaps the best Christian in town, being rebuked by the moderator for using a profane phrase: "We'll have no more of that." On the workload of the selectmen: Donny Crane quoted as having said, "The worst thing that could happen to Washington would be to have selectmen who had time to do the job." On the town's computer system: "It's a dinosaur, and was when we bought it, but it does a few things slowly and it's bulletproof." On the unpredictability of town meeting: "It's like you never know what's going to sell at a garage sale." Robert Crane, snapping his suspenders and lecturing a relative newcomer on the rules of Washington: "In this town you do not oppose God, the Shedd Free Library, or the Purling Beck Grange." Moderator Otterson on a question too extended: "If the question is longer than the answer, it's too long." On the noon recess: Whereas we used to break "for dinnuh," the motion in 1993 was to break "for lunch." Probably not a good sign.

Every town develops its own traditions about the shape and character of its annual town meeting. Always there is the tendency to think that there used to be more local color to relieve the beige of business as usual. Some towns still hold all-day meetings as we do. Ours often reaches far into the evening, and three times in the last decade we have recessed after about twelve hours to complete the business another day. Many towns meet only in the evening, sometimes two evenings. Some towns have a Budget Committee, with considerable authority to process spending proposals before they are presented to the full meeting. Every year we read of towns that romp through their work in a couple of brief hours. To our ears, that sounds scandalous, maybe even treasonous. What kind of commitment to democratic decision-making is that? I have never heard anyone in Washington express admiration for a town that does its annual business in a few hours.

We prolong the business by dispensing with certain standard rules. For example, we don't "move the question" if there is anybody who still wants to speak. The moderator follows the ancient rule that we are ready to vote when nobody has anything more to say. Our tradition of the secret written ballot may be the town's favorite fetish. When the voice vote is too close to call, it is never resolved by a show of hands but by a written ballot. The law requires a ballot vote if seven voters request it, but we have a standard of privacy seven times that high: we have a written ballot if one person asks for it, usually by just shouting "paper ballot." This quaint practice of a once-small town was elevated into a fixed principle of democracy by Donald Crane, our much-admired town moderator for twenty years, and it still sticks. People believe in it. With a secret ballot my neighbors are shielded from the dangerous knowledge of how I voted on the road grader. Usually it works: the meeting has to take a break now and then, and the "paper ballot" is one way to do it. Someday sheer numbers and the bother of it all may force common sense out of hiding and we might have to decide things by a show of hands. It will be warmly resisted.

. . . Equality is still the first principle of our town meeting, and patience is still its salient virtue. Perhaps it takes a special faith to believe that anything so simple and sophisticated, so enduring as town-meeting government could have derived from a haphazard process, something not thought up or written down. Some may prefer institutions to be invented out of whole cloth—the way the U.S. Constitution was all made up during one long hot summer.

Certainly there are cynics and others who say the town meeting is dated or outdated, that it doesn't work anymore. But those who speak this way are seldom citizens participating in the process. They are those, one native confided to me, who are paid to sneer. But some do quietly fear that the old meeting house stylistics are fading: gone or going are the wonderfully leisurely cadences of the day-long, night-long town-meeting decision-making of the 1960s; gone or going too are the "unimaginable patience" that impressed us two decades ago.

Maybe so. But we are not ready for elegies yet. We still meet for a dozen or more hours every year, and nobody expects or wants less. A larger and more diverse community, maybe we now have to *create* a consensus where we used to be able simply to *find* it. But we do it. Eventually most foolish ideas are flushed out; most half-baked ideas postponed for a riper day. Yes, it's monumentally inefficient as government; but it's very effective as education. Anyway, nobody around here thinks efficiency is the highest good.

Some of us are now and then concerned that the person who tries to take the measure of town meeting in Washington again in twenty years' time my be looking out upon a vastly different town. What if there is then only a short evening meeting attended by a tenth of the voters, and no hassle? Then it may be time for elegies. But right now our tradition is still free and proud and strong: three hundred and fifty years old in New England, almost two hundred and twenty in Washington. The institution is sill robust and sometimes eloquent, still widely praised and often disparaged, usually surprising and still imperfect, but deeply beloved and believed in, still our purest form of democracy.

8

Langdon: 208 Years and Counting

L angdon boasts the most consecutive town meetings in the same hall in New Hampshire, possibly New England—208 years without a miss and the tradition continues in the picturesque meeting house beside the picturesque cemetery at the picturesque town center. Built in 1803, the meeting house hosted town meeting that same year, though the building wasn't quite finished. Flash forward 209 years and the building is still under construction, undergoing substantial renovation and restoration guided by an active Heritage Commission.

Located close to the Vermont border and Connecticut River, Langdon sits (one might even say, nestles) between Walpole and Charlestown—each of which ceded land in 1787 to form the town, named for John Langdon, a Revolutionary War patriot and longtime governor. According to Frank Burnside Kingsbury's *History and Genealogical Register of the Town of Langdon, 1787 to 1930*, Governor Langdon was so pleased with the naming, he pledged to "present a bell if the town would erect a belfry to the meeting-house." Unfortunately, the town did not act swiftly to build its belfry. The wheels of pure democracy sometimes turn slowly—many voices to be heard and many votes to be taken. In the end, as "the governor died in 1819, and as the steeple was not erected until 1851, the town lost the much desired Langdon bell."

Originally part of Cheshire County, Langdon moved (without actually moving) to Sullivan County in 1827 when that county was created. The people of Langdon, evidently, wanted to stay where they had originally been; they voted four times in 1828, 1830, 1831 and 1832 to secede from Sullivan and return to Cheshire, but the state legislature and courts did not support their petition. So in Sullivan County they stay.

The population of Langdon approaches 700 (up from 337 in 1970), but it's not unusual for 200 voters—an unusually high percentage—to show up for town meeting, putting the old hall just about at capacity. I asked what

Langdon Town Hall

the fire department had to say about potential overcrowding. Not much, I was told. The firefighters sit with the police at the back and stay pretty quiet. In an era when many towns complain that their meetings are under-attended, Langdon is justifiably proud of its robust citizen participation.

The earliest town meetings in Langdon were held in private homes. The first meeting following incorporation took place on March 6, 1787, at the home of Captain Jonas Fairbank. Between 1787 and 1803, according to Frank M. Sellers' *History of the Town of Langdon from 1787 to 1987* (the bicentennial edition), seventy-nine meetings were held. Evidently, a lot of town business needed attention early on. For several years, the meetings alternated between Seth Walker's house on Winch Hill Road and Daniel Prouty's place on Ball Hill Road. This way if you lived on one end of town or the other, every other year you wouldn't have to travel so far. Fair is fair. In the 1790s, meetings moved to one or the other of two taverns—no doubt to accommodate a growing population. (No taverns are open for business in Langdon, today. I know. I looked.)

The village proper began to take shape in 1790 when, Sellers writes, "On 5 July, the town voted to approach Samuel Stevens regarding some of his land for the use of the common and 'burying ground'. There was considerable opposition to the choice of the committee . . . and, although the timber was cleared as early as 1791, it was not until the fall of 1795, after a survey had been made establishing that the common was, indeed, at the geographical center of the town, that it was finally accepted."

Evidently folks argued quite a bit over the location of the town-hall-to-be. The subject came up at each meeting from 1791 to 1801 when it was finally approved. More than two thousand dollars was raised for construction by auctioning off the pews to be built in the hall.

There's a lot to hash over at a Langdon town meeting. Road building and maintenance, for example, have always generated lively and often lengthy discussion. In his history of Langdon, Sellers describes the different methods of "working the roads" over time. The town did not use tax money for "breaking out the roads" in winter until 1935. Before that time, people broke the roads out themselves or stayed home. "Perhaps the most different method of working the roads," Sellers writes, occurred in those early winters. "Instead of scraping the snow off, as we do it today, they packed it down, so the sleighs would have a surface to run on. This caused an additional expense in the winter, as someone had to be hired to *put the snow on the road* when it ran into a covered bridge."

Prentiss Bridge, built in 1874, is billed as the shortest covered bridge in New Hampshire, in use until 1954, when a new one was built beside it. Covered bridge aficionados still seek out the original to photograph it. The new bridge, also a short one, was built offsite and hauled in. One resident recalls: "They came to Langdon and said, 'We've got a bridge. Where does it go?'" Knowledgeable citizens pointed them in the right direction.

Another resident said, "Sometimes we've had trouble replacing bridges. On the lower road, we had a little one-lane bridge, but the state wouldn't help fund the replacement unless we had a two-lane bridge. So it's a one-lane road with a two-lane bridge," providing another photo op and a source of some amusement to residents, who shake their heads and wonder when common sense flew out the window.

Those stories and many others emerged from a memory-sharing session held in May of 2010. A group of Langdon residents heeded the call of Carole Anne Centre of the Heritage Commission. Sure enough, fifteen or so generous souls took time away from their gardens on a glorious spring afternoon to reminisce about town meeting. We met at the Meeting House. If walls could talk, we thought, they'd fill us in on 208 years of history. Well, the walls didn't have much to say, but the people did. Dorothy "Dot" Campbell, "the oldest person that was born in Langdon," graced us with

*Dorothy
Campbell*

*James Cheeney
15th Generation
in Langdon.*

her presence as did James Cheeney, all of six months old, who spent the afternoon being passed from arms to arms. James represents the fifteenth generation of his family living in Langdon. Others at the session included:

- Caroline Cross, seventh generation in town ("on two sides, Ma and Pa"), who's served on the planning board, as supervisor of the checklist and on the Heritage Commission.

- Rodney Campbell, third generation, building inspector, planning board member.

- Eleanor Vanderpool, longtime Community Club member.

- Alvin Clark, seventh generation, owner of the first bison farm in town.

- John and Rita Gulardo, moved to town just five years ago, but are great town boosters and feel right at home. John, a professional photographer, serves as unofficial town photographer.

- Dennis McClary, Heritage Commission.
- Marilyn Stuller, who's served as selectman as well as on the planning board and zoning board.
- Katie Holmes Gallagher, Heritage Commission.
- Andrea J. Cheeney, tax collector and member of the Heritage Commission (also mother of little James Cheeney).
- Millie Kmiec, not a native but whose husband, Joe, was born in Langdon in 1922.

In anticipation of the meeting, Carole Anne Centre sent out an invitation for folks to "put on their memory caps" and write down their stories. Here's Alvin L. Clark's response in his own handwriting.

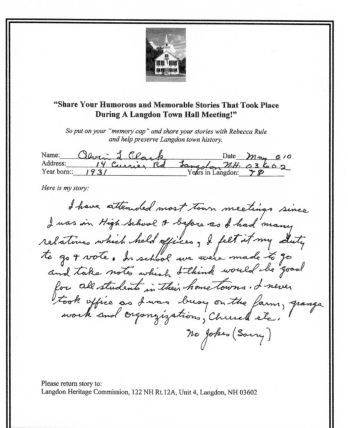

"Share Your Humorous and Memorable Stories That Took Place During A Langdon Town Hall Meeting!"

So put on your "memory cap" and share your stories with Rebecca Rule and help preserve Langdon town history.

Name: Alvin L Clark   Date May 0 10
Address: 14 Currier Rd   Langdon N.H. 03602
Year born:: 1931   Years in Langdon: 78

Here is my story:

I have attended most town meetings since I was in High School & before as I had many relatives which held offices, I felt it my duty to go & vote. In school we were made to go and take notes which I think would be good for all students in their home towns. I never took office as I was busy on the farm, grange work and organizations, Church etc.

No Jokes (Sorry)

Please return story to:
Langdon Heritage Commission, 122 NH Rt.12A, Unit 4, Langdon, NH 03602

Most people didn't write their memories down, but came prepared to talk. The town seemed well represented. I recorded the discussion on audio tape. It was hard, after the fact, to distinguish one voice from another—especially when folks got to talking all at once—which they did, a lot. But here's the gist, an affectionate picture of a close-knit community. My questions are in italic; the answers combine the comments of those present.

What do you value about town meeting?
— So many people come. A lot of people, town meeting is the only time you see them all year. And everybody talks. Some more than others.
— We do get together on other occasions—Memorial Day is always a big event that brings a lot of people out. There's a parade from the school yard to the cemetery—about a hundred yards. And a big display in the Meeting House, photos and write-ups about all the folks from Langdon who've served in the military, and those who died. For a small town an awful lot of young people have served their country.
— It's a participatory town. An extremely high percentage of registered voters participate in town meeting and vote in the elections.

To what do you attribute the high turnout?
— Not much else to do at the end of winter.
— Town meeting and sugaring time bring everybody out of the woodwork. We haven't seen each other through the long winter.
— Usually the best town meeting is the meeting the night after town meeting at the sugar house.

What happens there?
— We reenact town meeting (lots of laughter).

What are some of the traditions of your town meeting—things that happen every year?
— We raffle off the quilts. The ladies of the Community Club make a quilt each year and it's raffled off at town meeting as a fundraiser, though tickets are sold beginning in September.
— People were a little disgruntled when certain names were pulled and they weren't at the town meeting to get the quilt. They still won the quilt; we'd contact them after the meeting. Some who buy tickets aren't year-round residents. I was pulling the names at the time, so I decided next time to have a little child pull the name. The little child pulled a name. It wasn't mine! But it was the name of the president of the Community Club. People kind of lifted their eyebrows at that.

*Quilt at
Langdon
Town Hall*

Eyebrows were lifted?

— Eyebrows were lifted. Back along, the Community Club made pot holders. Mrs. Kendall always said every lady should make a hundred holders every year. I guess it was a hundred. She was quite strict about it.

— As a little kid I would go and watch the ladies work on the quilt at the parish house.

— It was against the law not to give something at a raffle. When people bought a ticket on the quilt, they'd get a pot holder, so it wasn't technically gambling. They were actually buying a pot holder—just one pot holder no matter how many tickets you paid for.

The Quilt Raffle

According to the town history, the Community Club evolved from an earlier organization, The Ladies Benevolent Social Society formed in the mid-1830s. The tradition of the quilt goes back to a time when chances for a raffle item couldn't be sold outright. Chance takers bought pot holders so their names could be entered into the raffle. The pot holders went for ten cents each until 1972, when the price was raised to twenty-five cents. May Holmes, age 94 years when Sellers wrote his history, was still sewing 100 pot holders a year.

What was and is the money used for?
— Now it's mostly scholarships.
— A lot of the money went to children who needed their eyes tested or needed glasses. The Community Club would pay for them.
— The club is still going strong. Getting stronger.
— We printed the town history.
— Remember, Caroline, we used to make aprons.
— We used to have a sale of the aprons and things we made. A bazaar.
— A long time ago the ladies didn't go to town meeting. They couldn't vote. The ladies would run a dinner down at the parish house. They'd spend all day singing and preparing the dinner.
— Miss Elizabeth Prentiss gave the parish house to the town on the condition that there would be no dancing and no playing of cards.

That goes today?
— Who knows?
— I don't think anybody would dare dance in the parish house.

How does town meeting run these days? Pretty smooth?
— Everybody knows how everybody's going to vote before you get there.
— I remember a discussion about purchasing a new police cruiser. Mr. Merrill wanted to know if the old cruiser was good enough to patrol in Vermont, why wasn't it good enough to patrol in New Hampshire? He'd spotted the cruiser in Vermont, I guess.
— Mr. Merrill hardly ever came to town meeting, but he did this year.

Was the cruiser approved?
— No.

How does the chief feel about that?
— He does the best he can.
— We had to put $2,000 into a vehicle worth $3,000 to make it go another year.
— Did it on a show of hands.
— We do voice votes for almost everything.

Was the cruiser the big issue this year?
— That, and we bought a dump truck.
— The meeting was packed this year. All the benches filled. Packed wall to wall.

Where was the fire department?

— Sitting in the back. Fire and police usually sit in the back.

— The road agent, he stays home.

— He was here this year. And he got his new truck!

Do you explain to newcomers about the process?

— No, they're on their own.

— They don't say anything the first year. They're pretty quiet.

Memories of town meetings past?

— About thirteen years ago, my wife was encouraged to run for selectman. One husband told her he'd never vote for a woman, but his wife winked at her. She served three years. Langdon's first woman selectman.

— I sent cards out. Men said they wouldn't vote for me, but the women kept the cards.

— We had a woman moderator before many towns had women moderators. Anne Newcomb was moderator in the late sixties, early seventies.

— We have had all kinds of different moderators. Who was before Jeff?

— Grampa was, wasn't he?

Grampa?

— Clifford Holmes. He was moderator for years. Bucket's brother.

How Bucket Holmes Got His Nickname

"Do I have to ask permission to call you Bucket?" the newcomer to the family asked.

"Only people from Langdon call me Bucket," Bucket said.

How did Bucket get his nickname? Folks say different things. Some say it has to do with sugaring buckets, but the story from Bucket's own lips goes something like this: He was just a kid out in the field with the men, haying. Someone asked him to go get a bucket of water. He didn't really want to get a bucket of water, so he said, "From now on my name's gonna *be* bucket!"

Darned if it didn't stick.

What else do you remember about meetings past?

— I remember one time at town meeting, we were raising money for a new fence down by the cemetery. This guy says, "I don't know what the hell they're putting a fence down there for. Those people aren't going anywhere."

— That's what you call town meeting humor.

— One of the older folks didn't think they should pay taxes because their children were out of school. I had ten children go through school, so I figure we're still in debt.

— The people who complained had already gotten their free education.

— We hold school meeting a couple weeks ahead of town meeting. We vote during the day for town officials, then hold the meeting in the evening. But we don't vote at the school meeting, we vote at the town meeting. The school has a deliberative session, then we vote on the articles on town meeting day.

— I think that's what Charlestown does too. Charlestown doesn't have town meeting any more.

— I remember some tremendous fights about the roads and the road agent. The road agent in Langdon is appointed by the selectmen. (In other towns he or she is elected.)

— A few years back, there were some tremendous pot holes on Holden Hill. Somebody took day glow paint and painted circles around them.

You have a lot of characters in town?

— A lot of good people. A lot of fun personalities.

— My wife's mother's cousin come from Connecticut—a purple-haired retired school teacher. Just before town meeting they were driving down Holden Hill in a pick-up truck, apparently it was a snowstorm. They did a few 180s, 360s, whatever, kinda scared her a little bit, kinda drops off. At town meeting she got up and asked if they could look into putting streetlights and guard rails on Holden Hill.

What did the selectmen say?

— Not much.

— People don't realize we'd have snow drifts up there eight feet high. We'd get men in there to shovel before the plow. Shovel it out, plow a couple feet, shovel some more.

— Nowadays, people expect a super highway, but back then it was a narrow road and not paved. They've been making the road wider and wider.

— Don't ever try to find Langdon on a GPS. I don't know what it is about Langdon, but we're not up-to-date on the road map.

— We're not even on some maps.

— We were so glad when our address changed back to Langdon. Alstead and Langdon have the same zip. That confused a lot of people. Langdon used to have a post office.

— The house I used to live in used to be the post office.

— The reason people have so much pride in Langdon, from an outsider's point of view, comes from the family connections. They have children the same age and grandchildren the same age. The Porters, Clarks, Bascoms, Merrills, Holmes's, Batchelders, Peltons.

— We bought a home in Alstead in the seventies. We knew maybe three people in Alstead. We moved here five years ago, we know all 700 people.

— We have some big families here. The Crams. The Holmes's.

Dennis McClary asked: Did town meetings used to be very different than they are now?

— They were smokier. The men smoked cigars. I don't think I ever went to a town meeting until I moved back to Langdon in 1945.

— The men didn't want us there, so they could go ahead and smoke.

When did the women start coming, Dot?

— Who knows? I don't know.

— In the 40s maybe.

— I think it was when the law was passed.

This old hall has seen a lot of action over the years, hasn't it?

— We used to have plays here in this hall—the old folks, the elderly folks, used to put on a play a few times a year here on the stage.

— We'd also have a Christmas party for the children.

— I think early on they held suppers here.

— They still have a food table at voting. And the food's pretty good. Chili, coffee.

— Sarah Porter used to come to Memorial Day and say the "Gettysburg Address." When I was a child I thought the first line of the "Gettysburg Address" was: "This is the seventeenth time I've said the Gettysburg Address in the town of Langdon." I thought that was the first line. And I thought Columbia was the jam of the ocean.

What are some things you can always count on at town meeting?

— We say the Pledge of Allegiance.

— People buy tickets for the quilt.

— Where people sit. People have their favorite spots. Anyone who's late coming in can generally find a seat in the front row or behind a post.

— The smaller the item the bigger the discussion. You can depend on that.

— Some of the people talk too much. It's like: "Oh-shut-up!"

— It's interesting to see everybody and get their different opinions. Hear about all the little things going on.

— It's a unique democracy. Town meeting is really how our democracy got started. It gives me a feeling of pride when I come here to town meeting.

Details from Early Langdon Town Meetings

Gleaned from Frank Burnside Kingsbury's
History and Genealogical Register of the Town of Langdon

The First Town Meeting—March 6, 1787

Freeholders (that is land owners) and other inhabitants of the township of Langdon qualified to vote in town meeting gathered at the dwelling house of Captain Jonas Fairbank. The warrant listed the tasks to be accomplished as follows:

To Chuse a Moderator

To Chuse town Officers for the year Ensuing

To See if the Inhabitants will Divide said town into Destricts for keeping School and fix the bounds and Limits thereof

To raise a Sum or Sums of money for the Support of the poor making and repairing highways and Other town Charges

To Vote for the president of the State and Senetors for the County

Hereof fail not Dated this Sixteenth Day of Feby

in the year of our Lord anno Domini 1787

John Hubbard Committee for Calling said Meeting

The tone and timbre of discussion, as well as who said what, are lost to history. But the results of that first meeting were duly recorded. Among them:

Chose Lut. Jonathan Willard Moderator

Chose Jonas Fairbank town Clerk

Chose Jonathan Willard first Selectman

Details (Continued):

Chose Samuel Prouty Second Selectman

Chose James Egerton third Selectman

Chose Levi Fairbank Constable with Samuel Prouty and Asa Walker Bondsmen for said Fairbank's faithfull performance—Voted to give the said Constable one pound and ten Shillings for Serving

Chose John Prouty Town Treasurer

Chose Joseph Willard and Asa Walker Surveyours of Highways

Chose Lut. (Jonathan) Willard fence Vewer

Chose Danil Prouty Hog Constable

Chose Samuel Prouty and James Egerton School Committee

Chose John Sartwell Cullor of Lumber

Chose David Rice Sealor of Weights and Measures

Chose John Woster (Worcester) tiding man

Nowadays, it's sometimes difficult to find volunteers to fill town positions, but in Langdon in 1787, it seems there was a man for every job—though some were called to double duty.

The voters of Langdon cast twenty-two votes for John Sullivan for President (Governor) and just four for the town's namesake, John Langdon. (In 1800, John Langdon got just one vote for governor, while his opponent garnered thirty. Just because your town's named after a person, doesn't mean you have to vote for him.)

They also voted to raise fifteen pounds to support the school, forty pounds to make and repair highways, and one pound and ten shillings for the town Book.

The town also voted "that Hogs be Keept Shet up."

Two special town meetings took place in Langdon in 1787. The subject of roads figured prominently and where to "fling" them up. One fellow, John Royce, asked for and received an abatement on his poll tax.

At the March 4, 1788 town meeting, voters discussed where to hold town meetings in the future, what to do about tax delinquents and paying a preacher.

Future town meetings it was decided would be held: "Every Either time at Seth Walkers and Every Either time at Daniel Proutys Begining the Next Meeting at Daniel Proutys."

As for those early tax evaders, it was voted: "To Set those that Did Not work out their highway tax the Last year to the town Rate for this year for the Same Sum which they the Delinquents are behind in Each Surveyors tax Bill."

That seemed to clear the matter up.

As for the souls of Langdon, six pounds were to be "Laid out in the town for Preaching the Insuing (year)." The following year voters decided to "dismiss" the article to "rais Money to hire preaching the year Insuing." Whether they couldn't find a preacher or didn't appreciate what the preacher had to say, we may never know. Meanwhile, school districts needed to be established and bridges built.

What kind of town is Langdon? It's the kind of town that represents the best of small-town community spirit and neighborliness. Here's a story from Frank Sellers' town history:

> On 4 October, 1931, the home of Kenneth Merrell was destroyed by fire. There was little firefighting equipment in Langdon in those days and the attempt to save the house, which in any case was too far gone to save, had to be abandoned in order to save the barns and cattle. Sidney Harris, a neighbor, suggested to the Selectmen, who were present at the fire, that the people of Langdon make an effort to rebuild the house. A special meeting was called the next evening and a committee was appointed to organize a plan for reconstruction. The committee met with Merrell and before the week was out, a plan had been agreed upon and the new house was under construction. Many of the people who worked on the house were not carpenters, but all of the work did not require it. People were needed to haul the logs to the sawmill and the finished lumber away from it. Most farmers, and Langdon was still composed mostly of farmers at the time, have some building skills. Each volunteer performed his own specialty and within a short time a very professional job was completed. This house stands today as a reminder of what can be done by friends and neighbors.

9 ⚖️

In Literature

In 1994 town officials in Wilmot asked longtime residents Donald Hall and Jane Kenyon—husband and wife—to compose a poem for the cover of the town report. Seldom has a humble town report been graced with original work by two such famous and accomplished poets. Hall and Kenyon, together, wrote "Words for a Warrant."

> When the stream by the Town Hall rushes
> with meltwater, and early sap drips
> into buckets until dusk; when the dirt back
> roads thaw by noon and freeze again at night,
> Bob looks for his gavel, and townswomen
> tuck the town warrant into knitting baskets.
> At seven o'clock on the second Tuesday in March
> we enter the warm room, with its loved
> and extremely uncomfortable benches, and settle
> to the business of governing ourselves. Once a year,
> for a couple of hours, we are civil and deliberate.
> Then we stand stretching, happy
> to go home, and step out into the clear,
> cold night, under the legislature of stars.

Town meeting is a natural subject for story, novel, essay, plays or, as Hall and Kenyon illustrate so elegantly, poetry. In "Words for a Warrant" they catch the essence of town meeting: the cold of early spring outside, with promises of warmth to come, contrasts with the warmth inside, the physical warmth provided by the woodstove (or furnace) combined with the emotional warmth of familiarity.

The image of the official town warrant tucked into the homely knitting basket—which also promises warmth to come—reminds us that we are a practical, hands-on people, equally comfortable knitting mittens and deciding how much money we need to raise in taxes to run our town in the coming year.

We step up or, in this case, sit ourselves down to do the work. We express our satisfaction with our efforts through a leisurely stretch at the end of a long sit and and an equally taxing think, happy that our civic duty has, once again, been fulfilled, and happy, once again, to go home. This town feels like home partly because of the work we accomplish together at each town meeting.

The naturalness of this process is beautifully wrought and its significance duly elevated in Hall and Kenyon's final image of that cold, clear spring night and its breathtaking "legislature of stars." What a phrase! Just three words that embrace the universe. No wonder when editors Rick Agran, Hildred Crill, and Mark DeCarteret compiled an anthology of New Hampshire poems in 1999, they appropriated the phrase in their title, *Under the Legislature of Stars.*

Poets Laureate

Jane Kenyon was serving as New Hampshire's Poet Laureate when she died of leukemia at age forty-seven in 1995. She met Donald Hall at the University of Michigan where she was a student and where he taught. Later, the couple moved to Hall's old family homestead in Wilmot to write full time. She published several collections of poetry to great acclaim, including *Let Evening Come, Constance,* and the posthumously published *Otherwise.*

Donald Hall has published many books of poetry as well as collections of essays, and books about poetry, writing, baseball, and art. He served both as United States Poet Laureate and New Hampshire Poet Laureate and received many awards and honors including the National Book Critics Circle Award for *The One Day,* the Los Angeles Times Book prize, and a Pulitzer Prize nomination. Among his best loved works are the children's book *Ox-Cart Man,* his collection of essays on rural New Hampshire life, *String Too Short to Be Saved,* and *Without: Poems* "written to and for his wife" and published three years after her death.

In 2011 Hall received the Presidential Medal of Arts from President Barack Obama "for his extensive contributions to American poetry. Through an illustrious career and as Poet Laureate of the United States from 2006–2007, Mr. Hall's work has inspired Americans and enhanced the role of poetry in our national life."

It's not much of a stretch to say that town meeting and poetry have a lot in common. Each pays close attention to language and the rituals of language. Each embraces repetition. At town meeting, our rituals connect us to our history and steady us in the moment. Whatever surprises we encounter on the way, we know where we're headed and have, over the years, become footfall familiar with the path that leads us there. Dudley Laufman of Canterbury has been a keen observer of New Hampshire ways, including the rituals of town meeting, for most of his long life. At the time of this writing, he'd just celebrated eighty years on this earth. Best known as a fiddler, a caller for barn dances, and for his work preserving traditional music, in 2011 he received a National Heritage Fellowship, the nation's highest honor in folk and traditional arts. He's also an accomplished and widely published poet.

Laufman says he started collecting stories of the Monadnock Region of New Hampshire when he was a teenager. Along with the stories come the local characters, a few of whom appear in his poem "Town Meeting," set in the fictitious, but completely true-to-life, town of Sycamore.

> There is usually
> snow on the ground
> and mud season
> most likely started.
>
> One of the Ashley brothers
> walked by Quint,
> sitting in the sun
> front of his house
> beside the hall,
> snow melt
> dripping off the roof.
>
> "Going to the meeting?"
> greeted the Ashley boy.
>
> "Nope," says Quint.
> "Stand up to say anything,
> either a Hudson or a Gates
> vetoes it."
>
> Boys of North Sycamore were
> standing around the stove
> at the foot of the hall,

making small talk.
Floor wet from melting snow
that came in on boots.

"Whole town should be run
by electricity," said Jeff.

Someone asked the preacher
"Who you voting for?"

"GOD!" he yelled.

An issue came up on the warrant
that called for a secret ballot.
Folks lined up along the
right hand of the hall,
filed around in front,
dropped their ballot in the box,
went back to their seats or to
stand around the stove,
chew tobacco, smoke.

Jeff says to Grampie,
"Which way you vote on that one?"

Grampie points to the
right hand side of the hall and says,
"I went that way."

Laufman introduces us to townsfolk and their attitudes, shaped by time and experience. You stay in one place long enough, eyes open, ears perked, you get to know the lay of the land. Quint, who lives next door to town hall, ain't going to town meeting. He's been burned too many times by the contrary attitudes of the Hudsons and the Gates. Let somebody else fight 'em this year. He's not in the mood.

The preacher, feeling feisty, gives as good as he gets. He's voting for GOD. As good a candidate as any, as the Boys of North Sycamore would, no doubt, grudgingly agree.

Jeff, the whippersnapper, looks to the future, to a time when the wood stove that keeps the hall consistently too hot or too cool will be replaced by electric heat or some more modern method of melting the tracked-in snow to puddles on the floor.

Then comes the Laufman twist—Yankee humor at its most subtle.

When the whippersnapper, nosey, asks Grampie to reveal his vote, Grampie points to the side of the hall where he stood in line to cast his secret ballot. "I went that way," he says. He doesn't say, "None of your damn business."

Nuff, said.

Speaking of Nuff and what he said, Jody Wells of South Sutton, who traces his New Hampshire lineage back five generations, records the dialogue of town meeting in his poem, "Town Meeting," not to be confused with Dudley Laufman's poem, "Town Meeting." What Wells notes is not the formal language from the podium, or equally formal language from the floor when citizen legislators address town officials. His ear picks up unadulterated murmurings, complaints, tart observations, bitches and banter about the subjects that matter most come spring: ice-out, sugaring, frost heaves, black flies, and taxes.

> The first Tuesday after
> the second Monday in March,
> when winter's back has been broken.
> We post the dirt roads,
> vote in our Town Fathers for the ensuing year
> then bitch about our taxes as we file
> into the town hall basement
> for the potluck supper.

> "Will someone please tell me why we need six police officers
>   in a town of 1700 people?"
> "We need to import some criminals."
> "Don't you get it?"
> "We've got eighty miles of roads to patrol."
> "What we need to do is separate our wants from our needs."

> A time before ice-out on the Lane River,
>   although by now
> up at Bull Bridge Corner it's starting to break-up.
> Will be a while before we hear the peepers.
> Fred always says: *First the black flies then the summer people.*

> "Where is Fred Fletcher?"
> "He told me he ain't comin."
> "Says he's smack in the middle of sugarin and still lambin."
> "He's sick of bangin his 4 × 4 over them frost heaves
>   and he's sick of listenin to Gracie Alden sittin there

with her knittin and that other bunch who think
they're friggin experts on *Roberts Rules*."

"Plus ain't nothin on the warrant articles worth mentionin."
"They got their new pumper truck last year
and they're gonna pass everything anyhow."
"Might just as well walk down front
take my wallet out of my back pocket
and throw it up on the stage."
"Nuff said."

You might think this trash talk means these speakers don't value town
meeting. On the contrary, however much they complain, they show up,
most of 'em, most years. Actions trump words, and complaining is integral
to the democratic process. These folks show up, speak their minds to their
neighbors, and vote, because they know town meeting matters and their
participation in it matters, too.

Tythingman

In South Sutton, Jody Wells may be better known to locals as a tythingman than a poet. For fifty years he assisted his father, George Wells,
with tything duties for South Sutton's Old Home Day.

George Wells died in 2011 at the age of eighty-nine.

*Jody Wells, George Wells, and the Reverend Henry Flemming
at the South Sutton Old Home Day. George, with stick,
portrays the tythingman. His son Jody assists.*

Poetry and Town Meeting Have a Lot in Common

Poetry creates its own rhythms word by word, line by line, break by break. So does town meeting. The clock strikes the hour of 9:00 a.m. The crowd settles. The moderator calls the meeting to order, sets the rules for the day, introduces the articles, reads Article I: "I await your pleasure," he says. *Beat.* "Move the question as read," says the first selectman. "Second," says the second selectman. *Beat.* "Motion having been moved and seconded," says the Moderator, "I'll open the floor to discussion." *Beat.*

Town meeting *is* a poem.

Poetry strives for conciseness and precision. Town meeting strives for these things, too: let's get the work done, done right, and in a timely fashion. Though getting the work done right usually takes longer than we thought it would. As the home handyman says: If you think a job will take an hour, plan on three.

Come to think of it, three hours, or eight, or ten is little enough time to plan a town's future.

Poetry surprises not only with content, but often with structure and punctuation. Despite strict adherence to tradition, no town meeting is ever the same as any that came before; we expect and are usually rewarded with a surprise or two. The crack of the moderator's gavel punctuates discussion. The issue we thought would drag out through many stanzas gets dispensed with in a blink with a curt, "Table it!" The article we thought destined for easy passage generates epic controversy, ending with a twist nobody saw coming:

"The petitioners withdraw their motion."

"What?"

"Huh?"

"Can they do that?"

"Use the mic!"

"Move the question!"

"What's the question?"

"House be in order!"

Poetry honors economy—an economy of words. Town meeting? Well, we do our best to use tax payer money wisely. We seek that kind of economy, though it's hard. Some, it's true, do seek an economy of words at town meeting. They think their comments through before speaking, or read them from a prepared statement. Others . . . not so much. Others seem to see town meeting as the one time a year when they can talk as much as they want to a captive audience. The technical term is yammering. They yammer on so long as the moderator remains tolerant. So long as nobody calls the question. Town meeting is all about letting people have their say: we hope for and honor an economy of words, but understand that not everybody can achieve it. Those who do earn our respect and, perhaps, our vote.

In his poem, "Patience and Democracy," Epsom poet Neil English spins a scenario—truth be told, it might be called epic considering the three-year time span—of how long it takes to get things done when everybody gets a vote and not everybody has the same opinion. Democracy can be a very slow process. As the population grows a town or a school can get too big for its britches—new bigger britches are required. But new britches cost money, and, gosh, don't we hate to spend money. Hey, Epsom didn't have such a rough time of it as described in Neil English's poem. Back in the 70s and 80s an addition to the elementary school in Northwood took thirteen tries before it finally passed.

Patience and Democracy

By 1978 Epsom's old white clapboarded Town Hall
had obviously outgrown its usefulness.
Way too many people had shown up
for School District Meeting.
Registered voters spilled out the front steps
like so much over-ripe fruit cascading from a cornucopia.
At each open window a tippy-toed crowd had gathered
on the outside peering in, an attempt to
hear what was going on.
As soon as the meeting was gaveled to order,
one member of "the opposition" raised his hand and said,
"Not only is it hot as hell in here, but all of us
have already made up our minds. I move the question."

When the moderator tallied the raised hands, both inside and out,
the school addition went down in ignominious defeat.

Two years later the school addition was brought up again
but this time School District Meeting was held at Circle Nine Ranch
so all the voters could fit *inside* the building.
Although some chose to stand at the back of the hall to heckle the crowd,
this time the moderator set some basic ground rules.
Not until all the voters' questions were answered and
four hours into the meeting did he entertain, "Move the question."

The vote was tallied and then . . . tallied again . . .
finally it was announced; 286 for, 143 against, a perfect 2/3 to 1/3 split.

The moderator consulted his *Robert's Rules of Order*,
laid his gavel aside and cast the deciding vote.
Epsom Central School finally got that much needed addition.

Who ever said a single vote doesn't amount to much?

Former New Hampshire Poet Laureate Marie Harris writes often about nature from her little house in the wilds of Barrington, where she has lived for decades, where she knows the lay of both the natural and political landscape—she's served as a library trustee since the dawn of memory, and her husband, Charter Weeks, has served in many offices including, most recently, selectman.

Like most poets, Marie writes with admirable precision. Her prose poem "Actual Grace" appeared in her collection *Weasel in the Turkey Pen* and was featured in the Barrington Town Report of 1983—"one of my prouder moments, actually," she says.

Actual Grace

The earth is beaten into dull stuff. A smudge of sun rides under the bellying sky. Winter is finishing slowly, like sap over a wood fire. At Phil's Restaurant, breakfast customers hash over the Town Report. We still have our say. We still sing our annual hymn of republic and objection. Now, while sugar steam drifts, like March weather, eastward, we lift our chalices of syrup to the resurrecting light.

The poem begins at ground level, soil level, then looks up to the sun. In the third sentence, Harris introduces a human element—someone has harvested sap from the maples and now the sap boils over a wood fire. From the outdoors and the fire, she moves us inside Phil's Restaurant, where syrup from that sap might be served along with plenty of opinions stimulated by the newly issued Town Report.

"We still have our say," Harris writes wonderingly. *Still.* As if having our say is a tradition in danger of disappearing. "We still sing our annual hymn." *Still.* As though that hymn of "republic and objection," is also something sacred to be cherished and guarded. With the word "hymn," Harris again moves us from earth level up—to the spiritual, to the religious. Town meeting is an "annual hymn," as dependable as the steam that drifts from the sugaring houses and the eastward drift of March weather. The syrup on the table at Phil's Restaurant is not contained in pitchers but in "chalices," lifted in a joyous toast to spring, to community, to renewal. Up and up, this poem takes us, from "dull stuff" to "to resurrecting light." Like spring and a hearty breakfast, town meeting restores us. When it's not making us hopping mad!

As all these poems demonstrate, town meeting and the direct self-governance it represents amounts to more than the sum of its parts. Like a good poem. The recurring images, the memories we make and keep, the essence of this hardy institution reflect a greater whole encompassing our history, our present, and our future. Look closely at town meeting and its trappings, these poems seem to say, and see who we are, where we come from, and what we value.

Poets Aren't the Only Ones Inspired by Town Meeting

You don't have to look far or hard to confirm the notion that town meeting inspires creative writing of all sorts. It's a natural subject because it provides so many elements for writers to work with. Among them:

- A colorful setting in a historic hall whose very foundation, walls, and ceiling seem to pulsate with all they have witnessed over the years. The sills, the plaster, the beams have absorbed high emotion and impassioned rhetoric along with the pipe and cigarette smoke from a time when such indulgences were allowed. This hall has witnessed tears and fisticuffs. It has heard laughter, praise, insults, and shouting matches. Many a reserved gentleman or lady has lost his or her cool here. ("Take your seat, Ma'am, or I'll ask the constable to remove you." "Don't you ma'am me, Mr. Moderator. Don't you dare ma'am me!") The hall remembers it all.

- Characters. The people of the town, old timers and new comers, truth-tellers and agitators, pacifiers and provocateurs, the blunt, the sharp, the sly, the jocular—one of every type is represented, yet every one of them is someone the likes of whom the world will never see again. Write in the name of your favorite town character here: _____ Write several in the margins, if you wish. Love 'em or hate 'em, each is a treasure. Whether you speak of town meeting or the world at large, truth is: It takes all kinds.

- Structure. A Beginning (7:00 p.m. sharp on the second Tuesday of March); Middle (laid out and numbered: Article 1—To raise and appropriate . . .); and End (motion to adjourn). What could be simpler? And there's plenty of room for drama to unfold within that solid structure.

- Pomp, circumstance, and time-honored words, heavy with meaning: *Point of order Madame Moderator; the vote being in the affirmative; the house recognizes Mr. Eldridge; motion to indefinitely postpone.* No matter how controversial the question or how inflamed the emotions, the rituals and traditions can be depended upon to frame, contain, and ultimately bring resolution.

- Conflict and Drama. The conflicts are many and complex. They can be personal, political, generational, historic, or (frequently) all of the above. Some conflicts are immediate and immediately resolved, such as voting yea or nay on each article. Some have deep, twisted roots. These deep-rooted or underlying conflicts may date back generations: "His father cheated my Aunt Maybelle on a land deal in 1935, therefore I will not support improvements to his road—not now, not ever." Some conflicts erupt in shouts. Others hum just below the surface of discourse—in frowns, rolled eyes, grumbles, soft curses, shrugs, nods, twitching jaw muscles. If looks could kill, town meeting would be littered with corpses. Every town meeting roils with conflict, if you know what to look for, who to look at, and when. Listen between the lines—you'll hear it. Sometimes the drama screams. Sometimes it whispers. Sometimes it's an exchange of meaningful looks between two old friends or enemies. But it's there. Always. "If everybody got along and agreed on everything, what would be the point of town meeting anyway?" That's a line from my play, *Town Meeting,* a version of which you'll find at the back of this book. It may not be literature, but as those who've performed it and those who've watched it performed attest, it hits close to home.

All these elements combust in a short story, "Town Meetin' Day," by Sidney M. Chase printed by *Scribner's Monthly* in 1910. Chase propagates the myth of the ultra folksy townspeople with ultra folksy vernacular and wicked short fuses. He proceeds to hang that myth on the scaffolding of the formal process and procedures that endure even now. His liberal use of the local dialect makes the story fun to read aloud. (You can easily find the complete text on the internet, along with Chase's lavish illustrations; he was a well-known artist as well as a writer.)

To summarize the story: farmers Aaron and Hiram be ready for town meetin'. They be braced for trouble. They be, neither of 'em, pleased with the see-lickmen who "dumps our taxes onto them bogholes o' roads in the South Parish, with this turnpike fairly spilin' fer a few loads o' gravel." (Roads, again. Always roads.)

No women participate in the business end of this town meetin', just men—as was the custom in those days. The women be home cooking up a storm. Meanwhile, at the testosterone-infused meetin' house, the room fills, the "political temperature" rises, and "shrewd plots mature." First up, the election of a moder-ay-tor. Ichabod N. Peaslee wins the vote. As his first official act, he proposes a prayer to get things off on the right foot. Since nobody volunteers to lead the prayer, the meetin' moves on unblessed. Not an auspicious beginning.

Illustration by Sidney M. Chase for his story "Town Meetin' Day,"
printed by Scribner's Monthly *in 1910*

Election of a variety of town officials continues until lunch time. After a hearty meal of ham, beans, pies, and coffee, topped with the smoking of pipes and cigars, "the throng," once again, pours into the hall, "full of zest for the struggles of the afternoon." From the upstairs gallery, the women watch—having finished their day's work of cookin' and cleanin' up—but they do not speak to the issues or vote. Down below, man-talk turns to tramps, hoss sheds, and hosses. The "aggrieved Aaron" requests $100 to fix the Swamp Holler road, full of rocks and near impassable with mud. But Mr. Higgins speaks vehemently agin it. Tricky maneuverin' amends the $100 to $50 and then to $49.99. End result: indefinitely postpone. Article sunk.

Discussion of the dog officer's honesty or lack thereof sparks spirited exchanges. Then talk turns to the the uselessness of the library which ain't, according to Aaron, "wuth a tax on kittens, let alone dogs. I ain't took a book out to read in ten years n' when I do, one I want ain't never in!" (Dogs and libraries—ever controversial. They have their supporters and their detractors. Especially dogs.)

Discussion of a centralized school leads to suspicions of deviltry, and the sorry state of schools that need fixin' up, which leads, in turn, to the notion that a fella wouldn't throw his wife on the street, just 'cause he could get a better one. If you're gonna abolish school districts, you might's well abolish families, too.

Debate takes a fiery turn when the subject of the fire department comes up, with the revelation of the exorbitant amount of pay collected by fire-fighters. "I knowed a fireman once in awful danger," one voter snarks. "He almost got wet!"

Somebody calls somebody a liar. Somebody picks up a chair and threatens to flatten somebody with it.

Now we're cooking with gas.

The tension builds in this fictional town meeting, just like real life. Starts out at a simmer. Gradually reaches a soft boil. Then, as the heat increases, it erupts into a full boil: sharp voices; harsh words; lines drawn in the dust of the old floor boards. Sometimes the pot boils over: puffed chests; accusations of being uninformed, gullible, ill-intentioned, disingenuous, deceitful, selfish, none-too-bright. Rarely, the words "lie" or "liar" are invoked. The knitters look up from their work and murmur, "Uh-oh."

After that emotional and political climax, more often than not, a gradual calming prevails. The vote is taken and that settles that. Citizens leave the hall satisfied at having said their pieces, whichever way the vote went.

We may not all be friends, but we're neighbors, and we tolerate one another, and one another's funny ideas. Try to, anyhow.

In the End—the denouement—the articles are dealt with and the town business settled. This is how it goes. We expect it. We accept it. We move on.

As Aaron and Hiram head home from their "Town Meetin'," Aaron observes: "They don't hev no sech town meetin's nowday's they ust to hev, Hiram, when you 'n' me wuz boys." Hiram agrees.

Each town meeting *is* a story. A story that repeats. It is a story that many of us hope will never end.

Town Meeting Takes Center Stage in *Coniston*

Winston Churchill, the New Hampshire author not the British statesman, used town meeting to advance the plot and reveal the nature of his characters in his 1906 novel *Coniston*. The novel presents two love stories—a short one and a long one, as the narrator explains in the opening chapter. It also offers a penetrating look at the social and political workings of a small town called Coniston in a small New England state and, ultimately, in the nation. The novel begins "some little while after General Jackson had got into the White House and had shown the world what a real democracy was." It continues through the presidency of Ulysses S. Grant. It's a big book, a national story with a small New Hampshire town smack at the center. Coniston is New Hampshire. New Hampshire is the nation.

We meet our hero and anti-hero, Jethro Bass, as a young man and follow him through his life, loves, and clever political maneuverings into the beginnings of old age. He's quite a fellow, this long drink-a-water in the coonskin cap. Jock, the town sage, says of young Jethro: "He's an all-fired sight smarter than folks in this town think he be. They don't take notice of him, because he don't say much and stutters. He hain't be'n eddicated a great deal, but I wouldn't be afeard to warrant he'd make a racket in the world some of these days."

Jethro, a patient man, slowly builds a power base by discretely lending money, here and there. And when he's ready, when he's built his economic, social, and political foundation one mortgage at a time, he stages a shocking coup at town meeting. It seems, the man who holds the mortgage on a person's farm can influence a person's vote.

"Through the winter, rumors of an upset in town government festered." Fletcher Bartlett, the rumor mill suggested, would be nominated as head selectman. People scoffed: Fletcher Bartlett? He was an "easy-going farmer of the Methodist persuasion who was always in debt." The other rumored members of the Bartlett ticket "were remarkable neither for orthodoxy or solidity." Could these rumors be true? Folks doubted it. Such a ticket made no sense at all.

Still, come town meeting day, the old guard felt uneasy. Something thickened the air. Was it spring springing or was it change a-coming? Maybe both. No one seemed to know who'd incited this potential shift in the status quo. Sure, the name of Jethro Bass came up, but folks didn't believe he had much to do with much of anything. Jethro kept to himself. He'd shown no overt interest in town politics. And yet . . . ?

Sleet slicked the roads that Tuesday, but the "staunch old deacons and selectmen, who did their duty by their fellow citizens as they saw it," failed to see "the trackless roads over the hills, now becoming tracked, and the bent figures driving doggedly against the storm, each impelled by a motive strengthened by a master mind until it had become imperative."

Uh-oh.

Yup, men turned out for that meeting in surprising numbers. Teams of horses filled the sheds, barns, and tannery. The "orthodox" worried. The moderator sat "aghast in his high place as they came trooping in, men who have not been to town meeting for ten years." Jethro Bass sat near the ballot box, watching, silent. Then came the bombshell, burst "from the lips of Fletcher Bartlett himself, inflammable as gunpowder." Fletcher says: "Gentlemen, I withdraw as your candidate, and nominate a better and an abler man—Jethro Bass."

On that day Jethro becomes head selectman. He will hold that position for the next several decades. Over time and over the course of the novel, he expands his power from Coniston to the state house to the White House— wielding control inconspicuously and becoming—some of the characters believe—one of the most powerful men in the country. Jock's prediction comes true.

Is Jethro Bass, at heart, a good guy or a bad guy? Will his wealth and power bring him happiness? These questions form the center of the novel. But in the process of answering these personal and philosophical questions, Coniston reveals the battles for power that underscore town meeting. On the face of it, the community gathers to hash out a budget and a plan for getting through the next year, or the next several years. As a body, voters assert local control over local matters. In the earliest town meetings, this might have meant what roads were to be built and who would build them. Often, the job fell to a landowner who would benefit from the road, and the town thanked him by forgiving him that year's taxes. In the days of travel by foot or horse, this might have meant five one-room schools in a town that was small in population but large in area. It meant raising money to pay the teachers, buy wood to fuel the stove, and books for the children to read. All well and good and a clear benefit for all.

But as we see in *Coniston*, political organization and savvy pays under the table as well as over it—even in a town of a few hundred people tucked among the hills of New Hampshire. Jethro Bass invested his money in mortgages. And those who benefited from the mortgages, why, they were inclined to cast their votes his way. When somebody ran for state office, maybe they could depend on a block of Coniston votes. When railroad entrepreneurs decided where to lay their tracks, maybe their friends at the state house or in Washington would put in a good word for little Coniston, because that would please Jethro Bass.

Jethro overthrew the good old boys to become selectman, but it wasn't long before he became the leader of another set of good old boys. The old guard, they're called sometimes. You see it today. New folks move into town. They notice that so-and-so has been selectman since 1984, owns a lot of land on the mountain and a real nice house in the village, and her cousin Mitchell is more often than not contracted to renovate town buildings. Maybe she's been taking advantage. Not only that, but when the building inspector inspected the new folks' house, he noticed some problems that needed fixing before he would sign off on the occupancy permit. And he was kind of blunt about it.

He's one of the old guard. And so's *she*. And so's her cousin *Mitchell*.

The old guard must go. And a fresh battle breaks out.

This scenario plays itself out over and over. Those with power are suspect and resented. Those without power want it. And believe they'll do much better by the town (or the world!) if they had it. The beautiful thing about democracy: On any given Tuesday in March, a power shift can be neatly accomplished. Without bloodshed.

Yup, we got that figured out.

In the "Afterword" to *Coniston*, Winston Churchill quotes James Russell Lowell on the state of democracy in America: "We have begun obscurely to recognize that . . . popular government is not in itself a panacea, is no better than any other form except as the virtue and wisdom of the people make it so."

Then, in an eery premonition of our own times, he writes that as Americans we must believe that our democracy "goes down in its foundation to the solid rock of truth." Since 1776 so many nations, he writes, have tried to "rule themselves, and are still trying, that one begins to believe that the time is not far distant when the United States, once the most radical, will become the most conservative."

Recalling the San Francisco disaster that occurred the year the book was published, he cites the theory that earthquakes are caused by "a necessary movement on the part of the globe to regain its axis." He then connects that notion to the politics of his time, not so different from ours, as the globe and the people of America attempt to "regain the true axis established for us by the founders of our Republic."

Some might say nothing brings us closer to that axis than town meeting.

Winston Churchill

Winston Churchill was not, in fact, a native son, having been born in St. Louis, Missouri. But he did make his home in Cornish for a number of years. He wrote many popular novels, including *Coniston, The Celebrity, Richard Carvel, The Crisis, The Dwelling Place of Light*, and *The Crossing*.

His novels addressed matters both historical and political—as well as romantic. And his interest in politics led him to serve in the state legislature and run for governor in 1906. Despite his fame and literary popularity, he did not receive the Republican party's nomination. Several years later, he ran again—this time as a Progressive—but lost in the general election. Like Jethro Bass in *Coniston*, Churchill had friends in high places, including Presidents Teddy Roosevelt and William Howard Taft. Like Jethro Bass, he was deeply involved in railroad politics and policy.

An Outsider's Perspective.

French aristocrat Alexis de Toqueville (1805–1859) was a traveler, writer, philosopher, and politician. He is best known for his classic—and still widely read—*Democracy in America*. The book is written in two parts, the first published in 1835 and the second in 1840. His travels in America, including New England, and his study of our history, particularly the development of our government, made him a vocal admirer of democracy, so different from the monarchies of his home continent.

He writes about all things American—from our geography to the free press. He writes passionately about the immorality of slavery and the mistreatment of Native Americans. He writes about American honor, pride, morals, and education. And, of course, he writes about all levels of government, including—of particular interest here—town government. New England's town-meeting-centered democracy, "more perfect than any of which antiquity had dared to dream," he writes, "sprang full-grown and fully armed from the midst of the old feudal society" the colonists knew in England. How that happened he is at a loss to explain, but he can and does describe, wonderingly, how it works: Suppose the selectmen want to start a school. They "summon all the voters to a meeting on a fixed day and place." Once gathered, town leaders "explain the need felt; they state the means available for the purpose, how much it will cost, and the site suggested. The meeting, consulted on all these points, accepts the principle, decides the site, votes the tax, and leaves the selectmen to carry out its orders." Really, he seems to be saying to his French audience, this is how it's done in America. Can you believe it?

Power and ambition thrive at the local level, he writes. "It is in the township, the center of the ordinary business of life, that the desire for esteem, the pursuit of substantial interests, and the taste for power and self-advertisement are concentrated; these passions, so often troublesome elements in society, take on a different character when exercised so close to home and, in a sense, within the family circle."

Americans, he writes, "rightly think that patriotism is a sort of religion strengthened by practical service," which makes perfect sense, considering the close ties between town and church in the founding of these towns, and the theocracy from which our democracy sprouted so naturally and from which, naturally, it evolved.

Sometimes it takes an outsider to see the forest for the trees.

Town Meeting Extreme in Shirley Jackson's "The Lottery"

Professors Maura McNeil and Inez McDermott teach a course on town meeting at New England College in Henniker. Their extensive syllabus includes Shirley Jackson's famous horror story "The Lottery." McNeil and McDermott recognized that at the heart of this disturbing tale is a kind of town meeting. Except at this meeting, instead of a vote on culverts or teacher salaries, the legislative body decides who will live and who will die.

Jackson's story begins on the morning of June 27, a sunny day in a small village, which might well be in Vermont, where Jackson lived at the time she wrote the story. Or it might be somewhere entirely different—in a parallel universe, for instance, like New Hampshire. The villagers gather just as they would for a regular town meeting, except they gather in the town square instead of the town hall . As we listen in on their conversations, we understand that these are regular country folks, taking time away from their work-a-day lives to participate in a civic ritual.

The children have come too, little boys like Bobby Jones and Dickie Delacroix piling stones and stuffing a few in their pockets. Mrs. Tessie Hutchinson is almost late because she "clean forgot what day it was." She dries her hands on her apron. "Thought my old man was out back stacking wood," she says, sharing a laugh with her neighbor, Mrs. Delacroix. Then she realized the kids were not in the yard, remembered the date, and "came a-running."

The lottery has been held in this village for as long as anyone can remember. It ensures, we come to understand, good crops, good living, and prosperity. In an old black box, town leaders have placed many slips of paper. Long ago, chips of wood were used, but now that the village has grown to more than 300 souls, paper ballots are more practical.

At a regular town meeting, voters slide their ballots into the ballot box. In this meeting, the reverse is true. It's town meeting upside-down. Heads of households are called forward one at a time, names read from an alphabetized checklist. Each draws a folded slip of paper from the box and keeps it folded until all the slips are drawn. Then all-at-the-same-time, the slips are unfolded and the result revealed. The one who has chosen the slip with the black dot "wins" the lottery.

On this day, Mr. Hutchinson draws the slip with the black dot, eliciting immediate protest from his wife: "You didn't give him enough time to take any paper he wanted. I saw you. It wasn't fair!"

Neighbors remind her that they all took the same chance. They don't appreciate her poor sportsmanship, but Tessie insists the drawing was unfair. Her complaints fall on deaf ears, and the process moves forward to a second drawing. This time all the members of the Hutchinson family,

husband, wife, and the three children—Bill Jr., Nancy, and little Dave—
must draw a paper from among five returned to the box, four black and
one with the black dot. Tessie draws the black dot.

Jackson's matter-of-fact tone and her description of the lottery as business as usual—something that must be done; that's always been done; that's
practical, efficient, and for the greater good—this is what makes the story
so brilliant and what happens next so horrifying:

> *Although the villagers had forgotten the ritual and lost the original black
> box, they still remembered to use stones. The pile of stones the boys
> had made earlier was ready; there were stones on the ground with the
> blowing scraps of paper that had come out of the box. Mrs. Delacroix
> selected a stone so large she had to pick it up with both hands and
> turned to Mrs. Dunbar. "Come on," she said. "Hurry up."*

Tessie, trapped in a nightmarish circle of her neighbors, continues her
protest even as the first stone strikes her in the head. Then comes one
of the most chilling final sentences in any story in American literature:
"'It isn't fair, it isn't right,' Mrs. Hutchinson screamed and then they were
upon her."

Even as we appreciate the civic ritual of our own town meetings, we
also appreciate Shirley Jackson's depiction of how civic rituals can, in her
imagination at least, go to the dark side.

When "The Lottery" first appeared in *The New Yorker* in 1948, people
didn't much like the story. Shirley Jackson, for one, was taken aback. In her
"Biography of a Short Story" from *Come Along With Me* she writes: "Things
began mildly enough with a note from a friend at *The New Yorker:* "Your
story has kicked up quite a fuss around the office." The fuss escalated. She
received more than three hundred letters, only thirteen of which "spoke
kindly to me," and those were from friends. Even her mother and father
disliked the the story. Jackson writes that if she thought the letters truly
represented most readers, she would have stopped writing. To her, those
hateful responses seemed to suggest that "people who read stories are gullible, rude, frequently illiterate, and horribly afraid of being laughed at."
They seemed to say, in part: How could a writer turn our beloved town
meeting on its head like this? Does Jackson really think New Englanders
are barbaric? Or could be? What perverse meaning are we supposed to
draw from this story?

Some (and this is scary) didn't care what the story meant. They wanted
to know "where these lotteries were held, and whether they could go there
and watch."

Luckily for readers who admire Jackson's work, she concluded that these letters did not, in fact, represent most readers. She continued writing and publishing to much acclaim. "The Lottery" remains her best known work, still widely anthologized and widely read. High school kids, bloodthirsty little buggers, love it!

Shirley Jackson

Born in San Francisco in 1916, Shirley Jackson grew up in California. She raised her family of four children with her husband, literary critic Stanley Edgar Hyman, in Vermont, where he taught at Bennington College. Her novels include *The Haunting of Hill House* and *We Have Always Lived in the Castle*. She also penned two memoirs, *Life Among the Savages* and *Raising Demons*, as well as collections of short stories and books for children.

Passions Unleashed in *The Dogs of March*

In his acclaimed Darby series set in southwestern New Hampshire, Ernest Hebert exposes small-town, close-to-the-bone conflicts with harrowing honesty made even more harrowing by the grace of his language. He writes lyrically, and, yes, lovingly, about a place and a people as far from the quaint Currier and Ives New England as they can possibly be. No one reveals the inner workings of a troubled character's mind and heart as starkly as Ernest Hebert.

In his debut novel, *The Dogs of March*, Hebert takes on what he calls *the* New England story—the cultural battle between newcomer and native. In this book, the battle turns ugly. Real ugly. Which of course makes for riveting reading. Of particular interest to us is the town meeting scene just past midway of the novel, a fulcrum for the actions that came before and those to follow. Tense? Oh yes! Accurate? Indeed. At stake: Passage of a junk-car ordinance.

Doesn't sound like such a big deal.

But it is. It is *us* verses *them*—and those junk cars symbolize the canyon that separates *us* from *them*. Newcomers take offense at junk cars cluttering up other people's property. They offend the eye. And probably aren't that great for the environment, either. Natives see no harm in the practice, and furthermore, believe their old cars are nobody else's beeswax. In fact, an old car sitting in a field can be a thing of beauty and practicality, especially if you are able, from time to time, to scrounge a belt or a radiator and keep your new old car running.

But what's really at stake?

Howard Elman, whose story connects all the others, is enmeshed in a bitter feud with Zoe Cutter, the newcomer who maneuvered the junk-car article onto the warrant, with the help of selectman Harold Flagg. She wants Howard—her next-door-neighbor—and his kind gone, or at least out of sight. One way to do that, she thinks, is to buy him out. She makes offers. Howard rejects them. This infuriates her.

Meanwhile, she has to look at his junk cars every single stinking day. They infuriate her. War is declared—and town meeting becomes a battleground.

Howard's thoughts on the coming clash surface during a long drive with his daughter, Heather, to visit his wife, a patient at Dartmouth-Hitchcock Hospital. Hebert's characters have lots of problems. As the old saying goes, "If it's not one thing it's another." Or in Howard's world, "If it's not one thing, it's several."

Howard's thoughts during that ride reveal his deep-seated anger along with chronic distrust of the political process, his neighbors, and the way the world runs in general. Howard despises town meeting as much as he loves old cars:

> [The junk-car ordinance] didn't make much sense to him. "Cars ain't like cows that go wandering off soiling other people's yards," he said. Heather ignored him; she could tell when he was talking to himself. He could not imagine that anyone was actually offended by the sight of his derelict cars. They were as natural and varied and pretty to him as trees. He was convinced that Mrs. Cutter had circulated the petition for the junk-car law for no other reason than to harass him; furthermore, he was convinced she wanted his land merely to deprive him of it. He carried a picture in his mind of himself shouting her down at the meeting, and it was this picture that tempted him to attend his first town meeting in many years.
>
> He didn't believe that anything he could say would change the outcome of the meeting. Indeed, he believed that the meeting was rigged. The world was run by certain powers—committees of communists, big businessmen, and the Vatican—which, though they might seem to be at odds, in fact were in league. Issues, debates, wars, great movements,

*governmental changes—all were elaborate shows put on by the powers
to keep ordinary men like himself busy. Howard's conspiracy theory did
not upset him; rather it set his mind at ease, because it answered a question he sometimes posed for himself: If the world were run the way it
appeared to be run, by governments and leaders who were seemingly as
baffled, wrong-thinking, blind, stupid, and greedy as ordinary men like
himself, why had it not destroyed itself by now? It was either believe in
the "powers" or in the hand of God. He rejected the second alternative
because it didn't make sense to him that a superior being should want
to invent a world based on chance and struggle. The idea was as absurd
as building a car that drove only backward or an elevator that went in
only one direction or a ball that did not bounce.*

*Town meeting was a silly game, Howard believed: long, pointless
speeches by men sweetened by the sounds of their own voices; old
ladies complaining about the road agent; the moderator—was it Vic
Copley?—rapping for order on a wooden table; farmers smelling faintly
of their barns; their wives crocheting, stopping only to vote. Still he was
tempted to make an appearance. He could see the Cutter woman flush
with anger as he stood over her, shouting, and then they were taking
him away and he was fighting them and they were falling and he was
strangling the woman.*

Will Howard attend town meeting? And if so, what will he do? To
whom?

By way of contrast, Hebert offers a second view of town affairs, town
meeting, and the human motivations that complicate them. As much as
Howard Elman hates Zoe Cutter, Harold Flagg—selectman—loves her (in
his way). He might even want to marry her. He fantasizes how and when
to break the news to her.

Readers understand that proud, sophisticated Zoe wouldn't give Harold
the time of day (unless she had something substantial to gain from it).
Harold is hapless all right, and hopeless when it comes to romance. But
he does understand how town meeting works. He knows this from long
experience and study. For all his blindness to Zoe's real feelings toward him
(indifference, disdain), he understands a great deal about the motivations
of his neighbors. One thing for sure: the legislative body is unpredictable.

To please Zoe, he tells her the junk-car ordinance might just pass, when:

*Actually, he had no idea whether the ordinance would be approved by
the voters. He had long since given up anticipating how they would act.
So much depended on luck, on weather, on where people sat in relation*

to one another, on the mood of the moderator, on chance comment, on
an overheard phrase, on a joke. All these and a hundred other things
could swing a question one way or another. Democracy was at once
predictable and as fickle as a flock of birds.

Before this tension-fraught scene plays out on the page, Hebert estab-
lishes who's present—not individually, but by type, four of them. Each
earns a page or more of description: what they value, how they relate to
those in the other categories, what they bring to and expect from town
meeting. Basically, the four types are these:

- Farmers: *whose families had been in Darby for generations and whose*
  attendance at town meeting was habitual. The farmers were plain, frugal,
  independent, literate, deep, and as narrow as the furrow made by a plow.

- Commuters: *whose homes were in Darby but whose work and play*
  were in the city and whose family roots might be anywhere, and who,
  as a group, were made uneasy by a vague awareness of the divisions in
  their lives.

- Shack people: *who lived in shacks and trailers and nice houses they had*
  transformed into shacks out of a kind of reverse interior-decorator men-
  tality. . . . From the rough, complex order of the forest floor they derived
  spiritual sustenance and messy habits. Shack people were stunted trees.

- New people: *who were full of vitality, bubbling with ideas, hypnotized*
  by the beauty of the countryside, greedy for the secrets of self-knowledge,
  self-sufficiency.

Having established the who's who in a general way, and more specifically through a host of characters developed in the first half of the novel,
and having set a number of tangled conflicts in motion, Hebert lets the
scene unfold.

The community gathers at town hall. The moderator, Victor Copley,
slouches at the lectern. The three selectmen sit at a table on the stage, facing their constituents: Frank Bridges "worried about his wife, who was so
strange and nervous these days that they had to give her pills"; Arch Sawyer
"thinking about his will until he wasn't thinking at all"; and Harold Flagg,
board chair, "of whom it was said, 'If Fatty Flagg decides he don't like you,
boy, you got troubles in this town.'"

Harold Flagg's point of view anchors the scene. We see the hall through
his eyes. He's surprised when Ollie Jordan (one of the shack people) enters

the hall; he'd never seen Ollie or any of his kin at town meeting before. Ollie is trailed by his sons, "the hunchback and the crazy one," as well as Howard Elman, "who stood with his sleeves rolled up and his arms folded in front of him like the blade of a bulldozer." Harold's love interest, Zoe Cutter, strolls in just as the meeting is about to begin. He's disappointed. He was hoping she'd arrive earlier so they could strategize.

Harold spots the fire chief, Elwyn Bell, lobbying for votes for the fire department budget. In fact the whole fire department is on hand, seems like, thirteen of them, a block of votes in favor of the fire truck that Harold opposes. The discussion of the proposed fire truck illustrates how that flock of birds changes direction on a wisp of a breeze, on a whim, on a turn of phrase. The chief pleads his case:

> "This pumper we're asking for is going to put this town in the twenti-eth century."
>
> "And our pocketbooks in the nineteenth century," squeaked a voice from the crowd that everyone recognized as Alexander Keeler's.

A well-timed jibe can derail an argument quick as that. A clever man might have had a clever comeback to Alexander Keeler's jab; the chief is not a clever man. The chief plods on: Maybe Mrs. Chapman's house could have been saved if the old pumper hadn't broken down at a critical moment. Which was a good point. The crowd absorbs it. But the chief doesn't know when to shut up. He goes on too long and makes the critical mistake of boring the crowd. In the end too much information poorly presented confuses them. When the legislative body is confused, it votes no.

Harold thinks the chief has dug his own hole and is standing in it. He knows he should say nothing, but can't resist rubbing it in. So he takes a shot of his own: "I think now maybe the people can understand why the selectmen cannot support Mr. Bell's efforts to buy a new toy at the taxpayers' expense."

The discussion turns again, this time in the chief's favor. Harold's "sarcasm had snapped the audience's attention to the issue." The audience began to ask the chief questions:

> Slowly but inexorably, the questioning allowed the chief to present his case so that it could be understood. Eventually it became clear to nearly everyone in the hall that the town needed a new fire truck, and that by buying a new truck, homeowners would reap an insurance benefit.

Harold tries to shift the focus by conceding that, yes, maybe a new truck was in order, but there should be more study on which truck would suit the town best and save money. He proposed that the vote on the fire truck be postponed. His amendment failed by one vote. The truck would be purchased. On to the next article, as the volunteer firemen slipped quietly out of the hall.

The next article faced by the voters of Darby asks them to accept federal revenue-sharing money. Boiler plate. It passes every year. And yet an old timer named Russell Pegasus dissents:

> *"This town was on its own for two hundred years," Pegasus said. "Now this town is a prisoner of the federal buck. In ten years it will be dead from all that money. You won't recognize it, and your children won't remember it." The voters nodded with sympathy, as though mourning an old friend, and then they voted unanimously to accept the federal funds.*
>
> *Harold wondered whether Zoe Cutter had caught on to what this was all about, whether she had figured out that the town-meeting form of government was nearly impotent, that it was democracy without real power, that most voters did not even come to town meeting, that the only ones who came did so out of nostalgia or because—like herself—they had a special interest or because they were new in town and curious.*

For a selectman, Harold Flagg's pretty cynical about town meeting and town government. Or maybe he's cynical because of his position, because he knows how the power works, recognizes that with so many state and federal mandates about how tax money must be spent, decisions on the local level are drops in the bucket. He echoes the nay sayers: town meeting is an anachronism.

At last we come to the junk car ordinance, the one of utmost importance to this cast of characters—Harold Flagg, Howard Elman, and Zoe Cutter. Zoe, recognized by the moderator, dives right in. Darby is changing fast, she asserts. Citizens must preserve the beauty of the place; they must maintain its attractive "essence." Junk cars, she implies, taint the essence.

Some in the crowd cheer. Zoe takes her seat. Howard's anger surfaces. He knows her comments are directed at him. Hell, they're an assault on his way of life. He shouts something that people don't understand, strides to the front of the hall, flails his arms, and the crowd—alarmed—goes still. The moderator asks if he wants to speak. Howard ignores him, circles the hall until he's standing directly in front of his enemy, Zoe Cutter. We witness the encounter through Harold's eyes.

> She stared straight ahead. Her mouth was set. Harold shook his head to make this image go away. Howard began to raise his hands slowly, as though lifting something heavy. The silence was appalling, embarrassing. . . . Harold was on his feet now. He sensed danger; somehow he knew Elman was about to strangle Zoe. Then there was a terrible gasp. A tingling ran up Harold's spine. He felt too much alive. And then relief. The gasp came from the back of the hall. It was Willow Jordan. Harold watched Ollie's hand go up and come down, strangely without sound, it seemed, on his son's face.
>
> "Is it possible that we can have order here?" the voice of Copley, sardonic, in command now. "Mr. Elman, if you wish to speak, speak now, and then sit. I can't have people browsing up and down the aisles. This is not a department store."
>
> Harold relaxed. He could see that whatever had come over Howard Elman had passed. Elman was now merely confused. He shook his head, coughed on a word, gestured to no purpose, and finally moved off.
>
> It turned out that a fatuous argument put forth by Russell Pegasus ruined any chance for the ordinance—at least for this year.
>
> "We never had anything like this before," he said. "Why do we need it now? Might as well pass a law that says no pigs allowed in church."
>
> The junk-car ordinance was defeated by voice vote. Only the new people favored it.

And so it goes at town meeting. What we're arguing about may not actually be what we're arguing about. Despite the moderator's cautions against personal attacks, the possibility of personal attacks—verbal, or in this case, physical—looms. One thing for sure about those who attend town meeting: We care! Intensely. We care about that junk-car ordinance. We care about the fire truck. We care about taxes. We care about our town. We care about what our town was, is, and is apt to become.

That's what gets us so roiled up. That—and his own mental and emotional problems—is what pushed Howard Elman toward assault.

And yet, a gasp, an admonition or joke from the moderator, a silly suggestion, a shouted "move the question," once again redirects the flock. And off we fly to the next meadow.

In this classic novel, Ernest Hebert spirals from the formalized surface of an institution to the depths of emotion and meaning for those who participate. He scrutinizes one town, one town meeting, and offers his gritty take on what motivates the people to whom the outcomes truly matter.

Finally, Town Meeting as Museum

In his collection of essays *In the Memory House*, Howard Mansfield—an elegant writer, deep thinker, and skilled synthesizer of ideas—takes on the question, What is a museum? Embedded in that question are many others: What do we save? What do we discard? What do we choose to remember? Or forget? All of which adds up to, "What do we value?" One of the museums he walks us through in this collection of essays is "The Museum of Democracy: Town Meeting."

Mansfield is a fan. His historical studies and firsthand experiences have made him a fan.

> *I go from town to town to sit for hours on hard benches and harder folding chairs, to watch debates late into the night: impassioned speeches about snowplows, dry hydrants, fire engines, schools, death, taxes and dogs.*
>
> *It is theater . . . I go to as many towns as I can schedule; hill towns with populations of five hundred that gather in meeting houses smaller than the garages on some suburban homes; and towns of five thousand that assemble in the high school gym. All those odd little towns. It's like walking into family discussions. Part of me can't help but see town meeting as a ritual family gathering, each town a republic of families.*
>
> *I go to see, each time, if democracy works. The discussions are sometimes heated and sometimes lethargic, good decisions and bad get made, but it all seems entirely natural. This is the way government should be: you get together with your neighbors, discuss and vote.*

Theater. Family discussions. A republic of families. Mansfield nails it. This institution is unique, and it works in its own and "entirely natural" way. Mansfield's one-line description of what goes on at town meeting is the shortest and most accurate I know: "You get together with your neighbors, discuss and vote."

Why then, do some call town meeting old-fashioned, outdated, inefficient, even unfair? For one thing, it's hard to understand how town meeting works unless you participate. To get it, you really have to be there. For another, Mansfield writes: "Town meeting has always suffered under the burden of expectations." Sages of the ages have called town meeting "the most perfect school of self-government" and "the ideal social compact." That's a lot to live up to in practice. And yet, Mansfield writes, "Town meeting when it works is really ordinary. Neighbors on hard chairs figuring things out. Democracy is in the details."

Differences get worked out. Problems are solved. It's the gathering of the people, and the face-to-face debate that allows this to happen. Marking an X beside Yes or No and sliding a ballot through a slot at the polls, just doesn't make the grade. At none of the meetings Mansfield attended "does someone say: It's Catch-22. It's insolvable. A conundrum. Just a plain mess. Beyond hope. At no time do people feel overwhelmed."

In our little republics, self-governance works. It ain't pretty sometimes. It ain't ever easy. But it works. Tax revolts, Mansfield writes, are expected. "You're taxing us out of the town. . . ." This lament is heard every year. And yet, every year, those same tax revolutionaries return to complain again.

In three short paragraphs that read like a poem or a call to action, Mansfield caches the essence of town meeting:

> So, yes, it is mythic, and it does work. It is an antique and an anachronism.
> But the antique is democracy.
> And the anachronism is the word 'citizen.'

"Town meeting is a collection of individualists.
When a man arises and cries, 'Mr. Moderator!'
and is properly recognized, no man living
is big enough to make him sit down."

JOHN GOULD, NEW ENGLAND TOWN MEETING:
SAFEGUARD OF DEMOCRACY

"One institution is ambivalently cherished more than any other in Washington, and that is the annual town meeting. Here is the community in a nutshell—democracy still pure and proud and free."

RON JAGER, *LAST HOUSE ON THE ROAD*

10 🔨

Humor

Some of us attend town meeting for the greater good—out of responsibility to our community and a sense of civic duty. Some relish the privilege of participating in pure democracy. Some attend for the drama, oh yes, the drama. Some attend to socialize with neighbors we haven't seen all winter and catch up on the news. Most attend for a mix of all of the above. My favorite part of town meeting is the humor—yankee humor, dry as beech leaves in January.

Town meetings may run four hours or twelve. And over a lifetime, a person may attend twenty or forty or, with luck, sixty plus. Nothing stands out more than the moments of humor: those illuminating and inspired exchanges, quips, comebacks, arched-eyebrow observations, spot-on summaries of the situation at hand, or flashes of wit that make us laugh out loud together. Some of these moments become legend. Together they are town meeting at its best.

Here are some favorites—observed, heard-tell-of, or read about in various official or, even better, unofficial documents.

Just Making Sure

"Can you hear me in the back?" the moderator says.

"No!"

Moderator: "Count your blessings."

Little of This, Little of That

Gordon walks in late. There's a stranger at the mic with a cowboy hat on. Gordon pokes his buddy Mike. "What's up with the cowboy?"

Mike says, "He's been talking for about ten minutes."

"What's he talking about?"

"He ain't said yet."

What Say?

During a debate in Seabrook (for many years, home to a race track), folks were complaining about how the poor recycling program was a waste of resources.

A latecomer, who caught just the end of the rant, pipes up: "Those racehorses ain't wasted. They turn them into glue."

Problem Solved

Debate raged over a warrant article to raise and appropriate $2000 to have the village sprayed against mosquitos. Some worried about the health risks of the chemicals. Others, like Catherine, just couldn't stand another mosquito infestation. Catherine said: "I was holding a cookout and the mosquitos were so thick we had to move everything inside. I couldn't even enjoy the outdoors around my home. It was terrible!"

Vin spoke up. "Mr. Moderator, I'd like to propose an amendment. Amend down from two thousand to a dollah ninety-eight. Buy Catherine a can of bug dope."

Didn't I See You at Breakfast?

The moderator's significant other rises and begins to speak.

Moderator interrupts: "Would you state your name for the record please?"

I Was Ned yesterday, I'm Ned today, and I'll be Ned Tomorrow

Old timer gets permission to speak. Moderator: "Would you state your name for the record please?"

Old timer: "You know damn well who I am."

Moderator: "Would you state your name for the record please?"

Old timer: "I've lived next door to you for forty-seven years."

Moderator: "Would you state your name for the record please?"

Old timer: "I give you that beagle dog of yours, named Nipper, from my bitch's first litter."

Moderator: "Would you state your name for the record please?"

Old timer: "My boy Lorus is married to your youngest girl, Penny."

Moderator: "Would you state your name for the record please?"

Old timer: "Edward Thomas Huckins."

Moderator: "Thanks, Ned."

Everybody Does Business with Grover Farwell, Eventually

A legendary exchange out of Brookline. Some say this happened every year. Some say only once, well remembered.

Newcomer: "I see we're expending $500 a year for a sexton? What's a sexton?"

Grover Farwell: "I'm the sexton. And I'm going to bury you."

Who Dat?

At town meeting in Deerfield, so many turned out that half the crowd had to assemble upstairs. The overflow was provided a speaker so they could listen in and a microphone so they could address issues. Jack Hutchinson moderated downstairs. His assistant upstairs monitored who'd raised their hand to speak and alerted Jack accordingly. During a heated discussion, Jack asked the assistant if anyone upstairs had a comment. Sure enough, a voter took the mic, and in a rich, deep, booming voice said: "This is John Pfeiffer, speaking from on high."

If the Chief Were 5'2" the Vote Might Have Gone the Other Way

The police department requested funds to purchase a radar counting device. It had been cut from the budget in an earlier proceeding, but an amendment was made to restore the amount. Among the reasons for a yes vote: a grant would pick up 50% of the cost.

The police chief explained that information generated by this device— how many cars, how fast they were going—would be used to support cases for lower speed limits and help out with decisions about road maintenance.

"How high on the pole will you mount this machine?" a concerned citizen asked. She worried that somebody might take a baseball bat to it.

"I'm 5'9", the chief replied. He stood on tip toe and stretched his arm to show how high he could reach.

The amendment passed anyway.

It Snows a Lot in Lincoln

Jim O'Donnell told this story, which I believe to be absolutely true. And if it isn't, it should be. The warrant article to purchase a new snow plow caused some controversy. It cost money, that's why. After much discussion someone proposed a solution. He happened to know that the neighboring town of Woodstock also had a new snow plow on the warrant. "Why can't we split the cost and share the plow?" he suggested.

The road agent said: "Far as I know, when it's snowing in Lincoln, it's snowing in Woodstock."

If Only

A resident of New Boston recalled the 1964 town meeting during which the fire department proposed the purchase of a brand new 1964 Ford fire truck to replace the 1937 model currently in use. After much discussion, the much-respected Fred Chaney banged his walking stick on the floor and was recognized by the moderator. Fred said: "I could support this truck . . . if it was an International."

That 1937 fire truck was eventually sold to Deerfield. "Last time I saw it," the resident told us, "it was in Raymond with a dump body."

Don't Blink

Some folks thought the one street light on the main drag was costing too much in electricity and ought to be turned off. "But if you turn off the light," a resident queried, "how would anybody driving through town at night know they've been here?"

Getting Hosed

The fire chief proposed buying 100 feet of new hose. The chair of the budget committee objected, claiming fifty feet would be sufficient. So they compromised: Wait until there's a fire and see how much we're short.

Not Buying Votes, Just Transporting Them

During one special town meeting, great effort was made on both sides to bring out the vote. Carlton had no car, but somebody fetched him. After he'd cast his vote, Maizie—who'd been in line behind Carlton and might have cast a glance at his ballot—said to the one who'd done the fetching: "If I were you, I wouldn't bother giving him a ride home."

No doubt, someone from the other camp made sure Carlton got home in good order.

That's One Way To Explain It

During a break, an irate citizen approached the selectmen's table and accosted the first selectman. "What, sir," said the irate citizen, "stands between you and a goddamn fool?"

"Just this table," replied the selectman.

Win Some, Lose Some

Mrs. Smith made a presentation of some length regarding a warrant article she supported. Then came time for questions and comments.

Mr. Smith had a comment. He addressed the voters: "Don't believe her. I'm married to her and she's never right."

Mrs. Smith replied: "I married him fifty years ago. And, it's true, I haven't been right since."

Agree to Disagree

By some miracle everybody agreed that it was a good idea to erect a new and updated veterans monument. Seems the old monument was a few wars behind. Discussion ensued. The monument was a fine idea, but should it be erected in Town Center or The Flat. The vote tied at eighty-two for the Center, eighty-two for the Flat.

So they didn't build it.

Sometimes You Feel Like a Nut

Jean Lane always bakes brownies for election day. She bakes Republican brownies and Democrat brownies. "What's the difference?" we asked her. She said, "The Democrats are the ones with the nuts.

That Town Just South of Freedom

Q: What would be served at the town meeting supper?
A: Effing-ham and beans.

Just Because It Happens, Don't Mean We Have to Like It

The venerated town elder was retiring from the school board after having served for more than fifty years. When it was suggested that he must have witnessed many changes over those years, he said, "Ayuh. And I was agin' 'em all."

Strategies and Options

During a discussion of cemeteries and the rising cost of plots, a newcomer asked how one went about procuring such a plot. "Well," said the sexton, "I'll tell you this. You don't just go in cold."

Someone asked, "What is a plot going for these days?"

Sexton explained: "You used to be able to buy a four-body plot for fifteen dollars. These days it'll cost you $1,500 or $2,000 depending on whether you want the lower or upper cemetery. Course," he added, "you can get scattered for nothing."

Additional discussion: "Why does it cost more to be buried in the upper cemetery than the lower?"

Sexton: "Better view."

Riot Averted, Barely

One neighbor says to the other: "Did you hear what happened after town meeting?"

"I did. I heard it was practically a riot."

"Ayuh. Ken Whitney, Hazel Cready, and Jim Havershan were all standing around the town hall yard. Glaring at each other."

A Dry Year

A sharp-eyed taxpayer noted that, according to the records, the road agent had failed to take any social security out of her pay the previous year. Why was that? And what happened to the money that had been budgeted for her social security?

The road agent explained: "It was a tough winter. No snow. Didn't have much work or money, so instead of taking social security out of my pay, I spent it."

You Don't Miss What You Never Had

Frank Case recalled a Raymond school meeting during which discussion escalated about whether the district ought to hire a part-time art teacher. One voter rose and said with conviction, "Raymond ain't never had no Pikatzo, and it ain't never gonna have no Pikatzo."

Come to Think of It

The annual report lists the vital statistics for the previous year—who was born, who got married and who died. Good thing. It's hard to keep track of that stuff. I asked a resident of a small town what the population was. "Three hundred forty-two," she said confidently. Then, on second thought. "The Osterman's moved away—there were five of them. And there's a young couple renting the apartment over the general store." Subtract five, add two: "Three hundred thirty-nine," she said. Then, "Oh—I forgot. My husband died. So it's three hundred thirty-eight!"

Ask a Good Question, Get a Good Answer

Thanks to Jack Hutchinson for passing on this story, which he heard from Richard Gale, regarding a terse exchange at a Deerfield School District Meeting. This story goes back a few decades. The president of the PTA posed this question to the school board chair: "Madam Chairman, the PTA wants to know if the Board of Education appreciates the PTA."

The crowd rumbled, then erupted into pandemonium. (Which in Yankee terms means chatter, a snort or two of laughter, and maybe a burst of applause.) The school board chair looked to the moderator. The PTA president persisted: "Madam Chairman, I want an answer."

The school board chair whispered something in the moderator's ear, then announced, "I've asked the moderator for a short recess. I want to confer with the board."

The PTA president responded: "I want the moderator to promise that when we reconvene I will have the floor." It was agreed. Short recess. Reconvene. The PTA president reiterates: "Madam Chairman, the PTA wants to know if the Board of Education appreciates the PTA." Uproar. Applause.

The chair responds: "Sir, I've conferred with the school board. Their message to you is that the Board of Education appreciates the PTA just about as much as the PTA appreciates the School Board."

Cattel, Horse and Swine Ordinance

I don't know if wry humor was the intention of the composers of this warning from *Nottingham-250—Anniversary Commemorative Edition*, but more than 200 years later, it makes me smile. It's the original "No Parking—Violators Will Be Towed" ordinance. Or maybe it's "No Trespassing (if you have four legs and are not a resident)."

Whereas it has been practised for a number of years past for persons not living in the Town of Nottingham to turn out in the woods, and on the commons in said Town a large number of Cattel and horses and Etc., by which cattle and horses the inhabitants of sd. Town are very much injured therefore voted in a Legal Town Meeting in sd. Town on the 1 day of June 1778 that all persons having any Cattel, Horses or Swine turned out in the Town of Nottingham are hereby immediately for to take care of them or they may depend on meeting with trouble in finding them where they have turned them out in sd. woods and commons in sd. Town.

Depends on Your Definition of Fine

At school meeting, it was proposed that a fourth counselor position be added at the high school. One fellow—known to be a heavy drinker and womanizer, didn't work much that anybody could tell, father to a passel of children but supporting none, having spent time in the county jail for a variety of infractions including the occasional assault—asked to speak to the article.

Recognized by the moderator, the fellow was clearly in a lather about all those counselors. After some ranting, he faced the crowd: "It's absolutely goddam ridiculous to spend all this money on four goddamn guidance counselors. We never had no goddamn guidance counselors when I was in school. And goddammit I turned out just fine."

Can't Win for Losing

Moderators don't generally vote during the proceeding, but they may if they wish. Occasionally, a moderator will vote to break a tie. I recall a tie vote on the hot topic of cutting or not cutting the proposed school budget (one or t'other, I don't recall). A ballot vote was called. We all marched past the supervisors of the checklist, who duly checked off our names. We marked yea or nay on the slip of paper and tucked it in the locked ballot box.

After everybody had voted, the box was ceremoniously opened. The ballots counted. A tie resulted.

In the case of a tie, the article or amendment automatically fails. But the moderator decided to cast his ballot anyway. He announced that he was voting no.

Todd said in my ear: "I don't know how anybody else voted on this except the moderator, and I'm mad at him!"

Though It Could Become a Problem Some Time Along

I have it on good (apocryphal) authority, that at the New London town meeting of 1959, a newcomer (possibly an engineer) announced that he'd done the research and to his horror discovered there were no maps of the water and sewer system in New London. Where, he demanded, was this information to be had?

Ira Littlefield, who'd been commissioner of water and sewer in New London since 1904, went to the mic. "I know where all the pipes are," he said.

"But what if," the newcomer said, "you should retire, or—god forbid—die?"

"Then," Ira said, "it ain't my problem."

How Many Police Officers Does It Take To Run a Computer?

In Gilmanton, the police department requested $7,500 for an IMC Multiple User License. At town meeting, the question arose: What the heck is an IMC Multiple User License?

Chief O'Brien explained that an IMC Multiple User License allowed three users to use the program at the same time. Mr. Goddard allowed as how he now understood that. His question was: Do we ever have three officers in the office at the same time? And if so, why?

Sometimes It Is Personal

No issue is too mundane to be discussed at town meeting—from the need to upgrade the bathroom in the town house to whether the milfoil problem in the lake might be solved by importing muskrats, since muskrats are known to eat milfoil. At this particular meeting, the dog ordinance caused a stir. One man spoke passionately about dogs barking at night and disturbing his much needed sleep—in particular the town clerk's dogs. They were a nuisance and there should be a law against such barking and the owner fined.

The debate turned personal. The town clerk defended her dogs and herself: "If you'd stay to home on the farm, Richard, instead of spending nights in the village with your lady friend, you wouldn't be bothered by my dogs."

No Brag, Just Fact

John Colburn sent this story. At the Weare town meeting, citizens complained because the drinking water in Weare Center was poor. Folks had to go to town hall and draw water from an outdoor faucet, which was darned inconvenient. During the discussion, one citizen rose to address the issue, prefacing her comments with: "I drink as much as anybody in Weare!"

Morbid but True

Frugal voter comment: "Why do we need to spend money on a traffic light for that intersection? Nobody's been killed there yet."

What Is It With Librarians and Books?

When discussion on the library budget got prickly, a fellow stood up, looked the library trustee right in the eye and said, with some hostility: "Didn't we buy books for you people last year?"

Someone else suggested maybe the library didn't need any more books. Maybe the patrons could be encouraged to read the same books twice.

Sure and Be Gorra

Everybody's Irish on St. Patrick's Day, they say. Similarly, on Town Meeting Day everybody's a road agent.

The Selectman's Funeral

The town turned out for the funeral of a popular resident who'd moved to town from Massachusetts after his retirement and lived there a good twenty-five years. He served on many town committees and had several terms as selectman. When it came time for people to speak of him, an old timer stood up, kinda misty-eyed: "Gosh," he said, "Jake was almost like one of us."

Maybe If You Squint . . .

A moderator said he attended a training session with Walter Peterson some years back. Peterson served as New Hampshire's governor from 1969 through 1973. He also served in the NH House of Representatives and as town moderator in Peterborough. According to an acquaintance, Peterson asked: "What do you do when a liberal raises his hand at town meeting?"

The moderator replied: "Walter, some days my vision is just not so good."

Division of Church, State, and Horse Sheds

The auctioning off of pews and horse hitches or even horse and buggy sheds was common when town halls and churches were being constructed. The money helped fund the construction.

Two hundred years later, give or take, the rustic sheds between the church and meeting house on one town square struck a concerned citizen as an eye sore. She went to the selectmen: "Those old sheds should be torn down. They're hazards and they're ugly."

The selectmen said, "We don't have anything to do with the sheds. They belong to the church. You need to talk to the pastor and the church folks."

So the crusader attended a meeting of the church committee. "Those sheds spoil the looks of the common and nobody uses them anyway," she said.

"They don't belong to the church," the committee chair told her. "They belong to the founding families. They were auctioned off as horse and buggy shelters for when folks went to church or town meeting. You'll have to talk to the owners."

The determined woman said that, indeed, she would, if she could have the owners' names. "I'll give you a list," the chair said, "But there's a problem. They're all dead."

The Shortest Story About Politics I Know

(thanks to J. P. Marzullo and Peter Beard)

Incumbent ran for selectman.

Unopposed.

And he lost.

Why?

He pissed off the road agent.

Problem Solved

Turnout for town meeting is fairly predictable, but sometimes when a special meeting gets called on a controversial matter, a whole lot of people show up—up in arms and armed for bear. If it gets too crowded in the hall, fire officials have been known to shut the meeting down and send everybody home. A great disappointment to all.

At one such meeting, we're told, the fire chief started counting heads, grumbling that the room appeared to be over its posted capacity. "I think we've got a problem," the chief said to the old timer.

"We wouldn't have a problem," the old timer said, "if you'd just go home."

Between a Rock and a Road Agent

An irate citizen brought a big rock to town meeting, and when the budget for roads came up, he placed it on the table at the front of the hall. He said to the road agent, "I've been driving around this damned rock for six months."

The road agent says, "Well, you ain't driving around that rock any more, are ya?"

That's Some Hard-packed Road

Robbie Robertson, as a kid, enjoyed going to town meeting to hear what the old characters would say. "My father was one of them," he says. "We lived on a dirt road between Greenfield and Bennington. They were hassling about the roads, and my father got up and said, 'My God, we take such poor care of the dirt roads, my tom cat has to go across the road and up to the railroad tracks before he can scratch.'"

Ginger and the Fuse

In that distant time before cell phones and digital cameras, if someone wanted to record town meeting they needed a video camera. Ginger let it be known that she intended to record town meeting and, according to the Right to Know laws she often quoted, town officials couldn't stop her.

Sure enough, she showed up early, set the camera up on a tripod at the back of the hall, plugged in her equipment. Did a test run. Everything worked fine.

Unfortunately, when the meeting started, she couldn't get the camera going. She pushed every button, switched every switch, checked the connections. Dead as a doornail.

Ginger was visibly disappointed.

After the meeting, the moderator had a quiet word with the select board chair. "Willis," he said, "I know Ginger had the right to record the meeting, but I'm kinda glad her camera didn't work."

"That reminds me," the selectman said, "I gotta put that fuse back in."

Hot Sauce and Bountiful Beans

"For years," Dave said, "I was the most powerful man at town meeting in Gilmanton."

"That so," I said.

"Yup," he said, "I controlled the meeting."

"Moderator?"

"No. I made the chili."

A Special Piquancy

In Brookline, I'm told, people at town meeting raved about the corn chowder. Best corn chowder to be had. Only a few knew that the pot in which the chowder was cooked every year was the same pot, housed in the church basement, that one colorful local (who didn't own a washing machine) used to wash out his undies.

We Don't Need No Stinkin' Map

For big money items like a new town shed or a school addition, committees may be appointed to look into the possibility of maybe hiring consultants to mull over the idea and formulate a report about how to move ahead. At one school meeting, an article proposed the establishment of a planning committee to hire a consultant who would be paid a considerable sum to develop a proposal for a new wing at the elementary school. Minnie stood to speak: "It seems to me," she said, "the school board is asking us to buy a road map for a trip we're not going to take."

House Be in Order—Please

This is a classic, maybe *the* classic town meeting story. The warrant called for $400,000 to build a bridge across a brook (some might call it a river—depending on the season). Old Zeb jumps to his feet in protest. "We don't need no bridge for that kind of money. It's ridiculous. Why I could pee halfway across that piddling little brook!"

The moderator bangs the gavel, "Sir, you are out of order!"

Zeb says: "Damn right. If I wasn't I could pee all the way across."

What Does "Miscellaneous" Have to Say on the Subject?

Another classic. Seems an unmarried woman got pregnant. The father was nowhere to be found, so the town helped her out with her medical bills. The expenditure appeared in the town budget under "Miscellaneous."

A budget watcher spotted the $250 and asked what it was for. The selectmen explained as delicately as they could. Another sharp-eyed local spotted $300 in revenues also under "Miscellaneous." Sure enough, the state had paid the town that amount to reimburse them for helping out the unfortunate girl.

Someone did the math: "It seems to me the town made a profit of $50 on this transaction."

The selectmen agreed that they had.

"Well, then," he says, "I make a motion to breed her again."

It Is What It Is

The citizen confronts the road agent: "Is there a plan for the maintenance of roads in this town or is it willy nilly?"

Road agent: "It's willy nilly."

"There is a special manner about the way a New Englander mounts the steps of his Town Hall on Town Meeting day. Unconsciously he remembers that he once went thus to help shape the life of a nation; dignity crowns his head."

ZEPHINE HUMPHREY, *A BOOK OF NEW ENGLAND*

11 🔨

Wisdom

Application of the collective Mind generates its share of wisdom. Reading town histories, town reports, and talking with folks unearthed some gems of common sense, plainspoken observation, and, yes, wisdom. Consider town meeting a microcosm for social and political interaction, and its wisdom can be widely applied. That is, what works at town meeting will probably work at the United Nations General Assembly, in a bar on a lively Saturday night, at the Red Sox game seated among Yankees fans, or at the dreaded family Christmas party. Former Moultonborough moderator Dick Wakefield defined his job this way: "To extract from the group something indicative of what the group wants that will stand up to legal challenges." And, he adds, "it helps if we're nice to one another."

Deerfield moderator Jack Hutchinson expressed his gratitude to his predecessor, Jim McIntyre, for sound advice. "Smile," Jim told Jack. "Let others get angry." Which seems like a good stance to take in many circumstances, especially at the dreaded family Christmas party. In my experience, smiling will always get you further and leave you with fewer regrets than getting angry.

Jim also advised Jack to keep his opinions and knowledge to himself. "You don't know any content, Jack. If someone wants the time, ask if there's anyone in the hall who can read the clock." It's the Sergeant Schultz approach to politics: I see nothing! I hear nothing! I know nothing!

Here's a collection of town meeting wisdom. Apply as appropriate.

Oh Behave!

From the beginning, the potential for trouble erupting at town meeting was recognized and addressed in *The Laws of New Hampshire, 1641*: "If any man shall behave himself offensively at any Towne meeting, the rest of the freemen then present shall have power to sentence him for his offense."

From John Gould's New England Town Meeting, published in 1940

"Town meeting is a collection of individualists. When a man arises and cries,

'Mr. Moderator!' and is properly recognized, no man living is big enough to make him sit down. As long as he speaks on the subject, uses proper words, and obeys parliamentary procedure he can say what he pleases. And every listening citizen in the hall knows that the same privilege will be extended in turn. So long as anyone wishes to speak, the matter at hand is held open for discussion. Knowing this, the Yankee carries the Town Meeting privileges over to his private life, and likewise into his state and national politics . . . Each voter brings his utter independence into the hall and from the congregation results a majority decision in which unity is attained without anyone's losing the least bit of his own separate self."

Given a Choice

I asked a longtime moderator what he liked about the job. "Better than being selectman," he said. His wife quipped: "You only get yelled at once a year."

Which Mr. Grace?

Mr. Grace was an astute thinker who cared very much about the welfare of his newly adopted town. This story comes from his daughter who recalled that the dignified man would often raise his hand at town meeting, *if* he had something he felt was important to share.

Unfortunately, another Mr. Grace, would frequently rise and share nonsense.

One day, the daughter writes, "my exasperated father raised his hand after this other jolly fellow had spoken. He stood up and said, 'Please let the record reflect *which* Mr. Grace made the previous statement.'"

What Clarence Webster Says

In his book *Town Meeting Country*, published in 1945, Clarence M. Webster traces the development and evolution of town meeting in New England. Among his conclusions: "The town stands alone; it is as strong and as perfect a form of representative government as has ever been built."

And:

"We are free men and women, doing as we please. We can also act as the town demands, for we are bound by its old and wise customs. That is why we can vote in the main wisely in town meeting. You have to be free before you can endure being bound by society; and you must be bound before you can build a society in which you can be free."

A Transplant's Perspective

In Bow, I asked Lori Fisher what she liked about town meeting. She said: "As a transplant, I think town meeting is what makes New Hampshire New Hampshire. It's the only place where you feel like you can really have your say. In New York it's on the ballot and you can vote yes or no. That's not having your say."

What to Do about Snow

No sense spending all kinds of money on snow removal anyway. As one Yankee sage said: "The lord brought it and the lord can take it away."

Thought or Opinion?

At town meeting, I was told, you learn pretty quickly that many people don't have a lot of thought, but do have a lot of opinions.

What T. J. Said

Founding father Thomas Jefferson made this oft-quoted remark. Over-inflated? Or right on the mark? Words like "wisest" and "perfect" are always dangerous, but they certainly reflect his conviction. He said: "Town meetings have proved themselves the wisest invention ever devised by the wit of man for the perfect exercise of self-government and for its preservation."

Longevity Counts

The *Concord Monitor* reported that George Condodemetraky lost both races he entered, one for selectmen, one for planning board. When asked why he thought he'd come up short, the candidate explained that he'd only lived in town thirty-five years. His opponents were natives.

Same Old Same Old

Asked how the new deliberative sessions compared to the traditional town meeting, a longtime resident said: "No different. It's the same personalities debating the same things."

No Sense Getting All Fancy

Cleve, who lived on the dirt road, asked if the plan was to "stripe it" after it was paved.

"No need," said the road agent. "Cleve, all you need to know is drive on the right and pass on the left."

Talk to the Hand

Marion Knox, former town administrator and selectman, summarized the dynamics of town meeting as follows: "Town meetings build a sense of community. It's a hard day if you're involved—a lot of preparation, so when it's over you say, Thank God it's over. But the people come. You see people you haven't seen since the year before. You renew friendships. If you're sitting up front, you know who is sitting where, and you almost know how their going to vote. That part doesn't change. A lot of people have made up their minds in the beginning. Some will raise their hand because the person next to them did. You can see the hand isn't up yet . . . but it's coming!"

Sometimes, Despite Our Best Efforts, Logic Prevails

The road agent put in a plea for a new snow plow. Yup, it was needed. No sense putting it off. But one old timer had his thinking cap on. "Wa'n't that the same snow plow we had last year?"

"Yup."

"And wa'n't last winter the winter we didn't get any snow?"

"Yup."

"If it was good enough last year and we never used it, why ain't it good enough this year?"

Motion for a new snow plow defeated.

Keep This in Mind

According to Dick Wakefield: "While it's true that people who disagree with us are generally wrong, sometimes they're not."

Geometry of Town Meeting

The length of discussion on an article is, usually, inversely proportional to the amount of money at stake. That is, the five-million-dollar school bond item passes in a voice vote after ten minutes of discussion. The vote on a $500 raise for the town clerk takes an hour.

Do the Math

Richard Snow of Candia stood up at town meeting and he *didn't* complain about taxes. He said, "The reason I don't complain about my taxes is because I had five kids who each went through twelve years of school. That's sixty years × $5,000/year, about what it costs to educate a child. That's $300,000. I will never pay that back. You'll never get it out of me."

Word to the Chatty

Sometimes you want to vote against a fellow, even if you'd normally agree with him, just because you're sick of listening to him. One such fellow was taken aside by a kindly moderator—word to the wise: "You'd probably be a lot more effective if you didn't talk so much."

Historical Heavyweight Alexis de Tocqueville Weighs In

From *Democracy in America*: "Town meetings are to liberty what primary schools are to science; they bring it within the people's reach."

Thin, Thinner, Thinnest

Horace Richardson, longtime Moultonborough selectman, always said: "You have to slice something awfully thin before there aren't two sides to it."

Store on Every Corner; Town Meeting Every Day

In her *Guide to the History and Old Dwelling Places of Northwood*, Joann Bailey writes of a time before automobiles when people walked or rode their horses to local stores, so small towns had many small stores within walking or riding distance. Such stores, she writes, provided time and space for being neighborly:

> In the summer much of this visiting was done on the shaded, front steps, but in cold weather the customers gathered round the wood-burning stove to soak up the warmth and the news. One of our selectmen once commented that he believed town meetings went smoother years ago because unofficial, preliminary discussions were held almost daily in the local stores all through the winter. By the second Tuesday in March the voters were well informed on the current issues, had made their minds up and were ready to vote.

Play Ball!

Frank M. Bryan wrote: "Voting after speaking is to governance what keeping score is to sports."

Where There's Smoke

A gentleman, unhappy with the new rule banning smoking in town hall, proffered this logic: "If the stove can smoke, we certainly should be allowed to."

Hey, Who's In Charge Here?

Lots of town meetings were heated by wood stoves. The hall could be boiling hot or bone chilly depending on how that stove was loaded and regulated—either extreme might drive voters to move on with the agenda. Regarding the wood stove, one moderator let this comment slip: "That stove has resolved more elections than any ballot counter."

Where There's No Smoke

Just before the vote on the new fire truck for Woodford, the beepers went off and the fire fighters, EMTs, and police officers made a dramatic exit from town meeting, dropping their official voting cards off with the supervisors of the checklist on the way out.

One woman leaned over and whispered in her friend's ear: "Do you suppose there *really is* an emergency?"

Sure enough, discussion on the new fire truck was not nearly as heated as it might have been. "Those volunteers do so much for our town," one speaker said, "as we just witnessed. The least we can do is provide safe equipment."

The new truck passed on a show of hands.

The Wisdom of Looking a Gift Horse in the Mouth

Peter Randall—writer, photographer, publisher—recollects a Seabrook town meeting at which "We were discussing whether to pass an article to accept a piece of land for a new town cemetery." Naturally, spirited discussion ensued. The New Hampshire Yankee looks askance at gifts. "What's the catch?" we say to ourselves. "What's it gonna cost us down the road?"

The article to accept the land looked like it was going to pass until one fellow stood up and said, "I heard tell the ground is so wet there it would be like buryin' someone at sea." That killed the article on the spot.

What's the Point?

One Nottingham historian, writing in the commemorative newspaper *Nottingham-250*, offered this insight into why so many petitions for road work were defeated at the 1835 town meeting: "The majority of citizens, having no chaise or carriage and able to walk or drive their ox carts or sledges where a modern tank might have trouble, had little sympathy for any highway improvement program and resented spending any additional monies."

When automobiles came along, no doubt the residents of Nottingham and every other town were whistling a different tune.

In that same publication, the writer offered this insight into the attitudes of the average resident: "Slow to accept change and loathe to abandon a project once adopted."

Why Be Selectman?

Dick Wakefield explained the job of selectman this way. "You get $2,000, functional indigestion, and all the abuse you can handle."

What Ralph Waldo Emerson Said of Town Meeting on September 12, 1835

"It is the consequence of this institution that not a school-house, a public pew, a bridge, a pound, a mill-dam, hath been set up, or pulled down, or altered, or bought, or sold, without the whole population of this town having a voice in the affair. A general contentment is the result. And the people truly feel that they are lords of the soil. In every winding road, in every stone fence, in the smokes of the poor-house chimney, in the clock on the church, they read their own power, and consider, at leisure, the wisdom and error of their judgments."

A Question for the Ages

From Pat Cummings: "Why are cemeteries plowed first?"

Things Happen

H. L. Mencken, satirist: "Some of the most idiotic decisions ever come to by mortal man were made by the New England town meeting."

A Letter to the Editor

Letter to the editor, with specifics altered because this young man will, as he matures, come to understand why this was not a wise political move:

> I am a newbie to the whole process of running for office. I have decided to run for town selectman and for the school board.
>
> As the new guy, I would appreciate it if you voted for me. The school board election is March 5 at the high school and the selectman's voting is March 10 at the town hall.
>
> I welcome any and all questions. Contact me at (e-mail address).

Defibrillate This!

Deb Schulte, New Castle town historian, passed on this true town meeting story. The town had put in a request for a defibrillator for the EMTs. Discussion included questions about the EMTs' qualifications to run the defibrillator and, of course, cost. Seemed kinda pricey to a lot of folks.

An older gentleman named Bill explained that he had a modest home. Would the selectman tell him how much the defibrillator would cost him in property taxes in the coming year?

Selectman said: "On your house, Bill, it'd be about $20."

Bill said, "My wife's worth $20."

The article slid right through.

What the Wise Man or Woman Does Not Say

- Where I come from, this is how it's done.
- I've only lived in town a little while, but in my opinion . . .
- This is the same point I bring up every year, but . . .
- I don't mean to belabor the issue, but . . .
- (shouting) Mr. Moderator, I wish to be recognized!
- I wasn't able to attend any of the budget committee meetings or hearings on this topic, but . . .
- Ms. Moderator, you can't have me thrown out! I'm a taxpayer.
- We're not proceeding according to *Robert's Rules*.

"As an enduring symbol of popular government, town meeting can't be beat."

JERE DANIELL

12

Heaves, Hoops and Earl Hadley: The Shocking Truth about What Went On at Town Meeting

by Ken Sheldon

Ken Sheldon is the brains behind the imaginary, but very real, town of Frost Heaves, New Hampshire. His variety show, "Frost Heaves," features stories, songs, and skits . It's a hoot, especially when Ken gets into character as his alter-ego Fred Marple. This story, which first appeared in New Hampshire Magazine, *is adapted from one of Ken's monologues. He catches the currents and undercurrents all right—and names names: Mavis and Avis, the Thompkins sisters; Millard Tuttle, who has access to dead raccoons and knows where to put 'em; Cecil Philmore, sports fan; Clara Franklin, interpreter of history; Mabel Pillsbury, inventive baker; and so forth. But it's Earl Hadley, Frost Heaves' "unofficial contrarian," who really gets things cooking.*

In Frost Heaves, New Hampshire, the same people generally run for office every year, so it ain't that interesting. We try to get people excited about the elections, but it's like trying to get a cat to laugh.

One year, we decided that instead of having an election, we would have a talent show, and the winners would get the office. The problem is we don't have much talent in Frost Heaves, so the bar was set pretty low. I ain't going to mention any names, but one of the local ladies, she really wanted to be a library trustee, so she did a belly dance. It weren't a pretty sight. You know how you get an image in your head and you just can't get it out? It's what you call Post Traumatic Stress Disorder. Anyway, we give up on the talent election idea after that.

This year, there was some controversy over cemetery trustee. Basically, Mavis and Avis Thompkins, they're sisters, trade off. One year it's Mavis, the next year it's Avis. Well, this year, it was Avis's turn, but Louise Mitchell decided she'd like the job. I tell you, it was the biggest controversy to hit this town since they moved the bingo game from the grange to the town hall. It was a bitter contest, and in the end, Avis edged out Louise. 'Course, Avis had an advantage, since she and Mavis keep the rolls of all the dead folks in the cemetery, many of whom actually voted this year.

Edith Wyer was reelected town clerk of course. And Albert Cooper was reelected as Supervisor of the Public Works. Basically, this means he takes care of the town plow. Now, the Frost Heaves town plow has got about one more year to go before it qualifies for the National Historic Register. Albert is the only person around who knows where to wham it when the cussed thing breaks down. A delicate piece of machinery like that, you can't just wham it anywhere, you got to know the specific location. He'll give it a couple of diagnostic whaps, and then deliver just the right whack to set it right again. Kinda like acupuncture.

There were some dirty tricks pulled during the election. I was helping out with the ballots, and Millard Tuttle come up to me and he told me he would put a dead raccoon in the back of my truck if Fred Kimball was elected to the board of selectmen. Well, what could I do? I had to report him for attempting to bribe an election official.

Then of course, right after election came town meeting. We still do town meeting, in contrast to some other towns around here. We ain't too lazy to do our duty and argue with our neighbors.

I don't know who first thought of doing town meeting in March, but if you want to guarantee that people are going to be cranky, just plan a meeting after a long winter. In other towns around here, people start out with a thin veneer of politeness, but in Frost Heaves we skip right over that.

The other downside to doing it in March: it conflicts with the college basketball tournament. Now, we never had a basketball player from Frost Heaves make it to the final 4 . . . or the final 64, or 1064 for that matter. But this year, there was a local boy named Jeremy Russell who plays for Millard Fillmore University over in New York, and last weekend was their conference tournament, and there was a chance they were going to make it to the big show.

This caused quite a dilemma for a lot of the men in town, who had been watching Jeremy play basketball since he was in junior high. They had to go to town meeting to make sure we didn't spend a penny more than we had to. But they sure didn't want to miss that basketball game. Then someone hit on a plan. Cecil Philmore has one of them old-fashioned hearing aids that runs to an amplifier in his pocket. He just replaced the amplifier with a transistor radio, so he could listen to the game and report to the other guys on the sly. The problem was that, although Cecil knew what was happening at the game, he had only the vaguest notion of what was happening at town meeting.

Which weren't that big a problem because town meeting is always the same, it's like a play that gets put on once a year. First they hand out the town reports. About the only interesting thing in there is that you can find out who didn't pay their taxes.

The Ladies Loon League always has a bake sale. This year, Mabel Pillsbury invented a new cake special for town meeting. She called it Democracy Cake, and it had equal parts of pineapple, chocolate, artichoke hearts, and beef jerky bits.

Generally speaking, I think segregation is a bad thing, but maybe not when it comes to food. Anyway, the cast of characters at town meeting is always the same. First you got Howard Everly, he's the moderator, and he follows the rules to a T, and always makes sure everyone gets a chance to speak. Consequently, getting anything done in Frost Heaves takes longer than it does for fossils to form.

The first item on the agenda every year is the financial report, given by Arthur Tidley, the town treasurer. Arthur loves to give reports, and he insists on reading every single line of the report. This is about as much fun as being awake during your own surgery and hearing the doctor describe each step. The only interesting part of the financial report was when Arthur mentioned that receipts for dog licenses had dropped 17 percent. Cecil Philmore shouted, "Whoa!" and folks who had been dozin' off kinda snapped to attention, wondering why he was so upset about dog licenses, but really, it was that the Fillmore Badgers had just taken the lead.

After the financial report come the reports from the town committees, most of which I missed because I had had some of Mabel's cake and I was experiencing democracy in action, if you catch my drift.

Finally, come the warrant articles. This year, you could basically sum up the response to the warrant articles as follows: No! Of course, these days, all the towns around here are pinching pennies, but we were cheap long before it become fashionable. In fact, I'm thinking that this recession could actually be good for Frost Heaves. Because, in times like these, people start to focus on the good old-fashioned virtues like honesty, integrity, common sense . . . we ain't got any of them, but we do have cheapness. It ain't exactly one of your classical virtues, but it makes a lot of sense.

When it comes to the warrant articles, the same people get up to speak every year. The town meeting is their big chance to hold the entire congregation hostage to their opinions, and they ain't going to miss it.

First you got Clara Franklin, who taught history at the Frost Heaves Academy for thirty years. I say "taught," but for the last ten years, Clara weren't exactly teaching from the book. A lot of kids graduated thinking the Gettysburg Address was a place you could send a postcard to. When the school board caught on, they held a quick retirement party for Clara, who looked a little stunned but managed to lecture her fellow teachers about the Peloponnesian Wars, the Taft-Hartley Act and the Gadsden Purchase, without which a southern railroad route to the Pacific would never have been possible before being drowned out by a chorus of "For She's a Jolly Good Fellow."

When Clara stands up to speak at the town meeting, you're never really sure what planet she's broadcasting from. And generally, there is only the flimsiest connection between the warrant article at hand and Clara's comments, which center around a few recurring themes: "The Way Things Used to Be," (better than they are now), "What Young People Need" (more discipline), and "those idiots down in Washington."

Clara was going on about the Federal Reserve when Cecil Philmore passed a note to Herb Cullen in the row ahead of him. Clara saw this and said, "Cecil! Maybe you'd like to share that note with the whole class!" So Herb passed the note to Clara — you don't want to cross Miss Franklin — and she read the note out loud: "64 to 60, second half" and a cheer went up, so Clara decided that was a good time to sit down.

Then Earl Hadley took the microphone. Earl is the town's unofficial contrarian. Earl is opposed to just about everything, on general principal, because he's kinda cheap. Actually, to say he's kinda cheap is like saying that Hitler was kinda pushy. And every year, he starts off the same way. "My family came to this town in 1790 . . ." and people start to settle in, 'cause they know they're in for the long haul.

This year the big argument was about whether to buy a defibrillator for the fire department. You know what a defibrillator is, it's like a jump-starter for your heart in case all that fried dough you ate at the Eastern States Fair over the years finally comes to roost in your aorta.

Nobody was too surprised that Earl opposed this idea, which he said was the stupidest waste of taxpayers' money he'd ever heard of. Of course that's what he says every year, no matter what it is. You'd think the town fathers just sit around all year coming up with a proposal that would top last year's for stupidity.

Well, Earl went on and on. Folks tried to reason with him, but after an hour of arguing about it, the guys from the fire department were pretty fed up, on top of which they were missing the game of the century. At one point, Mickey Edwards, he's the fire chief, he went off to the bathroom— we all figured he'd had some of Mabel's cake, too—and whilst he was in there, don't you know the fire bell went off. Mickey come running out of the bathroom and yelled, "Come on, men, let's go." And they all jumped up and ran out to do their duty.

Well, it was perfect timing. Someone hollered over to Earl, "You see, that's why we have to support our firefighters and give 'em what they need to do their jobs." For a moment, it looked as if Earl was going to crumble, but then he shook his head. "I don't care, I ain't voting for it."

By that time, everyone had just about had it with Earl, so someone made an amendment to the warrant, and before Earl could object, it was seconded and passed with a voice vote. And that brought the meeting to a close, to the thunderous applause of the gathered citizenry.

The cheering was so loud that the volunteer firemen heard it all the way over to the fire station, where they were gathered around a satellite hookup watching the last few minutes of the basketball game. And with just seconds left in the game, Jeremy Hudson made an astonishing shot from half-court . . . which didn't even come close. The Badgers lost by two points, but it's OK. We're from Frost Heaves, we're used to failure.

Oh, and about that warrant article. The way it read, as amended, was: "To see if the Town will vote to raise and appropriate the sum of Six thousand dollars to purchase a portable defibrillator for use on anybody who needs it . . . except Earl Hadley."

13 ⚖

Yankee Curse: A School Meeting Story

by Rebecca Rule

Town meeting and its twin, school meeting, move slowly, allowing participants plenty of time to visit, drink coffee, catch up on their reading, grade papers, balance their checkbooks, crochet, cross-stitch, knit, and sometimes think. The knitters are iconic —often appearing in newspaper photographs documenting the event. Little old ladies knitting—could there be anything quainter? These women (usually women) do their civic duty while creating warm things—mittens, scarfs, sweaters—in preparation for the next cold snap. The click-click-click of their busy needles punctuate the proceedings . The knitters ground us in homeyness and tradition. Though some might detect a hint of Dickens' Madame Defarge.

I always wondered what these sedate knitters were thinking, so I imagined it in a story called "Yankee Curse." Miranda, the knitter, and the other characters are based on no particular living persons, nor is the story based on a particular incident in a particular town. But, truth be told, I wish I were more like Miranda—able to hold my tongue until the time is right and speak clear truth. I also identify with Kaye Elbow, school board chair—newcomer under siege—and wish when I served my three years on the school board I'd been as spunky and prepared as Kaye.

"Yankee Curse" is my fantasy of what might happen. At the same time, I try to conjure the salty truth of what goes on in the roiling sea of small-town politics—on the surface, just under, and way down deep.

A t School District Meeting, Miranda knits.

May your neighbors steal from your wood pile, Mort Wallace.

The points of her flexi-needle slide in and out of the heavy burgundy wool.

May they incinerate their garbage in a barrel at your property line. And may the wind blow in your direction.

She counts seventeen stitches. She re-counts eighteen stitches. She recalls the musk of burning garbage, the red smoke blowing over, ash falling like snow.

May you choke on the smoke.

She maintains tension with her right index finger. That's the trick of it, isn't it, the pressure against callused flesh of wool flowing over.

May the ashes fall hot on your comb-over.

Miranda's thick hair—bands of gray and white—beehives in mysterious swirls that fascinate the young parents sitting one row behind her. When she lifts her chin, the back of her neck straightens, and the lines of her jaw smooth into youth.

She knits. Yarn loops her forefinger like a bloody slice.

Mort Wallace stands, but not to speak. He sidles to the PTA concession for a refill from the coffee urn—his fifth since the meeting started. The PTA volunteers are beginning to look at him askance. He throws coins on the counter, then opens his lips to suction the hot liquid, black and rainbow skimmed.

At the front of the gym Kaye Elbow, school board chair, speaks. The microphone amplifies the quaver in her voice. Mort Wallace will destroy this young woman if he can: Miranda has seen that in his cold, deep-set eyes—eyes that, over the years, seem to have sunk deeper and deeper into his skull. His hand tests the strength of the Styrofoam cup. His nostrils take in the steam.

Miranda knits faster, drops one stitch, corrects, knits on, drops another. She has hated Mort Wallace since childhood. Her parents hated his parents, so she in turn hated him. That is the way of it in these small towns—to hate by tradition. But make no mistake. Mort Wallace has earned his share. Even Miranda's Aunt Lou (who had a kind word for everyone) said of having been Mort's Red Cross swimming instructor when he was a boy: "I should have drowned him when I had the chance."

She was referring to Mort's meanness. He is an opinionated man. Everyone in town has opinions, most of them set in granite. Mort's opinions, though, are veined with meanness. He stands *against* on every issue; *against*, vehemently and with nothing but contempt and harsh words for those who stand *for*. He is a mean man. See it in his face. Hear it in his voice. Know it in the way his children leave home as soon as they graduate high school and never come back.

May your children spite you with their choices. May they abandon you in old age.

Know it in the way his first wife disappeared without warning—leaving her own babies, as though she saw in them what she loathed in her husband.

Know it in the way his followers—he has a few—peck at the grains of his meanness like chickens following the feeding pail.

May your chickens lay thin-shelled eggs, Mort Wallace. May skunks nest under the hen house. May raccoons scream at midnight in the tree that scratches your bedroom window.

Miranda does not invoke rabies—nor does she ever wish, even in the secret pocket of her heart, for the death of her enemy. "Curse them in this life," said her Gramma Annie, from whom she learned the art of the well-directed curse. Gramma Annie said death was an evil call and unworthy.

Though they've never spoken, Miranda has admired Kaye Elbow from the first time she saw her smiling down a heckler, too naive, it seemed, even to realize she was being heckled. Miranda admires Kaye Elbow's broad dark face and the way emotions skitter across it like bird shadows on the water. Though Miranda has no children, she has long been ripe with maternal instincts, which come on strong for Kaye Elbow when Mort Wallace's hand shoots up, raised stiff-armed from the shoulder, like a schoolboy in need of a bathroom pass. His shoulders round forward. His chest—under thick, checked flannel—appears to fold in on itself, yet there is enough air in those folded lungs to give his voice a boom that turns all heads: "Yes, I do have a question for you, Madame Chairman."

Miranda's husband Everett, God rest his soul, said this about Mort Wallace: "He's got two gears—neutral and steaming mad." When Mort speaks in public it is always in anger. Some in the crowd lower their heads, embarrassed, hoping the storm will blow though quickly. Some exchange gleeful looks: *Mort's gonna give it to 'em now!* Some want to shoot him down and watch him, winged, spiral splat into the water.

Miranda expects Mort acts even worse at home. She pities his second wife. They say she is an enthusiastic alcoholic who never leaves the house after 6 p.m. Mort, of course, is out practically every evening, stirring up trouble at selectmen's meetings, budget committee, planning board, Save-Our-Wetlands. (He opposes wetlands.) Wherever there is trouble to be stirred, he stirs it.

In summer, Mort Wallace's second wife tends a garden of annuals along the walkway in front of the house: ageratum, marigold, cleome, and masses of white petunias. Walking by, Miranda sometimes sees her kneeling on the bricks, dragging at the weeds with eager hands.

"Hello," Miranda says if their eyes meet. "Hello," Mort Wallace's second wife says back.

Miranda knits to the rhythm of her curse. *May your second wife find a sharp tongue in the bottle she loves and slice you with it.*

Miranda knits the left sleeve of a burgundy cardigan for the man in the old folks home who is still her father though he no longer knows her. This is a curse she would never levy, not even on Mort Wallace: to live too long. The rhythm of her stitches falters when she thinks of her good-hearted father, beyond suffering they say, but *they* don't know, do they? The rhythm of her stitches falters when she thinks of her own strong, kind Everett struck down by a weak heart before his time, and Mort Wallace, who never did a bit of good for anybody in this town, living on and on like some tough old bramble dug in so deep you can't kill it no matter how many times you mow it down.

"Mort Wallace was a bully as a child and he's still a bully," Aunt Lou said.

"Just like his old man," her father said.

"He's a phenomenon of nature," Everett said.

Mort Wallace didn't much bother Everett, not even during Everett's four terms on the Board of Selectmen. Though once, when Mort accused him outright and in public of fraud, Everett got riled. "You do get some funny ideas, Mr. Wallace," Everett said, out of his chair and advancing. "I'm not much of a one for lawyers and lawsuits, but you say that again, and I'm on the phone, misterman." Everett's thick finger pushed into Mort's concave chest, "And I'm gonna find me a lawyer."

It hurt her to see Everett attacked. She curls her knitting in her lap and lowers her head. So far the discussion at this School District Meeting has been civil, back-and-forth talk among good people trying hard to come to terms, trying to find a balance. Mort Wallace will attempt to change all that with his old trick of setting neighbor against neighbor.

May your neighbors' children BB your windows, cherry-bomb your mailbox, siphon your gas, and deflate your tires. May the little ones pierce your rest with their shrieks.

She studies the rich color of the sweater that will eventually be her father's but remains hers until the last tail is tied off. *May your dog bark on and on. May she someday turn on you. May she growl in your dreams when she's gone.* Miranda studies the fine, even stitches, row upon row, interlocking like the fingers of clasped hands. *May the words you are about to fire at Kaye Elbow turn like a boomerang stick and strike you between the eyes.*

Mort's voice carries, loud and sharp gunfire.

May your shingles curl and your clapboards peel.

She lets the hum in her head turn his words to gibberish. *May your sills rot under your feet.* She fingers her knitting, hefts accomplishment. She holds the sleeve out for scrutiny, a sharp eye for flaw. But she sees no flaw. She sees a perfect burgundy plain. *May ants turn your sills to powder.* A stranger in the next chair pokes her and whispers, "That's coming along good." Miranda meets the stranger's eyes, and he is struck by how beautiful her eyes are, like clear water flowing over mica-flecked ledge.

Kay Elbow smiles at Mort Wallace who is leaning hard into the cement-block wall, his arms crossed so tight it looks painful. Kaye is new to the board, chair by default (no one else would take the job). She has been warned about this old man and how he will try to influence the vote. "What gives you people the gall," he says, "to ask us hardworking taxpayers to cough up more money. You didn't manage your budget plain and simple. Maybe you didn't know how. Maybe you didn't want to. Maybe you didn't care. Maybe you're stupid. I won't say you're a bunch of crooks—I'd like to but I won't."

The moderator says, "Would you state your name for the record?"

"You don't know who I am? Tell 'um who I am, Robert," he says to one of the other school board members.

"You tell 'um," Robert says.

May a rat die between your studs.

Everett always said, "Mort Wallace has his followers, but they're none too many and none too bright." When Everett chaired the Board of Selectmen, he knew how to handle Mort's kind: "Sit down," he'd say, "we've heard enough," with a rap of the gavel. And if they didn't sit down, he'd suggest, mildly, "You want to step outside and settle it in the town hall yard?" No one ever took him up on the offer, including Mort.

"For the record, my name is Morton Wallace. Is that clear enough for you, honey?"

Kaye Elbow says in a high, steady voice: "Quite clear, honey. Now let me clarify something." She holds one white index card in her hand and reads from it. The School District, she explains, is not in deficit and cannot, by law, enter into deficit. The board is simply presenting the facts so voters can decide how to proceed, considering the special-education overrun, the hike in insurance, and the fact that the furnace is so far gone it can't be fixed.

She looks straight at Mort Wallace, tilts her head sweetly: "And by the way, I don't feel that any particular gall is required to stand before you. I'm just doing the job I was elected to do."

Mort Wallace's eyes darken. They are as dark as scorched pine. His face is gray, the hard lines deepened by his freshly inflamed anger and the artificial light.

Miranda watches the pulse in the cording of his neck. She sees how the cuff of his shirt hangs at his wrist, how his belt is freshly notched. He has smoked too many cigarettes and slipped too many shots of whiskey into his bottomless cup of coffee. More importantly, a terrible backwash of his own venom has poisoned him, is punishing him more than her curses ever could.

Now she raises her hand full of knitting. An umbilical cord of burgundy yarn trails into the tapestry bag at her feet. The sleeve is a burgundy flag. Recognized by the moderator, Miranda stands: "Mrs. Coffey—Miranda Coffey—some of you know me." She reminds herself to speak right up. "I realize you folks on the school board are doing the best you can. You're working awful hard and you've got figures to back up what you're saying. So I'm going to vote the money you asked for."

From the corner of her eye, she sees Mort with his hand in the air again. She turns to face him. She addresses her kind lie directly to him: "Mort Wallace, I know you mean well," she says. She holds her knitting to her chest and takes a long breath. "But there's no need for you to be talking that way to these good people. Sit down, now; we've heard enough."

Since he has no chair, Mort can't sit down. But Miranda sees that he would if he could. She sees it in the way his mouth opens and closes, in the way he flattens into the cement-block wall and fades like old paint. Everett would approve.

Miranda sits down. The stranger next to her touches her arm. The young mother behind her leans forward and whispers: "I'm glad you spoke up."

Miranda knits.

14 🔨

Town Meetin':
A Darius Wherry Story

by Deborah Whitaker

This short story appeared in the March 1936 issue of Yankee Magazine. *In it, writer Deborah Whitaker takes on the New England dialect with enthusiasm. She doesn't say, specifically, that the story is set in New Hampshire, but with a character named "Seabrook," one senses a Granite State connection.*

The narrator, Darius Wherry, comments candidly on his neighbors—who they are, how they act, and why they act like they do. He is, in a sense, the voice of the town commenting on itself. The meeting is contentious but quaint, despite roiling social undercurrents: some can't stand the city folks; some tolerate them; others, like Darius and his wife, sell them eggs and milk. In fact, Darius is describing the events of the day as a courtesy to city folk, so they can understand what really goes on: "Happen you city folk would like to hear about our town meetin'," the story begins. Darius tells all—warts, welts, and goiters included.

A disturbing reminder of the racial prejudice of the time (and the blinding whiteness of New England) comes when Darius explains that Mrs. Tarbell may be city folk, "but she likes country ways. She lives in a remade house and no one would ever know to look at it now that nigger Sam and his eight kids ever lived there. Posies and such like around the house, instead of broken chairs and bottles and old tires like when Nigger Sam and his kinky heads was in town."

Wow.

The slurs and racial stereotyping shock the contemporary reader. I considered cutting those lines in this reprint of the story. But this seems important: In 1936, racial prejudice was still so deeply ingrained in our culture that even a family magazine like Yankee *took no issue with Darius's hateful characterization of his black neighbors. "Times ain't like they was," he says later on, referencing the good service provided at the supper by the young folk. Looking back at this time capsule from the relative enlightenment of the twenty-first century, we can truthfully respond: Yep, Darius, times ain't like they was. Thank goodness.*

H appen you city folk would like to hear about our town meetin'. There wa'nt much excitement and goin's on up to the last minute, so to speak. Jim Haynes had his name on the Australian ballot—oh yes, we do things up citified—for selectman, and he didn't have no competition. He's been tryin' and tryin' to git that job for the last ten elections but he's such a jumper and a hollerer that folk don't seem to like him much, that is, fer a selectman. But he's got a lot of children and now what with the Depression and all, they've come back to live with papa, and a couple of grandchildren attained their majority this year, so he thought he was pretty well set. And besides all that, he didn't have any fight from the last selectman, seein's as how he's doin' time in the county jail for pullin' a gun on a feller for some little pifflin' thing. Course, we country folk don't stand for no Al Capone stuff. No siree.

Well, a few days before town meetin' there was a Granger meetin' to discuss the town warrant. Now remember, this Jim Haynes is a jumper and a hollerer and also a walker up and down the aisler. He got kind of excited about something or other and he did all his little tricks and he got another guy kind of mad at him. Used his name in vain he claimed. Well, the upshot of it was that this feller by the name of Joe Peavey, he says, by gum, he'll run on stickers. So he went to an old turncoat named Tobias Nelson, and he says, "Suppose I run for selectman, will you vote for me?" "Sure I will," says Turncoat Nelson, "and so will the missus." So he took cheer so to speak, and contacted several other people what owed him money and they was all agreeable.

Now Joe Peavey had bought eggs off the young squirt that was the chairman of the board of selectmen for the last couple of years, and he figures that seein's as how he'd allus paid him cash money, perhaps he'd vote fer him. So, he raises the price of eggs a cent and approaches him proper. Well, young Anson Seabrook, he thinks to himself, "now this feller is no jumper and no hollerer and he only gets drunk once in a while so perhaps he'd make a good selectman. The lesser of two evils." Then this young Seabrook was kind of sore at Jim Haynes anyhow because he made or tried to make so much trouble for the selectmen. Sort of an indoor sport it was to Haynes. He was allus runnin' to the state capitol to see if he couldn't restrain something. They spent too much money or not enough or in the wrong place.

This young selectman Seabrook, he don't do things halfway. He says he'll vote for Joe Peavey and he'll work for him too. Now young Seabrook's papa is the town clerk and treasurer, and his uncle is sexton and another uncle is a nice man, and they all got wives, so that makes eight votes to start on because the Seabrooks vote solid for the same man. And there's a cousin at the college that gets a tip to come home for town meetin'.

They gets out the old checklist and figures and argues and brings pressure to bear until they have enough votes to put this Joe Peavey into office. And then old Jim Haynes gets wind of what's goin' on an up to the state house he goes to find out if stickers is legal.

They ain't legal. That's a blow to the Joe Peavey party because some of the votes they counted on wouldn't or couldn't write a name on the ballot. It ain't exactly lack of ability to write, but lack of ambition. And besides, Joe's name turns out to be Johnathan, and that's bad.

Archie Turner, the second selectman, he's a yesser. He don't say no to nobody. He tells Johnathan Peavey he'll vote for him and he tells Jim Haynes he'll vote for him. He ain't exactly crooked but he anticipates. Either one of them might get in and then where would he be? If he sits on a fence now, he'll sit pretty then.

Well, when town meetin' opens, Turncoat Nelson, he's the moderator, says, "Brothers and sisters, you will please come to order." Now you must not think he is filled with a filial feeling for the citizens of the town, but he's a Granger and he gets kinda muddled. He's an auctioneer too and sometimes instead of sayin', "I await your pleasure," after the readin' of an article he hollers "How much am I offered?"

Young Seabrook sits up on the platform part of the time along with the moderator and clerk, and partly sits with his wife, who is kind of a nice young thing, and they laugh a lot. Things seem funny to them that don't seem funny to no one else. She knits during the whole meetin' on some pretty red thing and as none of the other fellers' wives do that, they think she's kind of stuck up.

To git back to business. There's twenty-two articles in the warrant, and all but two or three of 'em go off without much argument. Jim Haynes he walks up and down the aisle and waves his arms but he don't jump. And less he jumps he ain't very mad.

We voted to raise a hundred dollars for the liberry and young Mrs. Seabrook, she looks disgusted. But she's kind of highbrow about books. Can't see nothin' in them Zane Grey wild westers.

Then we come to the article about street lights. Well, we only got five and those don't do no good because no one lives within miles of 'em. We got a church and town hall, center school and five houses. That is the center of our town and no one lives there except summer folks. And in the summer what's the use of street lights anyhow? We voted the town into darkness unanimously.

Jim Haynes had sort of warmed up on the last article and when it came to article seventeen he jumped to his feet. This had to do with how much money should be spent on the repairs of highways and bridges. Well, young Seabrook got up and recommended $1,500.00, which was more than last year and enough to guarantee that the state would give financial assistance and he made a pretty good speech but he might as well have said nothin'. You see, the trick to this is that Jim Haynes has two sons-in-law that is road agents and five more either sons or sons-in-law or grandsons who work on the road. Now in order to get enough groceries for this mob, the tax payin' farmer has got to support these men, who only pay poll taxes—well, don't get me started on that.

Well, Haynes had a cause worth fightin' for now and he jumped and he hollered and waved his arms an' run up an' down the aisle. He shook his finger under young Seabrook's nose and he spit on the sawdust floor. Sure we got sawdust floors, we ain't that citified! "Why, you chislers," he shouted, "what do you suppose the NRA and the CWA and the PWA and the GOP—NO!—not the GOP, what am I thinking of? But all these grand unions that our great President has made up out of whole cloth. What are they for? Why to throw away money. And now I'm askin' you to quit yer chislin', throw away yer money and foller the example set by our great government. Chislers, that's what you are. And now worthy Master, I move you, that the sum of $2,000.00 be raised for the repairin' of highways etcetery." Well, of course he got his way because seventy-five percent of the voters work on the road or are married to them as do and there ain't but a hundred voters.

Young Anson Seabrook was hopin' that Jim Haynes would shout hisself hoarse on that last article because he wanted the next one to go through. This one read, "To see if the town will authorize the selectmen to administer or dispose of any real estate acquired by the town through Tax Collector's deeds." So young Seabrook got up on his feet and cleared his throat and made his spiel.

"Mister Moderator," says he. "Brother Seabrook," says Turncoat Nelson. Now young Seabrook ain't no Granger and Turncoat would have bit his tongue off rather than call that stuck-up young squirt Brother, but such is the habits of a Granger.

"I have a letter here from the state tax commission recommending the adoption of the article. Three fourths of the towns in the state have already done so." He read the letter. "Now aside from their recommendation you all know the Zackariah Kimball place. Several years ago the town acquired this property through tax collector's deeds. It's grown up to brush. It is valued at $100.00. It brings no money to the town and we have an offer of $150.00 for an immediate sale of the place. The people are from Boston and they want to put up a summer home and are anxious to start immediately. They are not transients, but fine people, and the value of the place would increase considerably, thereby bringing increased revenue to the town. The other land the town owns is valued at not more than $5.00 an acre and is worthless unless set out to forest. I make the motion that this article be accepted as read by the moderator."

Now you'd call that a nice speech, wouldn't you? Well, it was too good. Yessirree. It was too long. It give Jim Haynes a chance to git his breath. He jumped to his feet and strode up front.

"Brothers" sez he (that Grange agin), "you've heard what this feller had to say, now listen to me. Perhaps the Zack Kimball place is just wuthless brush land—on top. You git me—ON TOP. But what if ther's gold or granite underneath? Are you goin' to let three selectmen, whose heads are on no tighter than they should be, sell your property and mine? NO, I say, and no again. This is a matter in which every one of us should have a look-in. Why they may be sellin' a gold mine or a granite quarry or a golf course. Now I tell you, Brothers and Sisters, this is a matter for a hundred heads instead of three. And you look to your ballots."

Wall, he said a lot more too but what with the jumpin' and thumpin' and runnin' around and everythin' that was all I could git out of it. Didn't make sense no how. Then a lady got up and spoke agin it. Lucy Parsons sort of took young Seabrook by surprise 'cause she is chairman of the school board and has been a teachin' lady. She said that she didn't know anythin' about it really, but when these people come to live here they soon have children, which means transportation to school and an expense to the community. Then they'd want their roads plowed out right off first thing, and perhaps the lady smoked and that was a bad example to our dear little school children, and she really felt from the bottom of her heart that the more of these city folk that came to the country the worse off you were because anything might happen and thank you, Mister Moderator. Well, I couldn't make no head nor tail to that speech neither, but then I ain't prejudiced against the city folk like some be, seein's how I sell milk and eggs to 'em. They's just the same as us 'ceptin they say "how cher do," instid of "Howdy."

A few small punkins gits up fer and agin the articles and then Mrs. Tarbell, she ups and says, "Mr. Moderator."

Now I sells green vegetables and roastin' fowl to Mrs. Tarbell and m'wife sells her apple pie once a week, so I'm right special to her. Mrs. Tarbell, she's city folk, but she likes country ways. She lives in a remade house and no one would ever know to look at it now that nigger Sam and his eight kids ever lived there. Posies and such like around the house, instead of broken chairs and bottles and old tires like when Nigger Sam and his kinky heads was in town.

Well, like I was sayin', Mrs. Tarbell got up and says, "Mister Moderator." Turncoat Nelson, he gets it right this time and says, "Mrs. Tarbell."

"I just want to say," says she, "that I never heard of anything in my life as a gold mine in this town. I presume that three selectmen who know their business are capable of selling land, otherwise they would not be in office. May I suggest that if they do not administer the affairs of the town properly there are ways of ejecting them from office, though I would not recommend shooting. It is very well known that three wise heads are better than many full of ignorance. I thank you."

After that speech, everyone kind of laughed but some of the women folk were mad, because of that "heads full of ignorance" bit. And besides, no one ever talked about that shootin' business because too many folk were kind of mixed up in it. But Mrs. Tarbell, she was allus one to speak right out, and besides, she don't understand country ethics as well as she will after she's run for office.

Do you know, I got right surprised when that article went to vote. The selectmen had their way about it and old Jim Haynes and his gold mine was licked. Seems if he'd only said granite and let the gold lie, he might have made his point 'cause the whole town is built on granite if you only dig deep enough.

That just about closed the town meetin' except for an article that said reports of agents, auditors, committees etcetery, and there wa'nt no committees and agents and the auditors report was printed in the warrant so Turncoat Nelson called a recess until the votes for selectman, town clerk and treasurer and three road agents could be counted by ballot clerks.

The ladies rang the bell for dinner and everyone hustled upstairs to get closest to the lemon pie or blueberry, each to his own taste. As for me, I sat nearest m'wife's apple pie. Give me apple pie every time. Old Mrs. Seabrook, she was chairman of the dinner and some of the young folk waited on table and nary a drop was spilt down anyone's neck. Times ain't like they was.

Johnathan Peavey (seems like I can't git over Joe's name bein' so out-landish) was so nervous he couldn't eat no beans or brown bread. All he wanted was black coffee and doughnuts. Old Jim Haynes, he's a great tren-cherman, and all of the young folk were runnin' round for some o' Mrs. Seabrook's beans and m'wife's apple pie, and Nellie Bemin's cream pie. He chose the best and he ate 'em, and why shouldn't he? He's been runnin' for office for ten years now and if that ain't long enough to get over nerves, what is?

After dinner was over and some of the women folk were clearin' up, old Turncoat Nelson opened the meetin' agin. He harrummed and then read off the result of the ballot. Old man Seabrook was town clerk and treasurer again. He got in practically unanimously. Folks trust the Seabrooks 'cause they are so honest, but some fine day, mebbe next election, young Seabrook is comin' to grief with so durned much honesty.

Jim Haynes won out for selectman by three votes. Joe Peavey can't understand it and is good and sore. Someone double-crossed him and he knows who. But my bet is that it's because his name turned out to be Johnathan, and it takes it out of a man to write a word like that.

Jim Haynes' sons-in-laws got in as road agents and the third road agent is so thick with the Haynes tribe that he got in too.

Well, young Seabook, he's the first one to congratulate old man Haynes. There ain't nothin' mean nor small about that boy, and young Mrs. Seabrook, she shakes hands too, and he says, so she tells me, "Well, Mrs. Seabrook, I may jump and holler, but I don't mean nothin' by it, and you make sure your husband won't be comin' home all shot up."

So you see, Old Man Haynes ain't such a bad coot after all. Young Seabrook thinks he won't make so much trouble on the board as he did off.

"The object of all town meetings was to know the Town's Mind; whether it was for doing this, or for doing that, or for doing something else. In warrants it was written with capital letters, and was alluded to as if it were a distinguished person, slow to act, and to be consulted on every matter, small or great."

WILLIAM R. BLISS, *COLONIAL TIMES ON BUZZARD'S BAY*

"The town meeting has been not only the source, but the school of democracy."

LORD JAMES BRYCE

15 🔨

A Moderator's Address

by Jack Hutchinson

On March 26, 2005, Deerfield moderator Jack Hutchinson stood before those gathered for town meeting and gave this address, which he called "A Brief History of Town Meetings in Deerfield, New Hampshire." The town had just voted in SB 2, a fundamental change in how Deerfield would make its decisions in the future. Instead of town and school district meetings with binding votes, there would be deliberative sessions to discuss and vote on how the ballot would read—in preparation for the real vote at the polls to come some weeks later.

That day, Moderator Hutchinson spoke of early struggles to find consensus (just like now). He spoke of responsibilities the town took on, decisions made—caring for the poor, building a meeting house and schools, putting a bounty on the heads of wolves, setting rates of pay for town workers, paying soldiers to go to war. He spoke of dark times—the eighteen Deerfield soldiers who died in George Washington's army. He puts that particular dark time in modern context: Losing those eighteen soldiers then "would be like losing eighty of our sons and daughters today." He spoke of times when the town rallied. During the Spotted Fever epidemic of 1815, a meeting was called on one day's notice to plan a response and appropriate money for medical care.

Jack Hutchinson has been Deerfield's moderator for more than fifteen years; before that he was school district moderator, and before that he served on the school board. He takes his job seriously and appreciates the history of the annual meeting over which he presides—the opportunity for voters to deliberate together—acutely aware that he's "carrying out the legacy of Thomas Jefferson." In fact, he sometimes reads Jefferson in preparation for the privilege of our New England town meeting, "so rare in human history."

Here's the full text of what Moderator Hutchinson said to the voters of Deerfield on the occasion of the change from traditional town meeting to SB 2. Here's how he marked the letting go of old ways and establishment of new.

Thinking about our adoption of SB 2 and the changes we'll be making over the next year, I went to the archives to learn about Deerfield Town Meeting history and how our meetings have changed over the years. This morning, before we begin our 239th Annual Meeting, I would like to take a few minutes to share some of that with you.

The Parish of Deerfield was authorized by the House of Representatives of the Province of New Hampshire on January 7, 1766, "Chargeable with the Duty of Maintaining the poor . . . repairing all Highways . . . and Supporting the . . . Preaching of the Gospel." Three weeks later we held our first Town Meeting at which we formed a committee to "Look out for a Suitable Place to Sett a Meetinghouse."

Since 1766 each meeting has had a warrant, and minutes have been recorded and preserved. The language used then is familiar to us today. The warrant for our first annual meeting in March 1766 begins "This is to Notify and Warn all the Freeholders & other Inhabitants of the Parish of Deerfield Qualified by Law to Vote in Parish affairs to Meet at the house of Mr. Wadleigh Crams in Said Deerfield Tuesday the 18th of March at ten of the Clock before noon."

But we did not have an easy time learning to work together. The early minutes sometimes reported, "Voted to negative all the articles of the warrant."

And we did not have *Robert's Rules*. In a 1769 meeting we, "Voted that all the votes that was passed the twelfth of January past and the 24th of February last at the house of Mr. Henry Tucker was Reconsidered and Entirely Disannulled and Revoked and are of no force No More than if it had never been voted." How is that for a reconsideration? The Congregational Meetinghouse, the first project of our young town, was ready for the September 1771 meeting. It was also the home of the Congregational Society. It stood where we now find Old Center Cemetery.

In 1772 we set a wage rate for the town "a man is to have for a Days work two shillings the same for oxen the same for plough. Eighteen pence a day for Cart wheels."

In 1775 Deerfield volunteers joined in the Battle of Bunker Hill. Among them was John Simpson who fired the first shot. Three years later we "voted to allow each man that went to Cambridge at the time of Lexington battle one dollar per day" and "voted that fifty dollars be allowed to each man that enlisted into the Continental Services . . . without hire." In 1776 we voted a "Committee of Safety" responsible for loyalty oaths, identifying and disarming Tories and overseeing the men opposed to the revolution who were sent to New Hampshire under armed guard by the State of New York.

In 1777 we appropriated town funds to pay one of the two companies we raised for General George Washington's army. Eighteen Deerfield soldiers died in service during the Revolution—about 1 in 50 of our population. That would be like losing eighty of our sons and daughters today.

Eighty-five years later during the Civil War, President Lincoln called for 300,000 troops for the Army of the United States. Deerfield's quota was 23. We voted $300 each for the conscripts or their substitutes. That year the annual school budget was $1200 and the highway budget $1500.

We were still carving our town out of a wilderness. In 1782 a petitioned article sought to establish a bounty on wolves.

Education was an early concern. In 1783 we considered "the erecting of schoolhouses in the center of each District." There would come to be sixteen School Districts in Deerfield, each with its own schoolhouse and a single teacher who taught all grades.

When an epidemic of Spotted Fever struck Deerfield in 1815, we met on one day's notice. We voted "to supply such persons as may be attacked with . . . the Spotted Fever with such mediums and necessaries as may be prescribed by the Physicians," "that a sum not exceeding three hundred dollars be raised for the benefit of the sick in this town," and to "employ as many physicians as . . . necessary and pay them by the day."

Article 10 of the 1818 warrant reads "To take into consideration the Poor of this town and make such provisions for the year ensuing as thought most proper." A lengthy debate on this topic dominated the meeting.

The care of the poor, the infirm, the elderly, and the mentally unsound was entirely a town responsibility until 1868 when Rockingham County established the County Poor Farm in Brentwood.

Our 1845 meeting was the last in the Congregational Meetinghouse. We voted to dismantle it and reuse the material for a new Town House. We went on to "authorize and instruct" the selectmen "to erect such a building for a town house as they may think proper, the cost of which shall not exceed eight hundred dollars." That Town House was ready for the next Annual Meeting in 1846. We met there until 1990 when this school and gymnasium were opened.

From 1766 until 1892, the election procedure was deliberate and lengthy. Taking 1846 as an example: our first order of business was filling twenty-seven offices starting with Moderator and Town Clerk and ending with Cullers of Staves, Measurers of Wood, Hog Reeves, Field Drivers, Pound Keepers, and the Superintendent of the Town Farm. One office at a time, nominations were taken, ballots cast and counted, the result announced and, if there was a winner, the elected official sworn in. If no candidate received a majority of the ballots cast, then a new ballot was taken. Once a winner was declared and sworn, the process recycled with nominations for the next office.

We worked a day and a half that year to complete elections. Then we took up the other articles. On those, if a division of the house was called for, everyone exited the hall. Then as counters stood at each door, all in favor entered by the East Door and those opposed by the West Door.

In January, 1893, we voted twenty-one to eleven to "adopt provisions of Chapter 33 of the Public Statutes of New Hampshire for annual elections." That vote, by less than 10 percent of registered voters in a special meeting, ended the practice of conducting balloting one office at a time in open meeting. Now the polls opened at the start of the meeting and remained open until an agreed time, usually 3:00 p.m. Meanwhile we deliberated and voted the warrant articles in parallel.

In 1895 we voted to "Make arrangements with the Telephone Co. to put a Telephone in this town."

In 1933 we adopted the Australian ballot for the election of town officials. The following year would see the first use in Deerfield of a printed ballot listing all declared candidates.

Also in 1933 we addressed Depression unemployment by distributing road work among all men wanting it. "It was voted that the selectmen keep a list of the names of men who desire to work on the State Road Construction and employ a staggered crew of men working three days each week until all who wish have had employment."

In 1966 we moved to Saturday town meetings though in the following few years there was debate about Tuesday evening versus Saturday morning and we switched back and forth. And then by 1976 we see Absentee Ballots for local elections.

Deerfield began as a parish of 800 colonists. Travel was difficult, mostly by foot. Interdependence with our neighbors and commitment to community was much higher. We did not lack for candidates for town offices—the leading citizens of the community all served. Most of us rarely left Deerfield.

At first we met in the homes of settlers. The poor, the roads, and the church were our concerns. We met about six times a year as we struggled and often failed to make and sustain decisions.

During the period of the Revolutionary War, our meetings became more orderly and productive. In addition to responsibilities for the poor, the roads, the church, and the schools, we set a wage rate for laborers, paid soldiers who served in the Army, funded medical care, regulated trade, set a bounty on crows, and participated in the formation of state government.

For one hundred and twenty-six years the form of the meetings was stable, though participation varied widely. Some declarations report as few as thirty votes were cast.

We made our first big change in 1893 when we adopted a single prepared ballot for election to all offices. Then in 1933 we moved to an official ballot with declared candidates. In the years following we separated elections from our business meeting and later introduced absentee ballots.

Though many descendants of the early settlers continue to live in Deerfield, today we are largely a bedroom community of people whose work and families are in other places. Federal and State authority have increased and local responsibility and prerogative declined. We no longer have primary responsibility for the poor, pay Deerfield soldiers for their service, hire doctors in an epidemic, or elect Scalers of Weights and Measures and others to regulate trade. In fact now we sometimes have elections with no declared candidate.

But for 238 years we've been electing a moderator and selectmen and debating and funding roads and education as a citizen legislature in the Town Meetings Thomas Jefferson described as "the wisest invention ever devised by the wit of man for the perfect exercise of self government."

The Town Meeting is a New England invention which, though widely admired, has never taken root in any other soil. And it has been in decline in much of New England for some years now. We've been privileged to participate in this pure form of democracy.

It is our challenge to do as well with the next step we've voted to take under SB 2. We have a proud history as a community. I hope that we can work together to build an equally proud future.

Frank Case

"Voting after speaking is to governance
what keeping score is to sports."

FRANK M. BRYAN, *REAL DEMOCRACY*

16 🔨

A Moderator's Perspective: Frank Case

Retired pharmacist Frank Case believes in public service—as does his wife, Peg. He's a state legislator, as Peg was before him. He also served as moderator in the town of Raymond for ten years, from 1975 to 1985, when he and Peg moved to Nottingham, where they continue to be involved in civic affairs and organizations.

Frank and I sat for a couple of hours at his home on Pawtuckaway Lake. It was raining hard—chill outside, but warm inside. We sipped tea and looked out the floor-to-ceiling windows at the water. Most interviews, I'm lucky if I get a story or two, a few paragraphs that I can fold into a chapter. But Frank is so articulate and focused, his interview stands on its own. He covers a lot of country—the rules of town meeting, challenges that moderators face, changes he's witnessed over the years, outstanding moments, and, especially, his love for town meeting and his love for small towns with all their quirks and blemishes.

RR: Would you explain how town meeting works?

FC: What a lot of people don't realize is that, at least in New Hampshire, town meeting is a very free flowing forum. There are no real rules. There will be people who'll stand up and say, well, this is the law. The law states that, first, the town meeting will elect a moderator. And the town meeting will select the rules they're going to run by for that day. These rules do not carry on to the next year.

If you pay any attention at town meeting, the moderator will say, "Now we'll set the rules." He may have some preprinted like we do here in Nottingham. And he says, "Without objection, we will proceed by these rules."

There may be people in the audience who'll say, it's gotta go by Robert's *Rules of Order*. That's not the law. The people at that meeting will pick what the rules will be.

My first meeting as a moderator, 1975, I read a piece by a lawyer that said if you follow *Robert's Rules of Order* at town meeting you're breaking the law. The law says all issues at town meeting will be decided by a majority vote. That's not true under *Robert's Rules of Order*. Except for bond issues of course—they have to be two-thirds at town meeting. According to *Robert's Rules* there are things you have to have two-thirds, things you have to have thirty-three percent, well, that's illegal according to NH law. A majority carries any vote, except for bond issues.

My first town meeting as moderator, I'd read this article and I had the paperwork all together and had the rules—had a moderator who came to school meeting in Raymond and he used these rules. I said I wanted to do it by the simplified rules of order. Dave Bradley was the man, Bradley's Rules of Order.

This lady, who had served in the legislature, challenged that I could not do that because the state law says I had to use the same rules that was used in the legislature, *Mason's Rules of Order*. I said, "No that's not true. But what I'll do, I have an assistant moderator I've assigned. Have him come to the podium. I'll go down in the audience, because that's the proper way to do it, and I'll debate you on the floor."

So I just talked to the audience and told them what I read and what the truth is and they ruled that they were going to use my rules of order. We've used them ever since.

RR: It's not easy being the moderator, is it?

FC: It's a fun job, but there just doesn't seem to be a sufficiency of people who want to put their necks on the line to be moderators.

My first town meeting I was thirty years old, in Raymond. I was sitting in the crowd and thinking, *I'm not going to ask this question. I don't think I can.* And that was wrong. I thought if those rules stymied me, a college graduate, they must stymie other people. So I said, I'm going to find out about this and that's where I got that article. That's why I feel there shouldn't be any rules that make someone feel they can't stand up and speak.

RR: And yet some who stand up to speak can give you a hard time. How do you deal with difficult people?

FC: You just kind of slide with them. Most moderators have a way to handle them. What I do is I look like I'm making a really dumb mistake, then people start feeling sorry for me and that the person got the better of me,

---

Rules of Procedure for Nottingham Town Meeting

- No person may speak during the meeting without permission of the moderator and must speak through the moderator.
- There must be a motion and a second on the floor for each article.
- A reasonable amount of relevant and non-repetitious debate will be allowed.
- Any amendment to a motion must be submitted to the moderator in writing prior to a vote being taken on the amendment.
- The moderator will ensure that the contents of all motions and amendments are fully understood.
- Voting will be by:

  Voter Cards.

  You must be seated for the ballot clerks to count your vote.
- Secret Ballot requirements:

  The signatures of five (5) registered voters if requested prior to a vote.

  That seven (7) registered voters stand and request a secret ballot after vote.
- All votes are subject to reconsideration during the meeting, unless a motion to invoke RSA 40:10 is voted in the affirmative regarding the article.
- Any other question may be decided by the moderator but is always subject to overrule by a majority of the registered voters present.
- Results of all votes will be announced by the moderator.

---

and then they're all done. I'm their moderator, you see, and they don't want that to happen.

One guy, he wore a jacket, a sports jacket or a suit jacket, but underneath, he wore big red suspenders. And when they got into one of these real donnybrooks, he would step back, take his jacket off, put his thumbs into his suspenders and pull them out. I said, "Now *who's* the boss here." And that broke everybody up. If you can get laughter, you lose anger. Good moderators will do that.

One woman came to the meeting with a printed copy of the budget committee budget. She started asking questions about those figures, then one of her allies would ask questions. After a while I said, "I'm going to rule that you cannot use that budget book." She says, "Why?" I said, "Because nobody else in the room has that. Unless you want to supply one to every-body in this room, you're asking about something nobody else in this meet-ing has any idea what you're asking. I don't think that's fair. This is the people's meeting, not just yours and the school board's."

She challenged my ruling. I said something wrong when I was doing it. Anyhow, when it got all over, I announced the vote. I said, "I can't believe I really screwed this up that bad." Everybody just broke down laughing.

It turned the whole meeting. It was a hostile meeting. All of a sudden she was all by herself with her little cadre. I probably explained the vote wrong, so I screwed it up.

RR: But by admitting your mistake you got the room on your side.

FC: I loved being able to run a meeting—not even selectmen are over a moderator on town meeting day. Anything that happens here, you're the one that's gonna make it happen or not happen to some degree. If some-thing bad happens it's on your shoulders, so you shoot for something good.

There's satisfaction in getting people out to vote the way they want, to be able to get through it without a lot of haranguing and a lot of fighting, bad feelings. Get it over at a reasonable hour. A moderator can do those things. Not heavy handedly. Set a pace.

I loved the job. I looked forward to every town meeting. The thing I miss the most is that.

RR: You have to stay on top of the debate and the technicalities, too, so everybody leaves with the sense that, win or lose, the votes were fair.

FC: The one thing that could hurt the moderator more than anything else is the motion to reconsider. Particularly if it happens about five hours after the original vote. A guy says, "There never was a moderator who had to go to court because they refused a motion to reconsider." The crowd changes, you know.

Now we have a thing called 40:10. If right after the vote someone calls for a 40:10 and they vote yes, this means that article can never be recon-sidered again.

If I had a motion to reconsider and it was late in the afternoon, and it was apparent there weren't the people in the room there had been earlier, I would deny it. I could have gotten a challenge, but at that point everyone was probably too tired to challenge me. Someone could have challenged and won, but then it would be on them, not me.

RR: What changes have you seen over the years?

FC: SB 2 was voted in, they said, because of "democracy." Well, sure, that Saturday, everybody would get to vote (at the polls), but they had no idea what the hell they were voting on. They just go in there and put an X.

At a deliberative session (under SB 2) for the school two or three years ago there were thirteen people in the audience. I counted them. Course there were twenty or so officials up front. Thirteen people. Everybody in town gets to vote on the ballot, but it's set by the thirteen people. That's not an exaggeration, that's a fact. Last year was maybe sixty people.

I love town meeting. I hate these SB 2 bills.

We still have a town meeting in Nottingham, but we have SB 2 for the schools. Town meeting was a social occasion. People would be knitting. Some group would be selling food for a fundraiser. Good home cooking. The moderator would always break, so they could make their money. Even if the meeting got over at 10:00 we got a break before that.

Town meeting is true democracy. If you want to speak you've gotta be there. No other government form is as pure as town meeting.

RR: It's your job to give people the opportunity to speak. To make sure they understand the rules so they feel comfortable speaking. I get it.

FC: I didn't ever want to put anybody down, even if they were going to give me a hard time. I wanted them to know this is their town meeting. They have a right to stand there and say anything they want.

Sometimes you have to say, "Mary, some people haven't spoken twice on this and this is your fourth time. I think other people want to speak."

RR: Fair is fair. People understand that.

FC: Every year, sometime during the town meeting a Korean veteran— local boy, grew up in Raymond, got a ride from the local VFW—would ask to speak. He'd be three or four sheets to the wind and he'd say, "Mr. Moderator!" I'd say, "Yes, Mr. So-and-So?" And he would talk for about four or five minutes. Then I'd say, "is that all, Mr. So-and-So." He'd say, "Yes, it is. Thank you, Mr. Moderator." And he'd calmly walk off.

The sad part is, one or two years after I left, the new moderator wouldn't recognize him. And it got ugly. The police had to come in. It took five minutes of people's time for this man to speak. This man had been through a lot in the Korean War. He was in the 11th airborne, the 187th. Not many of those guys came back. He would never say anything hateful. Who knows

sometimes what he said. Sometimes I don't think he knew. Generally it
didn't have anything to do with the topic. He talked about life. I didn't see
anything hurtful in that.

Here was a person who had earned the right to speak. He fought in a
bloody war.

RR: What other stories stay with you?

FC: There was a warrant article in Raymond that said everybody in
Raymond had the right to carry a concealed weapon. Prior to the opening
of the meeting—people arrived, you're just standing around waiting—I'm
just making sure everything's working right. The woman behind the article
came up and said, "You're not gonna rule our warrant article illegal." I said
no. She said, "Oh good. Let me show you my weapon."

She lifted up her dress and she had a thigh holster with a pistol in it. I
said, "Nice gun." I was red in the face, I gotta tell you.

WBZ was there to film it. The guy running the video asked me if they
could film. I said, "It's not my call. It's the people's meeting. Once we get
going I'll ask and if it's all right then you can sit up here and do it. Only
one thing, just make sure you shoot it from my left side, because that's my
best side."

There was some discussion. Nobody said it was a bad article. Just let
it go. They voted it in. Maybe it's been rescinded. I've been out of there
since 1985.

RR: Other memorable incidents?

FC: This is history. There was a meeting held in the high school gymnasium
in Raymond. I don't think I was moderator then, but I went to the meeting.
The grist of the meeting was this: Governor Meldrim Thompson met up
with a man named Aristotle Onassis. They figured out a way to have an oil
depot at the Isle of Shoals and pipe it across the ocean and along a railroad
track to Raymond where they were going to put in a refinery. If you tell
people that now, they'd fall apart laughing, wouldn't they?

But that absolutely was the case. I don't think it ever came to the town
hall, but this was a meeting where people were hanging out of the balco-
nies. The place was absolutely packed. They all were against it. They didn't
want no refinery in Raymond. Raymond was too good for a refinery.

Oh Raymond. I loved Raymond. It was a tough town.

17 🔨

Snapshots: Town Meeting in the 21st Century

For a sense of what went on in town meetings, school meetings, and deliberative sessions in 2010 and 2011, I pulled together these summaries, highlights, and fly-on-the-wall observations as witnessed firsthand, reported in local press, passed on by attendees, or described in minutes—a mosaic of the whats, whys, hows, and wherefores of the contemporary town meeting.

Allenstown 2010

At the deliberative session on January 30, with sixty citizens in attendance (population around 5,000), all the articles were sent on as written to be voted on at the polls, except one. After considerable discussion, the house voted to amend the language of Article 19. Originally the article asked for $275,000 for the purchase of a New Medium Duty Rescue/Pumper Fire Truck to replace the 1976 Pumper Truck. The article was recommended by both the board of selectmen and the budget committee.

As reported in the minutes, Judy Silva asked why the article had received approval from town officials. Chief Hart responded that "he has been in fire services for over fifty years and has never seen a fleet in so poor condition." He said only one piece of equipment was less than twenty-five years old, and two were closer to sixty. Three vehicles failed inspection and one is out of service.

Fire apparatus, he said, needed to be dependable, but this "fleet is very old and costing the Town lots of money for repairs and is unreliable."

Jim Boisvert made a motion to amend the article to read "up to Thirty-five Thousand Dollars ($35,000.00) for a ten-year lease."

Others thought a direct purchase would make more sense. "Mike Ortisi stated that Article 18 may not go through and we could end up with neither truck." (Article 18 called for $300,000 for a tanker truck. It would authorize the selectman to apply for a grant for $285,000 with the additional $15,000 raised by taxes.)

Consensus was that the equipment was indeed old. There was a general discussion on applying for grants and whether the trucks being replaced had any value. Judy Silva proposed an amendment: "a.) To see if the Town will vote to raise and appropriate the sum of Two hundred seventy-five thousand dollars ($275,000) for the purchase of a New Medium Duty Rescue/Pumper Fire Truck to replace the 1976 Pumper Truck . . . If you are not in favor of Article 19a; b.) To see if the Town will authorize the selectmen to enter into a long-term lease/purchase agreement in the amount of Two hundred Seventy-five Thousand Dollars ($275,000) payable over a ten year term to purchase a New Medium Duty Rescue/Pumper Fire Truck to replace the 1976 Pumper Truck and to raise and appropriate up to Thirty-five Thousand Dollars ($35,000) for the first year's payment for that purpose. The lease/purchase agreement contains an escape clause. If both articles 19a and 19b are approved the New Medium Duty Rescue/Pumper Truck will be purchased not leased."

The amendment passed by a show of hands.

Then, on March 9, came the moment of truth. The twenty-five motions sent to the voters by the sixty people at the deliberative session were put forward on the ballot at the polls. Article 18 for the Tanker to be purchased with a $285,000 grant plus $15,000 in tax dollars passed (yes 314 to no 283). But both parts of the much discussed and amended Article 19 failed. This is a good example of why deliberative sessions are under attended—in the end, they don't amount to a hill of beans.

As for the rest of the warrant:

- Two zoning ordinances *passed.*
- The six million plus operating budget *failed,* forcing the town to fall back on a default budget.
- Three articles adding money to capital reserve funds and an expendable trust funds *passed.*
- New dump truck *failed.*
- *Failed* as well, all of the following: Money to be added to the Town Safety Expendable Trust Fund, the Police Computer Equipment Capital Reserve Fund, the Police Cruiser Capital Reserve Fund, the

Police Safety Capital Reserve Fund, the Special Revenue D.A.R.E Fund, the Recreation Capital Reserve Fund, the Fire Department Safety Equipment Capital Reserve Fund, the Fire Department Equipment Capital Reserve Fund, the Public Safety Facilities Capital Reserve Fund. In other words, voters said no to socking money away in anticipation of big expenses in future. They favored the pay-as-you-go plan.

- *Failed*: $150,000 to complete renovations to the second floor of the fire station and to authorize the selectmen to offset the entire appropriation by applying for a grant for $150,000, the article being contingent upon receipt of said grant. While 201 voters favored fixing up the fire station with grant money (no impact on their taxes), 394 were against it.

- *Failed*: Two petitioned articles rescinding the selectmen's authority to act as agents to expend from the Fire Department Equipment Capital Reserve Fund and the Highway Department Capital Reserve Fund.

The petitioned article to rescind SB 2 "as adopted by the Town of Allenstown on March 11, 1997, so that the official ballot will no longer be used for voting on all questions, but only for the election of officers and certain other questions for which the official ballot is required by State Law?" failed 197 yea, 381 nay.

The school deliberative session was even more lightly attended, attracting just thirty-seven registered voters. At stake, an operating budget of $9,803,971 plus $20,000 for the Building Maintenance Trust Fund, raises and increased health care for paraprofessionals as negotiated between the school board and the paraprofessional association. Discussion was minimal and the meeting lasted just forty-one minutes. In an article in the *Concord Monitor*, Principal Terri Kenny heartily supported the raises and benefits for paraprofessionals, including special education assistants and kitchen staff, since those folks had not seen a raise for two years and were apt to leave for districts which provided better compensation. "If everything else is a 'No,'" she said, "that's the one thing that has to go through." School board chair Tom Irzyk lamented the poor attendance at the deliberative session. "It comes with the SB 2," he said. "It's not like the old town meeting where you got 400 people to pack the room and work through the articles."

Results: At the polls a few weeks later, the operating budget was defeated by twenty votes, triggering a default budget about $100,000 lower. But the building maintenance article passed, as did the article benefitting the paraprofessionals.

Andover 2010

For forty years the rescue squad served the town as a private, all-volunteer operation with no charge to those who made use of its services. Now those same volunteers were requesting a change. They asked that the squad be financially supported by the town. More than 150 town meeting attendees decided to make it a town department from now on, with those who use the emergency services or their insurance companies to be billed for them. Not everyone thought it was a good idea. Peter Zak said, "If (the ambulance ride) is going to cost $200 or $300, I'd rather take a taxi."

Far as I know, Andover doesn't have any taxis.

A happiness article recognized Dennis Fenton, select board chair, who was retiring from town service after fifty-two years.

Barnstead 2010

A petition to increase the board of selectmen from three persons to five was defeated. Guess Barnstead voters thought three was ample sufficiency of selectmen.

Bartlett 2011

This didn't happen at town meeting but it just as well could have. Julia King of Bartlett passed on this story:

At a candidates' forum in Bartlett, the Moderator, Norman Head, asked the road agent, Travis Chick, how many miles of road the town currently had to plow. "Fifty," was Travis's short reply.

The fire chief, Pat Roberts, was sitting next to where Travis was standing. He leaned over to a friend on his other side and whispered, "Don't he know you have to come back?"

Without missing a beat Travis corrected himself: "That's 100, 'cause you have to come back."

Bow 2010

I sat in the nonresident, nonvoter section of the auditorium at Bow High School, eavesdropped on a group of high school students behind me, obviously on assignment, who seemed baffled by the whole deal: How long will this thing last? Who are those people up front? What are they talking about?

The students had come, as had generations before them, to experience town meeting firsthand—the hope being that in the future they'd attend and sit in the voters' section, or even take their places among the citizens up front, guiding the business of the town.

I combine information from the minutes of that meeting with my own observations. According to the minutes:

> Moderator Peter Imse called the 2010 Town Meeting to order at 7:00 a.m. on a sunny but crisp morning. As usual, after the Pledge of Allegiance Susan Stevens checked the ballot box under the moderator's direction then the voting commenced. The polls were closed at 7:00 p.m. and the meeting adjourned until Wednesday March 10, 2010 at 7:00 p.m.

That's when I showed up to take in the spectacle, including the flag ceremony with the colors presented by the Girl Scouts. (They alternate year-to-year with the Boy Scouts.) Usually a patriotic song is played for the occasion, but the moderator admitted he'd forgotten to bring the CD. He suggested that the legislative body "hum a few bars in your head," then introduced town officials at the head table and thanked those responsible for PowerPoint pictures on the big screen.

Bow town meeting 2010—The legislative body stands to honor Raymond De Course, citizen of the year.

PHOTO BY THE AUTHOR

Imse also introduced the assistant moderators in the orange vests, directing voter traffic so to speak, and outlined the rules of the meeting. Voters received voting cards and wrist stamps. There would be no voice votes. "Everybody's free to speak," he said, "but speak succinctly."

When Charles Griswold stood to present the Citizen of the Year award to Raymond De Course, he allowed as how he'd "try to be brief, something many of you think is next to impossible." In fact, he succinctly described Mr. De Course's many contributions to town and country: serving in the Marine Corps in World War II, supervising the flu shot clinic, raising money for the trauma center at Concord Hospital, helping young people find low cost or free musical instruments. "He is," Charles concluded, "a good neighbor, citizen, and friend to all."

Leon Kenison, outgoing selectman, was honored for his long service, having attended at least 450 meetings on behalf of the town. Colleague Harry Judd thanked Leon for his expertise, especially concerning highways, and for "being a calm voice of reason."

While the meeting was still in its thank-you mode, Paul Hammond rose to thank the police, the fire department, and the highway department for the wonderful job they did during the recent wind storm.

The moderator read the results of the previous day's vote at the polls, noting that he'd once again been elected moderator with 1164 votes: "I ran unopposed and luckily the write-ins didn't defeat me."

The meeting moved briskly along. The general municipal operations budget (recommended by the selectmen 5–0, and by the budget committee 7–1) passed as written in the amount of $8,180,269. The fact that it was nearly $50,000 less than last year didn't hurt.

A petitioned article proposing to "rescind the authorization for the expenditure of any further bonded funds, and to rescind that authorization to issue any further bonds for the non-bonded balance of the approved 2002 ($12,500,000) Municipal Sewer & Water System Bond" that had been passed at the 2002 town meeting, stirred up a hornet's nest. Peter Emanuel, a nonresident, requested and received the right to speak by a show of hands. Seems the town had been slowly working toward a municipal sewer and water system with the idea that such a system would attract business and increase the tax base. Peter Emanuel and dozens of others believed the project should be shelved. The report on the discussion from the minutes reads:

> *(Peter Emanuel) introduced himself as a businessman in the area and expressed his opinion that the project was not feasible and too*

expensive especially since it is not a complete system at this point only a "foot in the door." He said we could never reach the break-even point and it would only mean more taxes for everyone. He did not feel it was justified and asked everyone to consider how it would change the nature of the town if large apartment complexes moved into the area because of having access to sewer.

When the selectmen were asked their opinion, Harry Judd explained they'd been working on the project for ten years. With permits in place, they were ready to solicit bids to build the system. If the funds were revoked "state licenses and engineer plans" would be jeopardized.

Jack Crisp, another selectmen, supported the project because he believed it would encourage commercial development.

A third selectman, Tom Keane, said this wasn't the best time to go forward with it and that the cost in the end might be forty million, a lot more than originally thought. He suggested that having gone this far, "we should at least develop one line down River Road," and the rest later on, while "aggressively pursuing" businesses to come into the area.

Others spoke of the danger of becoming a bedroom community. Nixing the sewer system would limit options for bringing in bigger businesses. Eric Anderson, chair of the Economic Development Committee, presented a slide show on progress and expenses to date. Don Berube worried about road salt contaminating the water.

It boiled down to a Catch-22: Businesses won't locate in Bow without sewer and water; Bow can't afford sewer and water without business. It's the age old question, as one resident put it, of putting the cart before the horse.

But which is the cart and which is the horse?

What to do?

The Mind asserted its collective wisdom and the article failed, yes 80, no 202. The sewer and water project moves forward.

Another lively discussion was generated by the definition of marriage article—To see if the Town will vote to approve the following resolution to be forwarded to our State Representative(s), our State Senator, the Speaker of the House, and the Senate President. Resolved: The citizens of New Hampshire should be allowed to vote on an amendment to the New Hampshire Constitution that defines "marriage."

Town Clerk/Tax Collector Jill Hadaway caught the words and, behind the words, the sentiments of the speakers in her minutes. Many spoke on both sides. Hadaway wrote her account of the discussion as one long paragraph in the minutes. For ease of reading, I've broken the long paragraph into shorter ones.

> ARTICLE #26 was moved by George Lagos and seconded by Deb Bourbeau. Petitioner, Scott Lucas addressed the article by stating that many other states have given citizens the ability to vote on a constitutional amendment defining marriage. He recognized that this article would not change the law currently in place but our democracy gives the people the right to vote and he felt we should have the ability to exercise that right.
>
> State Representative, Mary Beth Walz, voiced her opposition. . . . She said New Hampshire is not a referendum state and since we elect representatives we had to accept that they represent us when they voted. She said the NH House had voted against this motion in two different forms, so this article was mute and the majority of SB 2 towns had rejected it.
>
> Peter Imse (who stepped down as moderator in order to speak) stated his opposition by saying that the real purpose of the article was to oppose same-sex marriage and that this was a form of discrimination. He said that we as a nation had risen above many forms of discrimination and that it was necessary to rise above this one against gays. He expressed his desire that Bow not sanction religious dogma and those who want churches to impose religious beliefs on everyone. He asked that Bow not be a town that stands for religious intolerance.
>
> Mary Lee Sargent said she hoped she was not the only gay resident to speak up against this resolution. She agreed with the comments made by Mr. Imse. . . . As a professor of history she said the U.S. Constitution stresses the rights of the minority not the majority. She voiced her hope that we would vote for equality not prejudice. She discussed the financial difficulties of being in a same-sex marriage.
>
> Jean Geruiskis said she came to do the business of the Town and this was not a Town issue. She said she has twenty-two cousins and two of them are gay and that had not adversely affected any of their marriages.
>
> Tess Kuenning opposed the article and mentioned that since our representatives have voted for us we cannot say we have not had the opportunity to vote on this issue.
>
> Phyllis Benoit made a motion to table the article. Assistant Moderator Jim Hatem explained that a motion to table would require a secret ballot. However since there was no second to her motion it failed.
>
> Jonathan Bressler voiced his strong opposition to the article.
>
> Van Mosher disagreed saying that he had voted on many issues

regarding constitutional amendments. He pointed out that none of those elected as our representatives campaigned on this issue so he didn't know how they would vote.

Steve Coneys made a motion to move the question and Georgette Daugherty seconded the motion. The motion PASSED by a majority vote.

Steve Elgert was still at the microphone so he was allowed to speak. He said that historically we have continued to expand individual rights, however these laws wouldn't have passed if the populist was allowed to vote.

Scott Lucas spoke again and stressed his desire for an opportunity to vote on this issue and stated that as a community we pride ourselves on intellectual and critical thinking. He emphasized that historically marriage has always been between a man and a woman and should remain that way . . .

Article # 26 was DEFEATED by a ballot vote of: YES 75 NO 192

This same discussion went on in more than a hundred towns across the state. The article seemed important enough to voters in Bow that they moved it to the beginning of the meeting. Understandably (and delightfully) Jill Hadaway makes a typographical error in transcribing the words of Mary Beth Walz. The state representative asserted that the article had already twice been voted on by elected representatives. She implied that since the legislature had affirmed its support for gay marriage, sending a letter to them asking for more votes would be useless and, as the minutes read, the article was "mute."

Probably Mary Beth Walz said, or intended to say, "moot." But "mute" works, too. By voting down an article we silence it—with our voices. Especially on social issues like this one, we say, "Quiet down; we've heard enough."

In other towns, with a yes vote, people were saying, "We're not finished with this discussion."

The chance to have our voices heard—that's central to town meeting. Whether or not the vote goes our way, there's satisfaction in voicing our side, laying out our perspective. Sure, most people have their minds made up before they enter the hall, but because we are all in a hall together there exists the possibility that somebody might change somebody's mind. Oh, it's happened. A nudge and a wink from someone you respect; a quiet "slow down, let's think this over" from someone who seems wise and logical; a passionate "you may not think you're hurting anyone with this, but you're hurting me," and the ground you thought was so firm beneath your boots, shifts just a little. Maybe you won't vote for it. But maybe you won't vote against it either. Maybe you'll just sit with your hands folded this once, because you're not as sure which side is right as you were when you walked through the door.

These are the small miracles of town meeting.

A couple of points from the discussion that didn't make the minutes:

History Professor Mary Lee Sargent explained that other gay citizens in Bow might be afraid to speak, afraid for their jobs, afraid of prejudice. This, we expect, might have been hard for the town to hear. Prejudice? Here in Bow? Surely, not. And then she said: "I have been very happy in Bow. I will not be happy if Bow goes on record to support intolerance. I take this resolution very personally."

Jean Geruiskis made common sense when she said that she came to do the business of the Town and this article on the definition of marriage was not the business of the Town. She made more common sense when she personalized her comment: Twenty-two cousins, two of them gay, no adverse affects on the marriages of any of them. The business of the Town, as most of us understand it, is paying for schools, repairing bridges, buying a piece of land for a soccer field, figuring out what we need (used fire truck) vs. what we want (new fire truck), tightening our town belts so we can all afford to live here another year.

But a few minutes later when Phyllis Benoit takes Jean Geruiskis's point and makes a motion to table the article—that is, let's stop talking about it, put it aside, and move on—she can't get a second. Not even from Jean Geruiskis. On some level, voters seem to say, this *is* the business of the town. This matters to us and we want to talk about it. Hear us.

In other discussions I witnessed, no one who supported the article would say, "I'm against gay marriage." That was, of course, the elephant in the room. But proponents stuck to their script: We just want to vote. This is all about voting.

To his credit, Scott Lucas, one of the petitioners, acknowledged Jumbo: Historically, marriage has always been between a man and a woman and should remain that way.

The town disagreed.

And moved on with hardly a grumble to the next article.

Another small miracle.

Other highlights of Bow Town Meeting involved roads. Lots of roads:

- Approved 1.2 million ($800,000 of which comes from state and federal grants) to improve the intersection of Dunklee Road and Route 3-A. Also voted $450,000 to improve the intersection of Knox Road, White Rock Hill Road, and Logging Hill Road. The word "roundabout" in the article was removed. Maybe a roundabout would be the best way to go; maybe not. Some thought the changes would be a waste of money. Others thought the changes would avert disaster. Aversion of disaster won the day.

- Approved $350,000 for paving of roads on the logic that the more the roads deteriorate the move it would cost to fix them. Voted unanimously to replace the culvert over the Bow Bog Brook on Bow Bog Road.

- Approved $250,000 to fix the sink holes, pot holes, and divots on Ridgewood Drive, though Sandra Seney, who lives on the road, wondered if that would be enough. Evidently, those sink holes, pot holes, and divots are substantial.

And, with eyes still on the roads, voters approved the purchase of a dump truck with a plow, a sander, and other accessories. The old truck had been used for eleven seasons and needed repair. Time for a replacement. Those who knew about trucks asked for details. The new truck would be bigger than the old one and it would be four-wheel drive.

The dump truck discussion occurred after Article 16 and then . . . The minutes say it best (and this happens at many a town meeting): "At this point in time the town was eager to go home and discussion basically ceased on the articles." Eight more articles passed with barely a cough or whimper. The public works facility got garage door openers and new gutters. Parks and Recreation got a pickup truck with a plow. Several thousand dollars were added to various capitol reserve funds; the police got some computers.

And everybody, I dare say, went home satisfied that they'd done their civic duty in a timely fashion. Or as the moderator might say: "I know it's been exciting, but you best go right home."

Bradford 2011

The natives were testy. According to the *Concord Monitor*, a police officer had to step between two angry men in the hall "when one threatened to bury the other in his back yard." The meeting lasted until midnight, but somebody didn't go directly to bed. Instead, he or she painted a sign at Selectman Jack Meaney's house: "You're next (expletive)." What Meaney was next in line for went unspecified, though perhaps the writer meant that Meaney would be voted out in the next election, as incumbent Peter Fenton had been in this one.

As for the actual business of the meeting, nineteen of thirty-five warrant articles passed, with a bottom-line increase of $302,000. A last-minute $22,000 was requested and approved. It seems the Bement Covered Bridge on Center Road (built in 1854 and listed on the National Register of Historic Places) had developed a sag and a lean that indicated some structural weakness. At the time of the meeting, the bridge had been closed for a week, so residents knew the problem was serious.

Cornish 2010

J. D. Salinger moved from New York City to Cornish in the 1950s, choosing a quiet country life on the Connecticut River. Here he stayed, protected by the townspeople, who would *never* reveal to strangers where the author of *Catcher in the Rye* lived. And in Cornish, population approximately 2,000, strangers were easy to spot.

Salinger died in January of 2010 at age ninety-one. At town meeting, his widow, Colleen O'Neill, surprised her neighbors by rising to thank the town for respecting his privacy. "This was the best place for him to live," she said.

Katie Zezima, in an article for the *New York Times* published shortly after his death, described Salinger's close connections to the town. Residents didn't see him as a recluse, but as "a towns-person." In Cornish, Zezima writes, "Mr. Salinger was just Jerry, a quiet man who arrived early to church suppers, nodded hello while buying a newspaper at the general store and wrote a thank-you note to the fire department after it extinguished a blaze and helped save his papers and writings."

Zezima noted that Salinger "until recent years" regularly attended town meeting, although he didn't approve of some of the customs. The tradition in Cornish, as in other towns, was to appoint the most newly married couple hog reeves. "In the 1950s Mr. Salinger and his second wife, Claire, were given the honor," resident Stephen Taylor said. "By all accounts, he was not amused."

Deering 2010

I'd heard sludge might be a sticky issue. And sure enough, it was. The warrant article in question proposed lifting the ban on the use of biosolids, a.k.a., sludge, by local farmers. Sharon Farmer argued against lifting the ban because the sludge might contain cadmium, lead, and other heavy metals. "In the 1800s," she said, "sludge used to be just human poo. That isn't the case now."

The request to lift the ban was defeated by just three votes. A close call. But that wasn't the most hotly contested issue. The most hotly contested issue concerned a contract for youth services. Evidently, Deering had, for some years, paid an annual fee to Hillsborough's Youth Services Program and the selectmen sought approval to deviate from tradition and negotiate with other potential providers. Evidently, the selectmen weren't pleased with the terms of the agreement and were, perhaps, miffed that their business was being taken for granted. Resident Peter Kaplan summed up the gripe: "It's time for Hillsborough to prove that they value the relationship with our town and not just the bucks."

The town voted to allow the selectmen to spend $18,000 on youth services, not necessarily in Hillsborough. Same with recreation services. Traditionally Deering paid Hillsborough to provide a summer recreation programs to Deering children. Now the selectman would negotiate for those services or look at the possibility of Deering providing those services itself. "I have never said in public or in private that I don't think Hillsborough Youth Athletics does a good job with our kids," said selectman J. P. Marzullo. "This is again about contracts. It's about negotiation. We're all Yankees here—we like to look for the best deal."

Epsom 2010

At the Epsom deliberative session, Moderator Jeff Keeler explained the purpose of the session and distinguished it from traditional town meeting. The actual vote on the articles to allocate or not allocate money, to approve or disapprove would be by ballot on Election Day. "What we're really doing," he said, "is all getting educated so we can go out and educate our neighbors who were not able to make it here today."

By Epsom tradition, members of the Municipal Budget Committee introduced themselves as did the board of selectmen and town clerk. Then the legislative body took up Article 1:

> Shall the Town of Epsom vote to raise and appropriate the sum of three hundred fifty thousand dollars ($350,000.00) for the construction and original equipping of a new Town Office complex, to be located in the

"Oh, Boy Did They Have a Lot to Say."

Justine "Mel" Graykin wrote this synopsis of the Deerfield Town Meeting 2010, published in The Forum.

(Any resemblance to actual reporting is purely coincidental.)

It started out just like any other Town Meeting, er, excuse me, Town Deliberative Session. There was heated debate about the land next to the Fire House which the Fire Department purchased with money that did or did not come from the O'Neal legacy which needed, or maybe didn't need, to be reimbursed. An amendment to put deed restriction language in the warrant was narrowly defeated.

More stuff got talked about, and was generally rubber-stamped and will be passed on to the voters to vote down if it involves any substantial amount of money.

Meredith Briggs got up and gave the selectmen hell for, as she put it, "trying to make an end run around the bylaws of the Volunteer Fire Association" by appointing Mark Tibbetts permanent part-time chief. Words like "cronyism" and "back door deals" were bandied about quite freely, and the selectmen defended themselves indignantly.

Debate about the budget went back and forth with Harriet Cady doing her usual thing of pointing out RSAs which were generally ignored and proposing cuts which were generally voted down. They fussed and picked at nickels and dimes and then settled on the lovely whopping figure that they would be passing on to the voters to get sticker shock at. (Wait till they see the School Budget.)

Then something bizarre happened. It all had to do with the petition warrant urging legislators to turn that whole business of a constitutional amendment to stop the abomination of gay marriage over to the voters. Even though Chris Tidwell started it out with the gentle and reasonable appeal that it was just intended to give the voters the chance to weigh in on the issue, it was like the lowering of the checkered flag. Everybody was off.

It brought more people to the mic than any other single issue, and it brought people who hadn't had anything to say about anything else. And oh, boy did they have a lot to say. Cathy Shigo got passionate about her right as a taxpayer to have a say in the legislative process, to which several people pointed out that one voted to elect the officials involved. That was your chance to effect policy, and if you don't like what the official does, vote the bum out. Besides, one doesn't "buy" one's right to vote by being a taxpayer; it's the right of every citizen.

An amendment was proposed to change the language of the article to "To see." Just that. Moderator Jack Hutchinson was rather bemused by that. "That's the wording you want? 'To see. . . . ?' Nothing else?" It would effectively disarm the warrant article, but on the other hand, there were going to be some mighty confused voters come March, thinking there was a serious typo on the ballot.

Then a parade of people came up to the microphone to wax eloquent on the amendment. It essentially became a referendum on the subject of gay marriage, even though Selectman Andy Robertson tried to plead that this really had nothing to do with town business. Nobody listened. By god, this was a hell of a lot more important than a new dump truck or redoing the corner of 43 and 107.

Rebecca Hutchinson talked about her own family, and confessed she didn't understand about homosexual attraction. But then, she said, she didn't really understand heterosexual attraction either, to which the audience laughed and applauded. Bernie Cameron, among others, likened the gay marriage issue to the civil rights issue in the Sixties, warning that if, at the time, it had been left to the popular vote, blacks would still be required to use separate restrooms. Protection of the rights of a minority should not be left to the tyranny of the majority. Even Pastor Carol Meredith came out (so to speak) in favor of the amendment, characterizing it as a civil rights issue.

Interspersed between these righteous speeches were a few indignant individuals who protested that they weren't necessarily against gay marriage, and didn't favor taking anyone's rights away, they just wanted to vote on it. (One presumed, to vote against it.)

In the middle of all this Harriet Cady tried to argue that the amendment changed the purpose of the article and was thus illegal according to a Supreme Court ruling, and again, nobody paid any attention. And finally, in good Deerfield tradition, Jon Winslow got up and moved the question.

They voted by secret ballot on the amendment to change the wording of the article to "To see." The amendment passed by a staggering majority: Yes, 92; No, 28. Oh, say can you see.

Becky Rule was there, not as a voter, since she is from Northwood, but to gather material for a new book she's writing on town meetings. I'd say she got some whopping fine material that day.

*lower level of Epsom's Historical Meeting House, and to authorize
the issuance of not more than three hundred fifty thousand dollars
($350,000.00) of bonds or notes in accordance with the provisions of
the Municipal Finance Act (RSA 33), and to authorize the municipal
officials to issue and negotiate such bonds or notes and to determine the
rate of interest thereon? By petition, three-fifths majority vote required;
this is a Special Warrant Article and its appropriation is in addition to
the operating budget.*

In other words, would the town agree to borrow $350,000 to fix up the
basement of the meeting house—formerly a church, saved from demoli-
tion to make way for a gas station and moved to its current location next
to the town library a few years back? The article, as the warrant noted was:
Not Recommended by the Selectmen 0–3 and Not Recommended by the
Budget Committee 2–5–1. With both the selectmen and budget committee
in opposition, chances for passage didn't look good from the get-go.

But at the deliberative session, voters didn't get to say yea or nay. They
could only decide how the article would appear on the ballot come voting
day a few weeks later. What they did was amend the dollar amount from
$350,000.00 to $1 by a vote of 46–39. So on voting day, voters would get
to mark yes or no on an article *To raise and appropriate the sum of $1. . . .*

Cheap enough. If I lived in Epsom, I'd probably vote yes. Although,
sticklers will tell you if you leave $1 on a line, the selectmen can move
money from other lines to supplement that $1. Best to amend down to
zero if you're really against funding something. A budget item with zero
appropriations is dead. No money can be transferred to that line.

The deliberative session severely wounded (though it did not actually
kill) the possibility of town funding for the old hall. Restoration and repair
might proceed if they could be done real cheap. Or with privately raised
funds. Or if the selectmen did something underhanded.

The proposal to fix up the meeting house for town offices did not go
down easily. It twitched on the floor for a good half hour. Some demanded
information on exactly how the money would be spent. Others sputtered
that at a previous meeting they'd been promised specific information from
the petitioners, but that information was not forthcoming: "We were led
to believe there would be facts and figures at this meeting."

Others said the facts and figures were hard to determine because the
committee expected a lot of donations and good will. "We believe once
we get started there may be town spirit around the project." A lot of the

work would be done for free and materials donated, so an exact budget was hard to figure.

Bruce Graham took the microphone. He addressed the moderator, "Can I talk to the people?" then dramatically turned to the crowd. "We own the building. It needs to be set up for use in some way. You gotta pay attention to an old building. If we can figure out how to occupy that building for no money, bring it on." Pause. "I guess it's time for me to sit down."

And he did.

When a speaker demanded comment on the article from "each of the selectmen and all members of the budget committee." The moderator stepped in: "Speakers are not allowed to dictate who responds to questions."

Someone suggested that to "Just throw money at it and hope things come out right" was not an intelligent plan. Discussion covered L-Chip grants (state money for restoring old buildings), the limitations on use of an historic property (upstairs can be used only for assembly), what was to be done about a septic system, and why didn't anybody come forward to defend their proposal.

The town attorney, Tony Soltani, had the last word: Even if the people voted in the $350,000, the selectmen didn't have to spend it. "People can appropriate, but people cannot mandate," he said. "The selectmen could just say, 'We don't want to do it.'"

Article 2, the big one, the operating budget totaling nearly three million dollars, slid through without much fuss. Harvey Harkness pointed out that all the factual information needed for discussion was printed in the handout. Besides which, the budget "represented the concentrated work of a number of people including the select board and budget committee." He added that "Discussion was detailed and specific and spirited at the time." And, here's the kicker: "The bottom line of this budget is less than last year's."

This is music to voters' ears.

The operating budget did stimulate a bit more discussion on (you guessed it) the meeting house. Adding $5,000 to the repair and maintenance of government buildings might be a good idea, some thought. That money could be used as matching funds for grants to fix the meeting house, maybe some electrical work, painting, generally moving forward to make the building usable. Penny Graham said: "We need to show the grantors that the town has an investment in the building."

Then came Article 7. People had strong feelings about Article 7. Yes,

they did. Seems the dollar impact of each article on the tax rate was traditionally listed on the ballot, so voters could see in black and white how
much each item would cost them personally. They could, literally, figure
the value of their property, say, $100,000, multiply it by the impact on
the tax rate for an individual item, say, 2 cents/$1,000 valuation, and cal-
culate that the new cruiser or snow plow or cemetery fence would take
two bucks out of their own pocketbook. Then, based on that calculation, a
voter could determine whether the new cruiser, snow plow, or cemetery
fence was worth 2 bucks. This year, there would be no such listing of cost
per $1,000 valuation on the ballot. Town officials had been advised not to
do so by the Department of Revenue Administration (DRA). Listing that
information might be construed, the DRA said, as electioneering, so the
selectmen decided to end the practice.

The petitioned Article 7 asked: *Shall the Town of Epsom describe the
estimated tax impact for each appropriation question on the official town ballot?* An amendment from the floor added *"and school"* between *"town"* and
"ballot," to cover all bases. A further amendment added language that the
tax impact be listed *"for such a time in perpetuity until rescinded by another
warrant article or by superior court."*

After some prodding, Attorney Soltani declared that such an amendment (the *in perpetuity*, etc.) would not be binding. Which seemed to tick a
few people off. The language, the attorney said, is "absolutely meaningless."
Which seemed to tick a few people off even more. Especially the ones who
suggested the change in the first place. Finally, the attorney explained that
the language was redundant, since the article itself implied the *in perpetuity*
part. Ah, well. The amendment is withdrawn: "Now that the town council
is so *kind* to explain that the amendment is redundant."

After that clarification, much debate ensued about what can and cannot be put on the ballot and what electioneering meant. An example of
electioneering offered by a selectman: "Allowing a candidate to stand next
to you holding a sign with his name on it while you vote."

Don Bartlett said: "Those that don't want the impact listed are concerned that people are voting their pocketbooks. This town does not necessarily vote its pocketbook."

What the discussion seemed to come down to was self-rule. One voter
said, "Seems like the people should be able to do this. We are losing control
all over and we're starting to lose it right here."

The article passed on a unanimous voice vote.

Take that DRA.

Other highlights:

- The Moderator asked if the road agent was present and would like to comment on a point of interest. Response from bleachers: "He's out fixing the road."

- Discussion of the police budget raised the question of crime on the upswing. A handout from the police department explained that the department was handling more calls than ever. A woman queried: "I called the police one time and said there's a goat in my back yard. Would that be counted as a call?" Yes, it would.

Franconia 2010

Twenty-eight articles were put before the voters at the 2010 town meeting. Three generated more discussion than the others. One of those controversial articles passed. One was tabled. And one failed in a close vote.

One involved road maintenance. One involved an infrastructure change—moving the police department from one building to another. And one—Article 19—involved a shared and shattering tragedy.

Here are accounts of those discussions from the minutes recorded by town clerk Marilyn L. Knowlton.

> ARTICLE 9. To see if the Town would vote to raise and appropriate the sum of Sixty Thousand Dollars ($60,000.00) to be added to the Highway Improvement Expendable Trust Fund previously established. The Selectmen recommend this appropriation.
>
> Ron Taksar spoke from the floor asking to have Article 9 amended to add an additional $30,000. He gave a brief description of the current condition of Wallace Hill Road and listed concerns of safety for people traveling the road. Ron Taksar put the town on notice which would make the town liable for any accident resulting in the poor quality of the road. Ned Densmore asked where Wallace Hill Road was on the current list of road improvements. Scott Knowlton, Road Agent, spoke to the question and explained that Wallace Hill Road is going to be reclaimed this year along with replacement of culverts but due to limited funds it will be a 3–4 year process before it is fully complete. A question was asked from the floor about whether there is any stimulus money available. Scott said they are looking into it but most of these programs require matching funds. Ramesh Dave asked if the $60,000 allocation is enough. Jon Peabody asked who established the $60,000 amount that is put into road maintenance fund. Scott answered the

CIP and he also explained that back when this amount was established asphalt wasn't as expensive as it is today. He also explained that we do get money from the State in the Highway Block Grant Fund which is usually about $40,000 that also gets added to the fund.

Bill Mead called the question for amendment on amount increase to $90,000. The question was moved and seconded. The call for the amendment was voted on by hand and passed.

The amended article was read, moved and seconded: To see if the Town would vote to raise and appropriate the sum of Ninety Thousand Dollars ($90,000.00) to be added to the Highway Improvement Expendable Trust Fund previously established. A voice vote was taken and the amended Article 9 passed.

So a deteriorating road gets the attention it, by all accounts deserves, and drivers on Wallace Hill will be safer for it. Eventually.

The next article to inspire many to rise and state their opinions involved where the police department belonged.

ARTICLE 17. To see if the Town is in favor of moving the Police Department from the Safety Services building to the basement of the town hall providing the water problem can be resolved.

The article was read, moved and seconded. Rich McLeod spoke to the article and confirmed that they had spoken to State Dept. of Revenue and were given the okay to switch article order. Rich asked Jeff Woodward who served as the Chair of the Infrastructure Committee to speak on this article. Jeff Woodward reviewed the history of the Infrastructure Committee and the conditions of the current Safety Services building highlighting the need for more space for all three departments—Police, Fire & Life Squad. Architects recommended possibly moving the PD to the basement of Town Hall explaining this may be the most cost effective solution. The cost of fixing the water problems and refurbishing the town hall to bring it up to code would cost approximately $400,000. Jeff Woodward also reported that they had polled other towns who share police with town hall and, seems to be working. The Board of Selectmen decided to see how the town felt about the relocation.

Ruth Vail pointed out that this article is asking the town to vote on something that is not going to happen this year and that the vote is not binding from year to year. Lydia Cumbee asked how Police feel about the move. Chief Montminy spoke to the question thanking Jeff Woodward and the Infrastructure Committee for their work. The Chief said he is not currently aware of any plans that have been drawn up on *a new location and would hope that he would be part of that process. He voiced concern with the proposed location and confidentiality. He also voiced concerns about sharing the parking lot with the library, town rink and town offices. He thinks the parking lot is too small! He has safety concerns of only one way in and out of parking lot. He thinks Police should have their own entrance. The sloping driveway is a concern in winter and not enough room in the bay for 2 cruisers. PD is the Emergency Management Center for the town and would need a generator to operate all equipment. The current location is currently set up for a generator and is in a good location with plenty of parking and has worked well in the past when they have had to be activated. The Chief spoke to other police chiefs in towns that are combined and they are not in favor of the current configuration. Scott Knowlton asked if PD, FD & SS have a problem working together. Chief said he wasn't aware of any opposition from the other departments and that he would like to all work together. Ramesh Dave commented that they should not be split and agreed that PD should not be divided. Kathy Mead, a former member of the Infrastructure Committee, spoke about past research done from Infrastructure Committee and that a new building estimate was given from architect at a cost of $1MM. At the time this was recommended the town was voting on a new high school and the water project was looming. Kathy suggested that we review this more this year given different circumstances and maybe something could be done in line of a new building. Barbara Floyd asked about combining municipal offices with the PD and selling town hall and move the municipal offices and PD to a new location. Jeff Woodward said he brought this option up in the past but was told the Town Hall was a sacred building and couldn't be considered. Joel Peabody reminded everyone that this was a non binding vote and asked to table the article until next year and take a year to review it further.*

Bill Mead made a motion to table Article 17. The article was moved and seconded. A hand vote was taken and Article 17 was tabled.

Too many questions in the air, it seems, to determine the best location for the police department. The Infrastructure Committee no doubt made their recommendation for the move to town hall in good faith, but the fact that the chief of police was against it boded ill. And Ruth Vail's point that since the move wouldn't be made in the coming year and the vote wouldn't be binding in years to come put another spanner in the works. The Mind saw fit to avoid a vote on an issue that remained unclear, even after a thorough discussion. Table it!

This last of the three controversial articles is truly harrowing. In 2007, a tragedy occurred in the North Country. The bare facts are this: After a traffic stop followed by a car chase, Franconia police officer Bruce McKay was shot by Liko Kenney who then ran over the downed officer twice with his car. McKay died. A local man named Gregory Floyd happened on the scene just moments after the deadly incident. He shot and killed Liko Kenney on the spot.

Some said Liko Kenney was hot-tempered and a loose cannon who was out to get Officer McKay, a fine public servant, due to many run-ins with him and a long-standing feud. Some said Officer McKay was arrogant and mean. He was out to get Liko Kenney, who was a fun-loving, intelligent young man, due to that same long-standing feud, and that Kenney killed McKay because McKay had chased him down and he was in fear for his life. No one knew what to make of Gregory Floyd happening on the scene and shooting Liko Kenney. Floyd was acquitted of any wrong doing so fast it would make your head spin. The national press picked up the story, partly because Liko Kenney was a cousin to Bode Miller, a famous skier also from the area.

After the shootings, people in Franconia—in the whole North Country for that matter—took sides. Who provoked whom? Who escalated the situation? Who could have stopped it? The tragedy created a gaping wound in the social fabric. A lot of people just didn't know what to think. All were saddened.

In 2009, a bill was introduced at the state level to name part of Route 18 in Franconia after the fallen officer. At the 2010 town meeting, petitioners asked the town to support that bill, and, in turn, show its support for Officer McKay. Reading between the lines, and noting the request for a secret ballot, you can see how very painful this discussion and the decision that followed were to this community.

> *ARTICLE 19. Should the Town indicate its support for Senate Bill 154, which proposes to name a 2.8 mile portion of Route 18 in Franconia, which runs from Route 141 to Interstate 93 (Also known as 3-Mile Hill), after Corporal Bruce McKay, a police officer who was murdered while serving our community. (Ballot Vote by Petition.)*
>
> *Bill Mead prefaced that there would be opinions on both sides and that this could become a very emotional subject and that he would take limited discussion. A petitioned article cannot be voted on by ballot unless requested with a written requested petition with five signatures.*

Bill Mead had the written request with the five signatures so the vote was done by ballot vote.

The article was read, moved and seconded. Rich McLeod spoke stating Board of Selectmen recommend article. Doug Grant made a motion to table Article 19 for no further discussion. The motion was moved and seconded. A voice vote to table went to hand vote. 54 in favor, 100 opposed. The tabled motion failed.

Russ Cumbee spoke to the article recognizing Sharon, Bruce McKay's fiancée and thanked her for being there. Russ spoke in favor of supporting Senate Bill 154 emphasizing that the Town owed it to Bruce McKay and his family since he served for the Town for fourteen years. He also spoke about the importance of letting the current police officers know that we support them. Mary Brubaker asked if this is a Senate vote, what the town's say means. Rich McLeod answered that the Senate already passed the Bill. It will be heard in the House. Members of the House asked to get local feedback. David Schafer spoke in support of the Bill and stated that we are not holding a popularity contest on whether someone was liked or not it is about honoring a fallen police officer. Russ Cumbee also noted for the record that the mailing that was done to promote SB 154 was all his own doing funded by him. The ballot vote was cast. 73 in favor, 93 not in favor. Article 19 did not pass.

Russ Cumbee made a motion for reconsidering the vote of SB 154. There was a motion and a second. A voice vote was taken for reconsidering the vote. The reconsideration vote did not pass.

With seventy-three in favor and ninety-three against, the vote shows a town sorely divided, a town wearing its broken heart on its sleeve.

Gilford 2010 and 2011

While some town clerks record just the basics in their minutes—who moved/seconded, yea/nays, an occasional pointed comment—Gilford's Denise Morrissette paints a detailed portrait of the proceedings. She diligently reported Peter Millham's "moment of personal privilege," during which he reflected on his thirty-nine years as moderator. He said what an honor it was to have "been the beneficiary of voters' trust and confidence" over four decades. Then he got into a little history, going back to the town report of 1971, his first year on the job: "What was not printed in the report but was in his memory," Morrissette writes, "was that a lot of roads were not paved—hills would be paved but tops and bottoms would not be paved so that the roads wouldn't wash out. He noted that there are not many unpaved roads in town today."

Furthermore, "Original Town Hall had a small hall in it for meetings, plays, and all the offices were in that building. That building now is a part or a wing on the Gilford Church." That was one among many changes he'd seen, but a big change that directly affected him was the advent of the voting machine, which "saved so much work that it got everyone home four hours earlier at night."

When Millham began as moderator, Gilford had fewer than 1,000 registered voters, compared with more than 6,000 in 2010. The 1971 town report "reveals the effect of the population and demand for services placed upon our Town government." The number of employees has increased dramatically, along with the budgets, but Millham said, this "does not illustrate any wastefulness. What it does illustrate is inflation and increase of services that have been required because of the increase in population."

He went on to offer a tip of the hat to the three town clerks he'd worked with over the years. "The Moderator and Town Clerk have to work together for the preparation of these meetings, also on the balloting and getting everything ready. . . . It's a great resource to have the Town Clerk to lean on to get those things done. Some of the responsibilities with regards to the meeting are the Selectmen's, some are the Moderator's, and some are the Town Clerk's. Over that period of time the Town Clerk, who also started in 1971, was Lorraine Royce. She was Town Clerk for many years and then we had Debbie Eastman. Probably many of you can still remember Debbie because that was only five years ago; and of course we now have Denise Morrissette and all of them have been very conscientious and wonderful to work with."

"With that," he said, "I'm going to proceed with the meeting."

What Moderator Millham said and Denise Morrissette duly recorded provides a nutshell look at what's happened to scores of New Hampshire towns in the last few decades—growing population, more demands for town services, greater and more complex responsibilities for elected officials and town employees. No wonder old timers shake their heads at the multimillion dollar combined school and town budgets. What happened?

But here's something counterintuitive, with so much money at stake, at the 2010 deliberative session (Gilford is an SB 2 town) where Millham made his remarks, only fifty-nine persons were in attendance. Never, said Millham, had he presided over a meeting attended by so few.

Update, February 8, 2011

Moderator Sandra McGonagle called the meeting to order at 7:00 p.m. and asked Peter Millham, former moderator, to lead the salute to the flag and the Pledge of Allegiance, which he did. At the beginning of the meeting, good news, ninety-five persons were in attendance, including, Denise Morrissette notes: "the media, Department Managers, and other non-registered voters allowed to attend the meeting for information on social services. The Moderator identified these people and stated they were not to act/vote on any of the amendments."

The only article altered was the operating budget, and the alteration affected only the town band. The band had enjoyed a funding level of $1,500 for the past few years, but though the selectmen cut the amount by half in their budget, an amendment from the floor restored the $750 cut.

Seems the spike in attendance might be attributed less to the band controversy and more to the selectmen's decision not to recommend any petitioned articles for support of social services such as Child and Family Services, emergency mental health services, Community Health and Hospice, Meals-on-Wheels, protection for victims of domestic and sexual violence, and so forth. Their explanation: All the selectmen's office received were the petitioned articles and no back-up material justifying the expense, despite requests for such back-up material. With insufficient information, they just couldn't recommend funding any of those social services.

Not to worry, a month later at the polls, Gilford voted to support the services just as they'd just done in years past.

Sadly for the 2012 Bicentennial Celebration, a petitioned request for $3,000 to fund t-shirts, advertising, entertainment, and banners (with t-shirts sales returning "a significant amount" of the money) went down in flames, 305 yea, 463 nay. It didn't help that only one of the three selectmen thought the t-shirts and such were a good idea. And *nobody* on the budget committee was in a celebratory mood, 0 to 8 not to recommend.

Gilmanton 2010 and 2011

I was drawn to investigate the Gilmanton town meeting by a heartfelt letter to the editor from Allen Everett, who urged voters to support the repairs and erection of the cupola at the historic Academy building. "The Academy is the centerpiece of our town," he wrote." It has been a source of great pride since 1794," designed to be worthy of what one historian deemed one of "the highest, most healthful and most beautiful New Hampshire towns."

The building served many purposes: school, town hall, meeting hall, and community center. In 2010, the Academy's crown, it's cupola, was condemned, removed, and put into storage. It needs fixing and to be returned to its rightful place. Cost: The selectmen recommended $40,000; the budget committee, $30,000. The hope: Grants might defray some costs. Voters appropriated just $20,000 for the project.

The big issue at the 2010 meeting, however, was the library. Voters, after much debate, approved $41,300 to operate the new library, which is not owned or run by the town but by a private organization. Resident Daniel Webster said he never remembered "quite so much bitterness" as had been generated by the library issue.

The library opened in September of 2009. Supporters had spent years raising private funds to build it, but asked for the town's help with ongoing operation. Evidently, this request for support came as a surprise to some residents, who thought the library would continue to be funded entirely by private donations. Organizers claimed they never promised that. They got the library going, and now it was time for the town to pony up. Oh, yes, you did promise! some said. Did not! Did too! Daniel Webster capped that back and forth with: "I really don't give a damn what someone said ten years ago. We have a million-dollar building. It's great for kids. It's great for everybody. The issue is: Should we use it or should we abandon it?"

In the spirit of not looking a gift horse in the mouth, the town voted to use it—by just ten votes, 189 yea, 179 nay.

Follow-up 2011

Moderator Mark Sisti opened the meeting at the Gilmanton School Gymnasium on a somber note. After Daniel Webster led the crowd of more than 300 in the Pledge of Allegiance, the moderator asked for a moment of silence—a tradition that, he explained, was a little different this year. In addition to remembering "all those we lost in this town over the past year," recognizing those serving in the military, and praying for the ill, Sisti acknowledge "the tragedy of enormous proportion we are all witnessing live in Japan [devastation caused by a massive earthquake and tsunami] and I ask that we keep those people in our prayers with a moment of silence."

Many articles were presented, discussed, disposed of. But I was curious. What happened with the library? This time around the petitioned article requested $47,500 for operating expenses. The selectmen recommended $00.00 instead, but the budget committee supported the petitioners.

Robert Hyslop moved to amend the amount down to $20,000. Here's how Town Clerk Debra A. Cornett recorded the discussion. A sizzling one to be sure:

> *Ernest Hudziec asks if there is a contract between the GYRL [Gilmanton Year Round Library] and the Town of Gilmanton to provide services. Stan Bean states, "There is not a contract, there doesn't need to be a contract, and the selectmen have chosen not to have a contract." Mr. Hudziec states that, "Every year we are going to go through this up and down, up and down and would prefer to see some multiyear contract that would fix the Town's portion of the GYRL budget and spell out the services that the library will supply . . . instead of going through all this year after year . . . by petition . . . going back and forth . . . budget with a fixed amount that they can count on so that they can raise the additional funds . . . Sara Thorne stated her support of original article . . . incredible community service, wonderful programs, periodicals . . . Mr. Barry Howland, spoke in praise of the disclosure of funds listed . . . that the GYRL supplies a wonderful service to the town . . . we need to straighten this out so that the Town is not divided . . . Holly Nimirowski speaks in favor of the amendment . . . citing praises of personal use of the libraries but due to personal hardships and financially difficult economic times for many in town could not support the full amount . . . asks GYRL to make do . . . amendment is a wonderful compromise in bridging the gap . . . Elizabeth Strauss spoke to the positive services of the library . . . John Dickey on budget committee for GYRL . . . would not be able to supply the level of services . . . asks to defeat the amendment . . . Salvatore Sisti . . . asks to defeat amendment . . . lowering would decrease use of the library to Gilmanton's youth . . . George Roberts . . . states library trustees need to be voted for in future to get rid of controversy by electing trustees . . . public funds would be represented by a trustee for those funds . . . John Dickey explained that the $50,000 donation received was to offset utilities . . . Moderator calls amendment to vote.*
>
> *Amendment #1 voice vote too close to call, Moderator calls for a hand count.*
> *HAND COUNT: Yes–106 No–118*
> *AMENDMENT #1 DEFEATED BY HAND COUNT*

Discussion then returned to the original article and original amount of $47,500. Despite a plea by Laurie Sanborn that "we simply can't afford it . . . people are losing jobs left and right across the State of New

Tragedy Touches Gilmanton Town Meeting

Though the business of the town got done at the 2010 town meeting, it was marked by tragedy.

Shortly after discussion of the appropriation of the treatment of milfoil in Gilmanton lakes, in which Stephen Goddard participated, he fell from the third row of the bleachers. The minutes describe what happened this way:

> *At approximately 12:45 p.m., the Moderator asks the body to clear the gymnasium when one of our residents, Stephen Goddard, collapsed. Mr. Sisti asked for everyone to exit to the Cafeteria so that emergency personnel can do their job. They will be called back when the emergency is cleared.*
>
> *At approximately 1:20 p.m. before the Moderator continued with Article #31, Mr. Sisti asked the body to bow their heads for a moment of silence and for the respect shown; he then redirected the body back to Article #31.*

Later, the EMTs were given "praise and recognition" for the handling of the emergency. They had administered CPR and used a defibrillator at the scene before transporting Mr. Goddard to the hospital, as his wife, Mary, stood by.

Though the minutes don't say so, local newspapers reported the next day that Stephen Goddard, aged sixty-four, died. His obituary described him as a "respected member of the community, an honorary lifetime member of the Bemidji Jaycees" who "served on the Town of Gilmanton budget committee."

Stephen Goddard's untimely death at town meeting underscores how integral our community institutions are to our lives. Many of us attend town meeting every year for decades. Like anniversaries and birthdays, it marks our time on the planet. Each year in each town a familiar face or two has vanished, and often, the town remembers together those lost to illness or accident or old age. Each year in each town, new faces appear—young people just discovering their political inclinations or new families moved in. Town meeting is a vital, ever-changing entity as the loss of Stephen Goddard in its midst so dramatically shows.

Just as when in our own lives after loss we find a way to go on, so does the Gilmanton town meeting. Stunned, worried, saddened, confused by Goddard's collapse, the body pulls itself together and moves on to the next practical matter, the next article—a testimonial to communal strength and to the sustaining power of tradition.

Hampshire . . . that's the reality . . . I just say no," when Moderator Mark Sisti called for the vote, and the secret ballots were marked and counted, the library got its money, 156 yea, 139 no.

Hill 2010 and 2011

The town was feeling pinched for cash at the 2010 meeting and, as a result, cut $37,000 from the operating budget by a vote of 58 to 42. Doesn't sound like a lot, unless you realize the budget that finally passed was for $876,373, so the cut amounts to just over 4 percent. Maybe 4 percent doesn't sound like much either; but it inspired some strong rhetoric. Shaun Bresnahan, Sr., led the charge to level-fund town salaries and cut back on the hours for the town clerk's office, tax collector's office, and library.

He'd done his homework. He calculated that 6,500 patrons used the library in a year, which amounted to about four patrons per hour the library was open. If the hours were halved, that would mean eight patrons per hour—and the library was plenty big to handle that volume.

The selectmen pointed out that they were not bound to make the cuts suggested by Mr. Bresnahan. The $37,000 came off the bottom line and they'd have to cut somewhere but, as recorded in the minutes, they did not see their way clear to cutting wages or hours.

In 2011, with ninety-five voters present (representing 12 percent of registered voters) the proposed operating budget, recommended by the budget committee, chaired by Shaun Bresnahan, Jr., came in at $917, 48. It included a 3 percent across-the-board raise to town employees. From the minutes: "Concerns were expressed from residents about giving any raises this year due to the economy." Henry Osmer moved to reduce the amount by $47,482 to a nice round $870,000. Seconded by Bill Henry.

Here's how Town Clerk/Tax Collector Desiree L. Mahurin summarized that discussion:

> Similar comments were made as with the original motion.
>
> Resident, Bill Machado commented to the voters to be very careful and mindful of how much more the budget is cut. The cuts from the 2010 budget for example, resulted in reductions to town services including reduced hours at the Town Clerk Office, reduced hours at the Public Library as well as other reductions to other departmental services.
>
> Additional comments and questions were also made regarding the Library. Questions were asked about expenditures, hours & wages. A question was asked of the Trustees if the original budget increase was

for additional wages. Library Trustee, Gayle Seip responded by saying
that the budget increase was for additional hours being added to the
Librarian's wages. Other questions and comments were also responded
to by Mrs. Seip.

Other comments were made regarding the public hours of the
Library. It was felt that more hours were not needed but different hours
were (i.e. evenings & weekends). Examples were stated regarding sur-
rounding communities the size of Hill that do not have Libraries open
as many hours and had much smaller budgets.

The amendment failed. A second amendment proposed by Shaun
Bresnahan, Jr., to reduce the budget by $17,884 passed. From the minutes:
"Similar comments were made as with the original motion and amend-
ment. Mr. Bresnahan made suggestions to make cuts in the following areas:
Police, Highway, Town Clerk, Parks & Recreation, Library and other mis-
cellaneous areas."

Of particular interest was an amendment proposed by Rick Vincent to
take money from capital reserve funds for Fire ($5,000), Highway ($10,000)
and Revaluation ($5,000) and put it toward Archival Preservation. From
the minutes:

Rick Vincent felt that more efforts should be made to protect the Town's
historical documents. Currently documents are being exposed to array
of hazardous elements.

Selectman Brady did not feel that this was wise to change around
the Capital Reserve funding for this project at this time.

Mr. Brady explained that the Board of Selectmen has intentions to
create a committee to review the downstairs area of the Town Office
building and help develop a plan for its use. Town Clerk, Desiree L.
Mahurin offered the reminder that a committee was developed 6 years
ago and did present a plan to the Town but nothing has ever been done.
She suggested that if a committee is formed and a plan developed it
would be followed through this time.

The amendment failed.

On a brighter note, by a vote of 41 yea, 39 nay, the assembled appropriated $5,000 for Old Home Day. Old Home Day comes to Hill just once
every ten years.

One expects that the thirty-nine who voted 'no' will refrain from having
any fun at Old Home Day.

What a Small-Town Budget Looks Like

The town of Hill, incorporated in 1778, has a population 1,100 give or take. It lies in Merrimack County and shares boundaries with Bristol, Alexandria, New Hampton, Sanbornton, Andover, Franklin, and Danbury.

Hill is famous for being the town that moved. In 1938 the town center was designated a flood control reservoir under the Franklin Falls Dam Project. That was the bad news. The good news was town leaders found a spot on high ground, purchased the land, and by 1941 had built the "New Village," complete with a town hall, school, and water system.

Because Hill is so small, its budget is a little simpler than the budgets of more populated towns. Here's the breakdown of the Budget Committee's recommended 2011 budget presented to the voters for their consideration at town meeting.

Executive	$41,319
Town Clerk	$47,146
Tax Collector	$5,100
Reval of Property	$5,600
Legal Expenses	$4,000
Personnel Admin.	$19,775
Planning & Zoning	$2,000
Gen. Govt. Bldg.	$24,384
Cemeteries	$2,300
Insurance	$14,850
Police	$69,000
Ambulance	$20,065
Fire	$50,946
Emergency Management	$975
Highways & Streets	$281,795
Street Lighting	$3,600
Recon. of Highways	$54,660
Solid Waste Disposal	$78,405
Water Services	$143,849
Health Agencies	$5,038
Welfare	$5,000
Parks & Recreation	$9,200
Library	$28,000
Patriotic Purposes	$800
Conservation	$175
Int. on Tax Anticipation Notes	$500

TOTAL OPERATING BUDGET **$917,482** less $17,884 cut at town meeting **$899,598**.

(Continued next page)

Small-Town Budget *(Continued)*:

From the budget you get a sense of the town's needs and how it balances those needs with what the taxpayers can afford. The roads need to be maintained so people can get around. More than $330,000 (Highways & Streets, Reconditioning of Highways) goes to roads—the biggest portion of the budget. Public safety matters, too, with nearly $140,000 going to Fire, Police and Ambulance services.

Good water is a priority. The public water system sucks up about $144,000. And Solid Waste Disposal (the dump) runs nearly $80,000. It also costs a lot to administer these services and keep the town running, round about $113,000 when you combine expenses for Executive, Tax Collector, Town Clerk, and Personnel Administration.

The library chugs along with $28,000 and many grateful patrons willing to speak their appreciation for its services, despite—in both 2010 and 2011—being a target for proposed cuts. The rural nature of the town shows in the relatively low amounts allotted for Conservation ($175) and Parks and Recreation. Hill doesn't seem to feel threatened by unfettered development. And the woods, streams, and ponds provide plenty of room for what we know to be the recreations of choice in this part of the state—hunting, hiking, fishing, snowmobiling, cross-country skiing, and so forth.

We salute the town's contribution of $800 for patriotic purposes—flags, perhaps? Sprucing up the main drag with red, white, and blue banners for Fourth of July? And the most vulnerable citizens get some help with $10,000 in appropriations for Welfare and Health Agencies. No doubt the $2,300 for maintenance of cemeteries keeps those areas tidy out of respect for the departed.

This small-town budget reflects small-town values. New Hampshire values.

Hillsborough 2010

Voters said yes to a $600,000 price tag to preserve the historic Governor John B. Smith Mansion, which houses the Fuller Public Library—a truly beautiful library. (I've been there many times as a speaker for the New Hampshire Humanities Council, so I know.) Part of the money would be raised by taxes, but $200,000 would come from the library trust fund.

On a sad note, Selectman Joseph Collins honored Paul Haley, a former selectman, who had died the week before of cancer. Collins presented Paul Haley's widow, Babette, as well as his son, Paul Haley, and son's girlfriend,

Suzanne Decker, with a plaque commemorating Haley's term as selectman. Collins, tearfully, remembered Haley as "a strong-willed man and
an Irishman to the core," who served as long as he could until the cancer
forced him to step down.

Hopkinton 2010

Rejected SB 2 for the school district and the town by a landslide.

Nelson 2010

This jewel of the Monadnock Region headlines its website with "Welcome
to the Center of the Universe." I'm not going to argue with that. Nelson is
famous for, among other things, the longest running weekly contra dance
in the universe. They dance at the town hall every Monday night, usually
with music from Bob McQuillen (piano) and Harvey Tolman (fiddle).
Between them, John Walters wrote for *New Hampshire Magazine*, "They've
been playing music for about a hundred years." Walters poses the question:
How long have there been contra dances in Nelson? Bob McQuillin (on the
south side of eighty) says that fifty years ago "Ralph Page said it went back
250 years, and he was dead serious." Contra dances in Nelson have been
going on as long as town meeting itself. Maybe all that dancing puts people
in an agreeable state of mind; nearly all the articles at the 2010 town meeting passed, most unanimously. Among the decisions and appropriations:

- $286,000 to defray town charges.
- $30,150 for the library.
- $3,487 for social services: Home Health Care, Monadnock
  Family Services, Keene Community Kitchen, and Southwestern
  Community Services.
- $5,000 to repair the gate pillars and reset and repair the monuments
  in Section 1 of the Nelson Cemetery.
- $2,000 for Milfoil Prevention and Treatment.
- $11,242 to subsidize ambulance service (it being understood that
  residents will still be charged for individual calls).
- $500 to fight forest fires.
- $25,000 for the Fire Equipment Capital Reserve Fund, with the

stipulation that no withdrawals may be made from the fund except by vote of the town and recommendation of the fire chief.

- $680 for hazardous waste collection on twelve collection dates.

- $1,500 for emergency management.

- $37,000 for the Police Department (down from $37, 942 the previous year).

The purchase of a 2010 Ford Expedition ($28,861.02) to replace the 1993 Ford Crown Victoria police cruiser struck a note of discord. The original motion was amended from providing the full amount over three years to raising $10,000 to add to the Police Capital Reserve Fund. The amendment passed on a written ballot, 69 yes, 39 no. Money for roads and road equipment slid right through. The Town Clerk/Tax Collector didn't fare as well—a petitioned article to raise $3,840 to restore the salary to the amount appropriated in 2006 ($18,306.00) was passed over.

As for a petitioned article directing the selectmen to put a Conservation Easement on a parcel of land, allowing a house, garage, and dock (with no clear-cutting of trees), the selectmen didn't recommend it and the voters didn't go for it either. They voted no.

Newbury 2011

Voters objected to nearly all warrant articles, and voted no on most of them. They just weren't having it. True, the operating budget of $3.2 million passed without a murmur, but an expansion of the town docks on Lake Sunapee roiled the crowed. Some didn't think more boats in the harbor was a good idea. Ron Wolf summarized his objection, when, according to meeting minutes by Town Clerk Linda Plunkettt, he "pointed out that boaters will still have to walk over the sunbathers on the dock; they will just have a longer walk over more sunbathers. The people who jump off the end of the dock will still be jumping off the end of the dock, just further out and still near boats. Therefore, in Mr. Wolf's opinion, these changes do not enhance safety for swimmers or boaters." Parking was also a problem.

Mr. Bachelder didn't care for the plan either. He raised a number of concerns: "The existing dock system has been primarily used as a swim facility. This plan seems to change it to primarily a public docking facility and takes away the traditional use of the Newbury Harbor dock. The effect on the people of the town has not been well thought through. The east dock is widely used by families for swimming, diving, and fishing and as a substitute for a beach in town. There are many people that have no private access to the lake and use the dock instead. The west dock is always busy with people who like to sit in the shade and relax and enjoy the view. This plan takes away the opportunity for people to be able to swim laps in deep water for exercise." And so on.

When the results of the secret ballot were read, voters decided 40 to 76 that the docks would stay just as they were.

A veterans memorial to be located at the "property formerly known as the Bald Sunapee Garden Center" was "put in abeyance" for one year. Renovations to the veterans hall also sparked debate, but in the end the $35,000 went through, despite one resident's warning that those renovations would cost a lot more in the end: "I think this is the camel's nose under the tent," said Dan Wolf.

The ham and bean supper provided by the Newbury Beautification Committee was delicious and enjoyed by all.

New London 2010 and 2011

In New London, town meeting attracts a big crowd. At the 2010 meeting, Cotton Cleveland, one of just a few female moderators in the state, moderated her tenth and final meeting and was commended for her "dedicated and enthusiastic service." The big article that year was a hefty $5,200,000 to fund the town's share of the Sunapee Wastewater Treatment Project; the old plant needed upgrading. This article, which would have raised the bulk of the money through bonds, also stipulated that at least 35 percent must come from grants or other outside funds. Truth is, while most people in New London, aren't hooked up to the municipal sewer system, the downtown businesses, Colby College, and the hospital are. The businesses, college, and hospital provide an economic base for the town.

Gus Seamans supported the upgrade. Though he wasn't a sewer user, and the project would cost him about $35 in taxes, he said, "I'd like to think the $35 is going to help the major sewer users in town." The article passed 336 to 6 (about as close to unanimous as you'll ever get on a secret ballot).

Alas, the grant money didn't come through. So in 2011, a new vote had to be taken.

This time voters—without a lot of enthusiasm (nobody wants to spend that kind of money) but recognizing the need—approved the bond *without* the grant stipulation. Done and done.

While they were at it, they approved a bond to fix up the library. They also approved $149,000 to improve the sidewalks in Elkins village—but this was (kind of) free money, no impact on property taxes, because the bucks would come from a federal grant and a capital reserve fund.

In a big change, the legislative body voted to start the town's fiscal year in July instead of the traditional January; a tricky maneuver that involves establishing and paying for one 18-month budget during the changeover. To ease the pain to taxpayers, it was agreed that tax bills be issued quarterly instead of semiannually. Onward into the second decade of the twenty-first century, New London.

Northwood 2010

Lucy Edwards, summarizing the 2010 school meeting in *The Forum*, awarded the quote of the day to a voter, "who got up during the discussion of the school budget and said, 'Taxes are going up, I like my house and want to stay in it, and to hell with the kids.' The sentiment was not warmly received by the assemblage." It was one of those things that a person might think, but maybe ought not say out loud at a public meeting with a large contingency of the parents of school children, not to mention teachers, administrators, the school board, and so forth.

Warner 2011

The operating budget went up less than one percent from 2010, which pleased the crowd. Proposed work on the town hall required explanation, so public works director, Matt Waite explained it. He also explained why a bridge needed replacement and the dump truck needed repair. Evidently his explanations satisfied voters, because everything passed. Ed Mical asked for a public meeting on how money to fix the roads was being used. Folks, including the selectmen, agreed that was a good idea.

The town also tucked away capital reserve money for a new town truck down the road, and a fire truck or rescue vehicle some time along. By all accounts, this year's meeting was both smooth and informative.

Weare 2010 and 2011

Where is Weare? It's kind of in the middle of New Hampshire, about equidistant from Vermont and the sea, West of Concord, South of Henniker.

Last count it was home to just over 9,000 people. For many years, it was home to retired Supreme Court Judge David Souter, which is quite a claim to fame. But for purposes of this book, Weare's greatest claim to fame is the record it holds for default budgets. Under the SB 2 system, the voters in their wisdom have defeated the proposed budget *twelve times,* in fifteen years. With each defeat, a default budget (the budget from the previous year with exceptions for contractual obligations) kicks in.

At the 2010 deliberative session, resident Donald Burke pointed out that a town that votes down its operating budget year after year is like a person who doesn't maintain or repair his home. "It's going to come around and bite us eventually," he said. At that same meeting, Police Chief Gregory Begin attested that times were bad, but that the town was "in dire need of a passed budget."

Dire need or not, the town voted down the budget in 2010 and in 2011 as well.

Wilmot 2010 and 2011

The citizens of Wilmot seem to get along just fine, or, at the very least, seem to agree with one another over how the town ought to run and how much taxpayers can afford to run it. In 2010, town meeting lasted just a couple of hours and every article sailed through unammended. On top of the town operating budget, voters said yes to a new heavy-duty dump truck with a plow. Mary Kay Huntoon, chair of the select board, complained to the moderator that the meeting was going so fast, she wouldn't have time to take her usual nap.

In 2011, the trend continued. Voters, in a generous mood, agreed to increase the town budget by $5,405, approving all the articles on the town warrant, including a 2 percent raise for town employees.

The Big Social Issue of 2010

The New Hampshire legislature passed a law in 2009 that took effect in January of 2010 allowing gay marriage. This article, which popped up on a number of town meeting warrants (including Bow's and Deerfield's, mentioned earlier) expressed some people's displeasure with that new law: *To see if the Town will vote to approve the following resolution to be forwarded to our State Representative(s), our State Senator, the Speaker of the House, and the Senate President. Resolved: The citizens of New Hampshire should be allowed to vote on an amendment to the New Hampshire Constitution that defines "marriage."*

Proponents said they wanted the chance to vote on the rights of gays to marry, rather than let the legislature decide as they had in passing the 2009 law. The article, of course, had no teeth. All it required, if passed, was that a resolution be forwarded to various representatives who could, and likely would, choose to ignore it. ("Thanks, we'll take that under advisement.") The article if passed couldn't change the law, nor the fact that New Hampshire, unlike some other states, doesn't hold referendum votes to make or change laws. We just don't do it. There's no mechanism for doing so. No precedent. No method.

Nevertheless, folks on both sides—those who support gay marriage and those who don't—got wicked worked up. No wonder. Depending on how you read the article, it seemed to stand for voters' rights (that sounds good; voting is good; we like to vote), but also seemed to want to undermine the legislature's recent vote to allow the personal freedom (that sounds good; we like personal freedom; we're the live-free-or-die state) of marriage between gays. It seemed to pit democratic rights against minority rights.

In other years, a broad, controversial, socially charged article might have addressed nuclear power or global warming—national and international issues with little direct connection to the mundane business of running the town. These were issues, nevertheless, about which at least twenty-five citizens had strong feelings and opinions. According to Joseph Zimmerman in *The New England Town Meeting: Democracy in Action* the idea of placing non-binding questions on town warrants is a relatively new one as town meeting traditions go.

> *Commencing in the 1970s, national and regional interest groups utilized town meetings to obtain publicity for their respective causes by persuading the required number of voters in a town to sign a petition to place a non-binding question on the town meeting warrant. The issue was the Panama Canal Treaty in 1978; transportation, storage, and disposal of nuclear materials in 1979 and 1983; acid rain and El Salvador in 1983; and campaign finance reform in 1996. The acid rain resolution, for example, was approved by 197 town meetings in 1983.*

In 2010, when I was beginning to write this book, the send-a-message-to-America issue of the moment was gay marriage. The hot-button nature of the article—petitioned in many towns with identical language—was

clear. When the time for discussion came, the mood of the meeting turned
tense, even grave. Chatter subsided. Voters quietly lined up at the microphone to speak. The dueling abstractions of being *allowed to vote* and *definition of marriage* pitted neighbor against neighbor. Who would speak out?
What stance would they take? How does that stance affect me? My belief
system? My rights? How does this issue affect our community?

Prior to town meeting, letters to the editor turned inflammatory.
Homosexuality was sinful; opposition to gay marriage was bigotry. These
were among the milder assertions from either side. But at the meetings
themselves, in my experience anyway, discussion remained civil. Well, not
in all cases, but most. It's one thing to suggest in a letter to the editor that
someone you've never met is going to burn in hell for their sexual orienta-
tion, and quite another to stand among your neighbors and express the
opinion that this neighbor or that one is evil-minded, ignorant, bigoted, or
an abomination in the eyes of God. Town meeting requires us to face our
community, look our neighbors in the eyes, and stand up for our beliefs.
It's hard, but civilized, and often civilizing.

Frank Bryan called his book on the New England town meeting *Real
Democracy*. Part of what's *real* about it is that it involves *real* people deeply
engaged—people you know, people you've seen at the hardware store or
the dump or beach or post office—together in a room, talking to each other,
then voting. It's one thing to fill in a circle on a ballot and slide the ballot
into a voting machine, quite another to talk issues through in a forum
where, at the end of the talk, you vote and make it so.

Sharp edges get tempered in a situation like that. Your perceived enemy
has a face and feelings and kids and a job He makes delicious maple syrup.
She stopped to help when your car broke down. They painted their house
the most beautiful shade of blue. Just like you, they lost electricity for ten
days during the ice storm. Your perceived enemy lives a life similar to your
own. Your perceived enemy may even have a point.

Here are some of the comments made at town meetings around the
state regarding the so-called "Definition of Marriage Article"—as I heard
them in person or culled them from newspaper accounts or minutes.

Pro:

- I'm talking about we the people. We the people want to vote.
- This is not about whether to support gay marriage. It's about letting
  people decide instead of the legislature.

- No one who believes in democracy should be opposed to letting people vote.
- If people don't have the right to vote then they (our representatives) will get voted out very quickly.
- It's fair for every single person to vote, not just a few in our legislature.
- The article doesn't take a position on marriage. It's whether or not the people want to vote on this issue.
- I want a constitutional amendment so I can vote. It's scary that you won't let people vote one way or another.
- I pay taxes. I should have the right to vote.
- I have no problem with whatever transpires between a man and a woman or a man and a man. I'm a big data person. I am fine (with gay marriage) as long as people vote.

Con:

- I enjoy the comforts and security that come with marriage. I don't feel that the majority should be a part of refusing that right to a minority group.
- At first reading it seems like something we all ought to do. But the 19th Amendment was not voted on by the populace. The voters were all men. This is a question of civil rights and efforts by our elected leaders to expand rights.
- This town or any other town is not the place to debate gay marriage or any other type of marriage. The state of New Hampshire has already spoken. Granted, it was by people who can't even define an adequate education . . .
- Live free or die is only guaranteed when everyone has the same freedom. It's a libertarian idea: You don't bother me; I don't bother you.
- The legislature has passed a law recognizing the rights of a minority group. In the future do we want to vote on other rights—guns, the right to attend Catholic church?
- I grew up in the South and I am old enough to remember separate bathrooms for black people, them being relegated to the back of the bus, and blacks and whites being denied the right to marry each other. Discrimination hurts all of us.

How It Turned Out

When the dust settled, some towns voted yea, some nay, some tabled it, some voted to indefinitely postpone. Some SB 2 towns changed the wording. Instead of the full wording appearing on the ballot, the article was shortened in an amendment and would appear as simply, *To See*. Under the rules of SB 2, a petitioned article cannot be removed from the warrant, but—evidently—it could (at that time) be reworded. *To see* or not to see. That was the question.

A sampling of individual town results:

- Allenstown: Failed on a ballot vote
- Andover: Failed on a voice vote.
- Barnstead: Passed on a ballot vote 93 yes, 42 no.
- Boscawen: Tabled with little discussion.
- Bow: Failed on a ballot vote, 75 yes, 192 no.
- Farmington: Tabled on a voice vote.
- Franconia: Tabled.
- Hancock: Failed, 32 yes, 102 no.
- Nelson: Article passed over.
- Northwood: Voted to indefinitely postpone 66 yes, 49 no.
- Pembroke: Failed on a secret ballot 60 yes, 79 no.
- Pittsfield: Passed in a ballot vote 79 yes, 36 no.
- Salisbury: Failed in a hand vote 27 yes, 30 no.
- Stratham: Indefinitely postponed on a voice vote.

These are just a few of the towns that considered the measure. The results state-wide are tricky to tabulate with all the amendments, tablings, and indefinite postponements. Supporters of the article complained that a tabling or indefinite postponement was a dirty trick to prevent voters from voting on the right to vote. So did a tabling or indefinite postponement count as a nay? According to the website Granite State Progress, which offered the clearest tabulation I could find, eighty-eight towns gave a thumbs down, in one form or another, to the article; sixty-one towns gave a thumbs up. Despite organizers' efforts, seventy-three towns fell short of the twenty-five signatures needed to put the article on the warrant—so voters never saw it.

What does this say about attitudes toward gay marriage in New Hampshire? Your guess is as good as mine.

Point of interest: Plainfield, the northernmost town in Sullivan County, population 2,500 give or take, didn't like the article one bit. The legislative body voted no 185–40 and then went on to instruct town officials to write a letter to state officials "commending them on passing and signing into law legislation affirming marriage equality for all New Hampshire residents."

As reported in the *Valley News*: "We see this not as an issue of voting rights, but rather as an issue of civil rights," said Richard Atkinson, speaking on behalf of a coalition of Plainfield residents opposed to the article. "Rather than possibly sending a vague and misunderstood message to our elected representatives, we wish to send a message that states that we as a town affirm and celebrate marriage equality."

To See or Not to See Update:

As reported in the press, the first act of the legislature in 2011 was to pass HB 77, a time-sensitive vote since proponents wanted it to take effect before the first of the SB 2 deliberative sessions. The guts of the act are as follows: "No warrant article shall be amended to eliminate the subject matter of the article. An amendment that changes the dollar amount of an appropriation in a warrant article shall not be deemed to violate this subparagraph."

No longer will voters at a deliberative session be able to change the wording of a warrant article to "To see . . ."

No more messing around with the wording of petitioned articles. They must pass through as written—or close to it. What does this accomplish? It reinforces the right of petitioners to have their petitions voted on as written by ballot on election day, no matter what the opinions of those gathered for the deliberative session. It further codifies the impotence of deliberative sessions.

18 ⚖

SB 2:
Town Meeting Under Siege

Since 1995, towns have had the option of adopting the SB 2 form of town meeting by an act of the state legislature. A petitioned article—bearing the signatures of at least twenty-five registered voters—appears on the ballot at the polls. If three-fifths of those who cast their votes say yea, SB 2 is adopted for the following year and forever after, unless a petition to repeal it is submitted and receives the same super-majority. When the dust settled after the 2011 vote, sixty-seven towns had adopted SB 2; only three have adopted and subsequently rescinded it—though each year some towns try. The totals change annually, but there's a general creep upward, with more and more towns giving up traditional town meeting for this newer form. Someday, sadly, traditional town meeting may be nothing but a memory. Which is, in part, why this book needed to be written.

How is SB 2 Different from Traditional Town Meeting?

Both include dual sessions. One session involves marking a ballot at the polls, the other session is a sit-down and discuss together gathering. But their sequence is reversed and their content is very different. With town meeting, the first session is a 1) Ballot Vote for officials and limited other items like changes to zoning. This is followd by 2) a meeting at which all other items, including budgets, are discussed and decided.

Under SB 2, session 1) is a deliberative session for discussion and amendments, which cannot change the basic intent of the proposed articles, followed one month later by 2) a ballot vote on the articles as amended at the deliberative session.

At town meeting by the time folks leave the hall, the budget for the town has been set and decisions have been made about whether to paint the cemetery fence, fund an addition to the town shed, or support certain social service agencies. The sit-down town meeting day tends to be several hours long, and the ballots at the polls relatively short—a page or two listing those running for each office and the proposed zoning ordinances.

At the SB 2 deliberative session voters may discuss each warrant article. They may vote to amend the articles and adjust the money amounts up or down. But they cannot approve or disapprove the articles. That happens weeks later at the polls. Deliberative sessions tend to be short—one I know of in 2011 lasted just fifteen minutes. The ballots at the polls tend to be several pages long, making them cumbersome to handle and to hand-count.

Say the school board submits this article: *To see if the School District will vote to raise and appropriate the Budget Committee's recommended amount of Twelve million one hundred seventy-two thousand seventy-six dollars ($12,172,076) for the support orf schools, for the payment of salaries for the school district officials and agents, and for the payment of statutory obligations of the district. The School Board recommends Twelve million seven hundred forty-nine thousand six hundred sixty-one dollars ($12,749,661).*

At a traditional meeting, the voters would hash out the numbers, come to a compromise, and vote for that amount. Job done. Budget set. Under SB 2, the voters hash out the numbers, come to a compromise, and leave. Weeks later, lots more voters go to the polls, see the compromise amount on the warrant and vote. If they vote no, the school district still gets a budget, but it's not the budget the school board, budget committee, or voters at the deliberative session figured out—it's a default budget, that is, the budget from the previous year with a few adjustments (such as maintaining contractual obligations) as specified by state law.

Town or school officials, with approval from the superior court, may hold a special meeting and try again for the budget they think they need, but this is rarely done.

Some towns run on default budgets for years. One wonders why the school board or selectmen in those towns even bother to put their budgets together year after year, since the majority of voters pay no attention to them. Overtaxed voters understandably have a knee-jerk reaction and vote No on any money issue. And property owners in New Hampshire are, indeed, overtaxed; we have no broad-based taxes, so the bulk of the tax burden falls on property owners. The thinking seems to be: *Maybe if I vote No on all the articles my property taxes will go down. If I vote Yes, surely they will rise.* Oddly, in some cases the default budget was actually higher than the proposed budget—and people still voted no.

And in the meantime, towns and schools running on default budgets instead of budgets based on assessed needs and expenses must cut and cut some more, undercutting infrastructure. When the cries of, "Why are test scores down in our school?" or "How come the state declared that bridge unsafe and shut it down?" the answer could well be: "We've been running on default budgets for ten years."

Pros and Cons and More Context

I make no bones about being biased in favor of traditional town meeting—except when the towns get so big (population over 10,000) that town meeting is no longer viable. When that happens, a practical solution seems to be what some Vermont towns do: elect representatives (200 or so) who form a legislative body and on town meeting day hold a representative-based town meeting. The 200 speak for all the constituencies and only the 200 may vote—though the meeting is open to all. This representative town meeting, I discovered in researching this book, more closely duplicates the pure democracy of traditional town meeting than SB 2.

For the record though, here are some of the common arguments favoring SB 2.

- More people get to vote. Instead of 300 or fewer people voting at a sit-down session that might last all day and requires stamina, several hundred may take the time to walk through the polls and check off the ballot. Proponents of SB 2 say the elderly and people with small children have an especially hard time sticking out the long hours of traditional town meeting. (Though ideally, the deliberative session of SB 2 would stimulate equally intense and lengthy debate, which would again be hard for the elderly and people with small children.)

- It's more convenient for working people. Instead of spending a whole Saturday or staying up past midnight on a Tuesday, busy voters may simply show up at the polls and cast their ballots in a matter of minutes. Voters may make their way to town hall at any time during the day—typically 7 a.m. to 7 p.m.—read through the articles, check yes or no, slide their votes into the ballot box or electronic counting machine, and go on their way. Instead of spending the whole day on town business, they can make short work of it. In and out. Duty done, they can read the results in the newspaper or on the town website the next day.

- Just like at regular town meeting, voters may, if they choose, attend the deliberative session and talk issues over. They can even change money amounts and language (so long as they don't change the intent of the article). They just don't get to actually vote the articles in or out on that day.

- Once the articles are set at the deliberative session, people will have time to research and ponder them before voting some weeks later, as opposed to hearing the arguments and voting the same day in the heat of the moment.

- Some people may be too shy or insecure to speak at town meeting or even raise their hands in support or opposition to an article for fear their neighbors will judge them. Though these folks may request a secret ballot on any article at town meeting, even the act of requesting a secret ballot on, say, the new police cruiser may—they perceive—raise the hackles of the chief of police. Best to do everything in the privacy of the voting booth.

These arguments have merit, but the merits of SB 2 do not outweigh those of traditional town meeting. Not by a long shot. The fact is, if citizens want more articles on the official ballot to be voted at the polls, they don't need SB 2 to do that. The school board or selectmen may put any article they wish to on the official ballot if that's what citizens desire.

Joseph Zimmerman in *The New England Town Meeting* wrote that much of the vitality of town meeting results from the dialogue and discussion. "Ideas are exchanged, adjusted, and affirmed in an open democratic manner. We believe that a voter who will take the time to attend a town meeting has a vital interest in and is better informed about town and school affairs than the voter who is willing to cast a ballot but who has not attended the meeting and listened to the deliberations."

Deliberative sessions tend to be grossly underattended compared to town meeting. In towns where 300 people might show up to town meeting, the deliberative session is lucky to attract thirty, many of whom will be town or school officials. To those who say town meeting attracts special interest groups who may pack the house and tip the vote their way, well, it's clear that the smaller the group, the greater the chance of the special interest group to win the day.

For example, at a deliberative session the selectmen ask for $1.5 million to run the town. Thirty people show up. Twenty of them are mad as hell about their taxes and the rest are town officials or the spouses of town officials. The angry twenty reduce the budget to $1 million (or one dollar if they're in a real bad mood). And that $1 million (or $1) is what appears on the ballot some weeks later for approval or disapproval by hundreds of voters. Essentially, those twenty angry voters at the deliberative session set the town budget for the coming year.

At traditional town meeting, those same twenty mad-as-hell residents propose an amendment to reduce the budget. Discussion ensues among the 100 or 200 or 300 people present—where to cut? What would be the repercussions of such a cut? If the cutters make a good argument, the amendment passes. If the selectmen or other townsfolk make a better argument for keeping the budget as is, the amendment fails. Generally, compromise prevails, with the final budget falling somewhere between the selectmen's proposed budget and the budget proposed by the amendment. A vote approving the compromise is taken on the spot, with everyone in the hall knowing what's at stake and why.

Some say SB 2 is still town meeting, just a little bit different. I don't see it. If somebody substitutes a cat for my wire fox terrier, though the animals have much in common (fur, four legs, two eyes, hearty appetites, etc.) they are more than a little bit different—they are entirely different animals. Same thing with town meeting and SB 2: entirely different animals.

Gary Evans of Weare summarizes some of the pro SB 2 mythology and reflects the anger many feel when a town gets talked into SB 2 (usually by a small number of activists with money to buy signs, send out mailers, and oversimplify the nature of the change) in this letter to the editor:

SB 2 Built on Lies

The loss of town meeting is sad in many ways but mostly because so many people fall for the myth of increased voter participation. Instead of a meeting where you gather with neighbors to hear a presentation of what you are going to vote on, you have a closed booth and no knowledge of what is in front of you. You don't know why the fire department really needs a new truck or a certain road really should be paved.

This "deliberative session" is a farce attended only by a very few who want to make sure their wording doesn't change. Town meetings were a wonderful institution done in by lies of increased participation and more elderly people being able to attend. We all know that the real point of SB 2 was to prevent people from voting with a knowledge base so that they would just go and vote "no" on anything having to do with town spending and they wouldn't have to do it by raising their hands in front of their neighbors.

Battleground Mason

When Mason faced the SB 2 challenge, town meeting supporters fought back. In many towns, they don't. In Mason, town meeting supporters gave as good as they got. Even better it seems, since SB 2 was ultimately defeated. Mason is a small town on the Massachusett's border, population 1,400 give or take. Among Mason's claims to fame, it is where Uncle Sam grew up. That's right, *the* Uncle Sam. As an adult, Uncle Sam a.k.a Sam Wilson ran a meat packing company in New York. During the War of 1812, his company supplied meat to the army. He marked his barrels U.S. for United States, but he and his company were so well known, when people saw the U.S., they'd say, "That's Uncle Sam." In this way, U.S. and Uncle Sam became synonymous.

When Attorney Charles V. Moser expressed his opposition to SB 2, he invoked Uncle Sam.

UNCLE SAM WANTS YOU TO KEEP TOWN MEETING

I oppose adopting SB 2 in Mason. For well over two hundred years we have thrived under governance by town meeting. Uncle Sam, when he lived in Mason, enjoyed town meeting governance. Unless you are a selectperson or a board member, town meeting is *your* best opportunity to participate in direct, non-representative democracy.

"When, in some obscure country town, the farmers come together to a special town meeting to express their opinion on some subject which is vexing the land, that, I think, is the true Congress, and the most respectable one that is ever assembled in the United States." Henry David Thoreau, "Slavery in Massachusetts" (1854).

When one of our citizens stands up in Town Meeting, you know something important is about to be said. You learn the thoughts and feelings of a concerned citizen who has thought deeply and *cares* about Mason. Maybe you are moved to agree or perhaps vehemently disagree, but all the voters present benefit from the discourse. Most importantly, you can respond if you choose, and share you own passionate feelings about the issues with the folks that will, in a few short minutes, vote on that issue.

While SB 2 provides for a deliberative session, it is statistically proven that deliberative sessions have very poor attendance compared to town meetings. Many people do not see the value of attending the deliberative session because they will have the opportunity to vote on the same issues a month later. But there is one group of people that will always attend the deliberative session: those with a special interest in the election. And, because deliberative sessions commonly suffer poor attendance, those special interest groups can, by mustering a few of their number, take control of the deliberative session to modify the warrant to suit their personal or corporate wants. So, when you step into the voting booth a month later, you are voting on articles that, without your knowledge, may have been designed or modified to meet the needs of a special interest group.

Warrant articles can be modified by motion at town meeting. But it happens before the watchful scrutiny of all and the same people who will vote on the article. There is much less opportunity for a small group to manipulate the warrant in a true town meeting, where any special interests would be exposed for all the voters to see.

We have a small town. The population of Mason in 1850 was 1,626 people. The population today is estimated to reach 1,570 by the year 2030. The town meeting form of government has always worked for our town at the size it was and is now.

I understand that there are folks who fear public speaking and are loathe to speak their mind at town meeting. However, disagreement in politics is impossible to avoid. Thomas Jefferson said, "An association of men who will not quarrel with one another is a thing which has never yet existed, from the greatest confederacy of nations down to a town meeting or a vestry." If, after hearing the discourse on a warrant article at town meeting, a citizen fears recrimination if their vote is public, a secret ballot can be requested.

Let us continue to have meaningful debate and argument in Mason. Keep town meeting—it was good enough for UNCLE SAM and it is good enough for us. Vote against SB 2.

When SB 2 was first proposed for Mason in 2009, Garth Fletcher did his homework. He gathered information about where SB 2 had been adopted, proposed but not adopted, rescinded, and where failed attempts had been made to rescind. He also called the town clerks of the SB 2 towns "to gauge its effect on public participation." He recorded the information he'd gathered, including the number of voters attending each deliberative session and the percentage of registered voters that number represented, for comparison and analysis. He was particularly interested in how Mason fit the profile of the SB 2 town. Here's what he discovered:

- Fifty-nine out of sixty-two SB 2 towns are larger than Mason (969 registered voters)
- Fifty of sixty-two SB 2 towns are more than twice Mason's size
- Average size of SB 2 towns is 5,472 registered voters, almost 6 (5.65) times Mason's size
- The three towns that rescinded SB 2—Dorchester, Enfield, and Orange—had 270, 3148, and 209 registered voters
- One hundred thirty-one attempts to adopt SB 2 yielded sixty-five successes (50%) and sixty-six failures
- Thirty-seven attempts to rescind SB 2 yielded three successes (8%) and thirty-four failures
- Adoption of SB 2: 50% adopted in 1996, 71% by 1998, slower pace thereafter
- Of the ninety-six towns which considered SB 2, sixty-three have adopted it (66%)
- Average number of voters attending deliberative sessions=eighty-three including town officials
- Average number of voters attending deliberative sessions in the smaller towns (less than 2,000 voters)=seventy-three including town officials
- Voter participation in deliberative sessions average 2.5% (1 out of 40 voters)
- Voter participation in deliberative sessions in smaller towns (less than 2,000 voters) 6.3% (1 out of 16 voters)

Fletcher writes of his research:

> In calling the Town Clerks I simply explained that I was researching some data for our own Town Meeting and that I hoped they could provide a count (or good estimate) for voter attendance at their most recent SB 2 Deliberative Session. The majority reported their recent 2009 sessions, though some towns on later schedules provided instead their 2008 session attendances.
>
> A surprising number took pains to make sure I understood the count included all the "officials" who had to attend. Many made comments which made it clear they were unhappy with SB 2. Some asked why I was asking and I would reply that Mason had SB 2 adoption on

the ballot and I was trying to understand its consequences—uniformly they then counseled very strongly against adoption.

Some typical comments:

Candia reported that the final (ballot) votes had only increased by maybe 20% (going from 500 to 600) over what they used to get in Town Meetings, but that SB 2 had increased their meeting costs fourfold and caused many other problems.

Rye said "SB 2 was the worst thing that had happened to Rye;" and went on to say SB 2 is easy to vote in but almost impossible to vote out.

Plaistow said their attendance of thirty-five was actually pretty high (this year); usually just the town officials plus 5 or fewer "public" (attended), those often spouses of the officials who had to be there.

Merrimack reported that the most common voter complaint was "that a small number of people controlled the ballot;" in other words, that small group which attends the Deliberative Session.

Fletcher's research led him to form a strong opinion that SB 2 would be a bad choice for Mason. He posted his findings on his website to inform his fellow citizens. He also posted an essay called "In this I believe." The essay, he explains, "is a statement of belief, and of faith, rather than data, which I wanted to keep clearly separated from the factual information presented."

Following is Garth Fletcher's argument against adopting SB 2 in Mason, along with the spreadsheets of his findings.

This I Believe
My Personal Views on Why I Believe SB 2 Is Wrong for Mason
by Garth Fletcher

A dozen generations ago our predecessors proclaimed a radical ideal: *that ordinary people were capable of governing themselves, and that they should be free to do so.*

This notion flew in the face of common sense, for everyone knew that governing, for century upon century, had been work reserved for kings, aristocracies or theocracies. The notion that common people could have sufficient skills and intelligence must have seemed laughable to many.

And because that ideal denied the King's Divine Right to rule, it was high treason. Insisting upon this ideal meant taking on the world's great superpower, Great Britain.

But insist they did, and the 500 Mason residents were in the thick of it—conspiring with the rest, boycotting British goods, stockpiling gunpowder, sending twenty-seven men under Captain Mann to the Battle of Bunker Hill.

History of SB2 in NH Towns and its consequences in voter participation
(data collected & organized by Garth Fletcher, Feb 17…23, 2009)

Schedule of considerations, adoptions & Rescissions [a]

++:Adopted   II:Rescinded   A:failed adoption   R: failed revocation

Town	96	97	98	99	00	01	02	03	04	05	06	07	08	09	SB2	Nov-08 Regist. voters[b]	Town Clerk data Delib. Session Attend[c]	as %
Carroll		++		R	R										1	658	85	13
Danbury (1)											++				1	751	45	6
Grafton	++			R	R		R								1	892	60	7
Bennington	++														1	1,101	30	3
Newfields									++	R	R				1	1,228	93	8
Alstead	++			R		R		R							1	1,427	50	4
Ashland			++												1	1,457	54	4
New Hampton			++	R											1	1,639	60	4
East Kingston (1)											++				1	1,653	111	7
Kensington		++													1	1,753	110	6
Hampton Falls								++							1	1,789	125	7
Bethlehem					++	R									1	1,895	50	3
Canaan	++				R	R									1	2,565	85	3
Sunapee		++					R								1	2,704	95	4
Winchester	++														1	2,978	75	3
Allenstown		++			R			R							1	3,024	100	3
Newton	++														1	3,080	65	2
Danville	++														1	3,109	41	1
Milton		++	R												1	3,209	89	3
Candia										++					1	3,347	138	4
Charlestown	++			R		R									1	3,425	75	2
Epsom		++	R		R		R								1	3,455	77	2
New Ipswich			++		R										1	3,551	47	1
Deerfield								A	++	R					1	3,599	90	3
Wakefield		++	R					R							1	3,648	80	2
Auburn (2)												++			1	3,824	60	2
New Boston			++		R										1	3,989	80	2
Kingston	++														1	4,025	75	2
North Hampton		++													1	4,134	120	3
Alton								++							1	4,135	60	1
Newport (1)												++			1	4,173	70	2
Littleton	++														1	4,246	100	2
Sandown	++														1	4,290	123	3
Rindge								A		++	R				1	4,794	65	1
Epping				A	A	++									1	4,797	80	2
Rye		++													1	4,848	120	2
Belmont (1)											++				1	4,929	30	1
Swanzey			A					++	R						1	4,996	45	1
Peterborough (2)								A	A		++				1	5,456	89	2
Wolfeboro	++			R											1	5,550	200	4
Atkinson	++														1	5,756	137	2
Seabrook	++														1	5,786	50	1
Litchfield			++												1	5,903	55	1
Weare	++														1	6,196	50	1
Hampstead	++														1	6,299	43	1
Gilford									++						1	6,309	78	1
Plaistow	++														1	6,356	35	1
Barrington		++													1	6,357	100	2
Raymond							++								1	7,440	50	1
Newmarket	++								R						1	7,444	60	1
Conway	++														1	7,915	125	2
Amherst			++												1	8,849	167	2
Pelham			++												1	9,070	86	1
Hooksett	++														1	9,295	60	1
Windham				++											1	9,929	50	1
Exeter	++														1	10,716	127	1
Milford	++														1	10,894	83	1
Goffstown	++														1	12,832	120	1
Hampton	++														1	13,384	80	1
Hudson	++														1	16,305	72	0
Merrimack	++						R			R					1	19,442	207	1
Salem	++														1	20,654	60	0

Town	1	2	3	4	5	6	7	8	9	10	11	12	13	14	Reg. Voters
Dorchester	++		II												270
Enfield	++			II											3,148
Orange	++	II													209
Bow	A			A	A	A	A								6,278
Brentwood										A					2,717
Chester							A								3,455
Chichester								A							1,979
Deering								A							1,406
Dublin				A	A	A									1,266
Dunbarton										A					2,019
Farmington							A								4,551
Freedom				A											1,257
Freemont									A	A					3,009
Gilmanton							A	A	A						2,578
Haverhill						A									2,758
Henniker			A	A						A					3,276
Hinsdale							A			A					2,754
Hollis			A												5,754
Lincoln							A								1,218
Madison			A	A				A	A						1,808
Marlborough			A	A											1,574
Mont Vernon			A												1,896
Moultonborough							A								4,051
Northfield								A							3,517
Pembroke							A	A							5,613
Pittsfield			A												2,904
Plymouth					A	A				A					6,681
Sanbornton			A	A		A			A	A	A				2,447
South Hampton								A							630
Tamworth									A	A					2,114
Temple									A	A					994
Tilton									A	A					2,670
Whitefield								A	A	A					1465
MASON													??		969

	1	2	3	4	5	6	7	8	9	10	11	12	13	14	
SB2 voted IN	30	8	6	4	0	2	1	1	2	4	1	4	2	0	65
SB2 voted OUT	0	0	0	2	0	1	0	0	0	0	0	0	0	0	3
failed adoptions	0	1	0	8	9	3	5	8	8	14	10	0	0	0	66
failed revocations	0	0	0	5	3	7	6	4	0	4	5	0	0	0	34

SB2 TOWNS as of 2008........................... 62
Towns having considered SB2.................... 96
AVERAGE Size (# reg.voters) of SB2 Towns.......... 5,472
AVERAGE # of voters attending (*including Town officials*)........ 83
AVERAGE **Participation** in SB2 Deliberations, **% of reg. voters** 2.5

NOTES:

(1) In Sec of State 2008 list of SB2 towns, 2007 adoption assumed
(2) except towns known to have adopted SB2 last year
(3) Londonderry was on SB2 Town list, but Town Clerk says only its school district is SB2.

SOURCES:

[a] Adoption history: "SB2 Adoption and Rescission Votes: 1996-2006", NH Center for Public Policy Studies
[b] Registered voters 2008: Source: <http://www.sos.nh.gov/general2008/summarynames08.htm>
[c] interviews with NH Town Clerks, 2/19…23/2009. Phone # from list: <http://www.sos.nh.gov/clerks.htm>
  Asked for voter attendance at most recent Town, SB2 Deliberative Session. Most reporting 2009.

Comments & Analysis:

1) 59 of 62 SB2 towns are larger than Mason (969 registered voters)
2) 50 of 62 SB2 towns are larger than twice Mason's size
3) average size of SB2 towns is 5,472 registered voters, almost 6 (5.65) X Mason's size
4) the 3 towns which rescinded SB2 had 209, 270, and 3,148 registered voters
5) 131 attempts to adopt SB2 yielded 65 successes (50%) and 66 failures
6) 37 attempts to rescind SB2 yielded 3 successes (8%) and 34 failures
7) adoption of SB2 : 50% adopted in 1996, 71% had adopted by 1998, slower pace thereafter
8) of 96 towns which considered SB2, 63 have adopted it (66%)
9) of the 65 towns which adopted SB2, only 3 rescinded it (5%)
10) Average # voters attending = 83 *including town officials.*
  "   in 12 smallest towns (< 2000 voters) = 73 *including town officials.*
11) voter participation in SB2 Deliberative Sessions averages 2.5% (1 out of 40 voters)
  "   in 12 smallest towns (< 2000 voters) averages   6.3% (1 out of 16 voters)

The signing of our Declaration of Independence in 1776 began the war in earnest. Eventually, against all odds and through many privations and terrible losses (proportional to half a million deaths today), they succeeded.

They founded a new country in which ordinary people could and would govern themselves. They created a framework of rules, our Constitution, designed to ensure that the right could be retained by the citizens.

Four score and seven years later at Gettysburg, Abe Lincoln would describe their extraordinary creation as a government *"of the people, for the people, by the people."*

In the small towns this self-government took the form of Town meetings. Citizens would gather to hear and question the reports of those they had elected to serve as officials, to listen to their proposals for the coming year, and to discuss, debate, and then decide upon what would be cone.

This direct form of democracy still thrives in Mason, and in many smaller NH towns.

Mason's next Town Meeting will be its 233rd since 1776. It will be the 161st taking place on the worn boards under the sagging roof of our current Town Hall. Meeting after meeting has accepted the torch of direct self-government, held it high as a cherished gift, and proudly passed it on to the next.

There is now a proposal to lay down this torch, to break the compact which has linked us generation to generation, to declare our 233rd Town Meeting to be our last.

The proponents of the change to SB 2 cite its great convenience— *". . . at a time of a voter's own choosing in just a few minutes instead of having to fully attend an hours long meeting . . ."*

This I believe reflects a sadly diminished version of democracy; a bleak *"McDemocracy"*—drive through, hasty selection from the menu, and then onwards to the more important things in life.

The issues we decide are rather more important than simply buying a snack. They affect a big part of our taxes, determine the kind of education our children receive and the opportunities they may or may not have later, set the level of police and fire protection for our homes and selves, affect the safety of our roads, and so on.

We are the privileged inheritors of what our predecessors worked and struggled over twelve generations to create and preserve—*a right to govern ourselves.* That is an extraordinary privilege, but carries with it equally great responsibility—*to govern wisely.*

My great concern is that SB 2 will seriously damage our ability to govern ourselves wisely.

If you watch a stranger walk into a real estate office, read over its listings, select one, and then start to write a check—you might think them so incredibly rich that buying a house was "pocket change," or incredibly unwise; you certainly would not think them prudent.

If you or I were buying a house we would carefully inspect it, possibly hire in an expert, ask lots of questions about the septic and well and roof, enquire about the town and its schools, maybe negotiate a lower price. In short, we would invest a serious effort before deciding whether to take that final step of writing the check.

Voting is indeed a crucial step in self-government, but, like writing the check, it is only the final step. The heart and soul of self-government lies in the "heavy lifting" that has to be done before a vote.

And here lies SB 2's problem—how do we "inspect the house" before signing the check through our vote? Mason's self-governance issues are very important to us, but of little interest to the outside world. There will be no TV or radio programs discussing our problems; no pundits nor experts analyzing our issues. The coverage of our affairs by local newspapers is already thin, and seems to be shrinking.

In the past, Town Meeting has provided our final means of "inspection"—where we can listen to our officials' reports, demand answers to our questions, hear and provide opposing views and alternate suggestions, and make changes before deciding the outcome.

It has not been a perfect means—I would much like to see Town Reports mailed to every household two weeks beforehand, and I would like to see Town Meetings held Saturday so we are assembling in daylight at a more convenient hour under less pressure—but it has been an important means, often our only one.

Of course, governing a diverse community requires more than simple "inspection." We also need to find that elusive middle-ground which manages to balance our differing needs into a broadly acceptable compromise. *The process of negotiating that middle-ground is the crucial hard work required for a functioning democracy.* That work is accomplished at Town Meetings when conflicting views are discussed, defended and criticized, priorities rearranged, and compromises offered until we arrive at something most of us can accept. Our voting is simply the way we ultimately ratify the result of that hard work. As Thomas Paine warned, *"Those who expect to reap the blessings of freedom must, like men, undergo the fatigues of supporting it."*

Some hope that SB 2's deliberative sessions could provide similar opportunity; sadly they don't. Our twelve-year experience with SB 2 in the Mascenic School District and the information I gathered from the Town Clerks of the sixty-two SB 2 towns both show the same depressing result:

very low attendance—many fewer than attend Town Meetings. Even in the smaller SB 2 towns fewer than 1 in 16 voters attend Deliberative Sessions.

Sadly, that low attendance creates a stronger role for the small group which does attend (the "powers that be"); it also sets the stage for disturbing forms of mischief which would never sneak by a Town Meeting.

So I ask again, how do we "inspect the goods" under SB 2? How do we negotiate the compromises? I fear the answer is "we don't." And if we don't, then how can we possibly govern ourselves wisely?

SB 2 seems to me to be the wrong answer to the wrong problem. It decreases our supervision of our officials, it decreases voter participation in debating the issues and setting priorities, and it *increases* the role of factions, special interests, and small "in" groups.

Mason may someday become too large for Town Meetings and we'll then have to change to some other form of governance. Perhaps we'll use the solution that both our State and the Nation employ—a representative democracy in which we elect representatives whom we authorize to study the issues, negotiate compromises, and make binding commitments on our behalf. Our role will then be simplified to the electing of wise representatives.

I do not believe the time is yet, but when that time does come, SB 2 will not be a suitable solution for its results are "neither fish nor fowl." Under SB 2 we keep our "right to vote" on every issue, but decline to take part in the study or negotiations, so we vote without wisdom as isolated individuals, not part of a community.

I also sense a distressing intolerance in an SB 2 world. *Listen to what your Selectmen and department heads have to say, or ask them questions?* Can't spare the time! *Listen to the opposing view of other citizens?* Why bother! *Present your own opposing views or find someone else to do so?* Don't care enough to make the effort.

In such an environment who will be willing to serve as our officials? How will we motivate people to put in all the necessary effort for a public that can't be bothered to even listen to their reports, let alone to say Thank You?

So, I beg of you, don't lay down that torch. Don't take that rare and precious privilege handed onwards to you over 233 years by tens of thousands who attended Mason Town meetings and trade it in for just a few hours of extra free time once a year.

Instead, let us recommit ourselves to being proud members of that glorious 233 year tradition of Mason citizens who have been willing to carry the torch of freedom and self government. Come to meetings, ask questions, make your views known, propose better solutions. Be part of your government, not just a disgruntled spectator.

Addendum: Mason voters had, as Garth Fletcher mentioned, many years of experience with SB 2 while part of the Mascenic School District. Mason withdrew from that district and created its own SAU 89, voting in SB 2 for the new district in March 2010. The first deliberative session of SAU 89 drew just twenty-nine voters, four of whom were district officials. Attempts by SB 2 promoters to oust town meeting in Mason failed in 2010 and 2011 by four votes and nine votes respectively.

The Last Word Goes to the Youngest Voter

Student Chaloe Tyler researched SB 2 for a course on town meeting at New England College. Here's what she has to say:

> *I think my favorite part about Town Meeting is that we come together—bound by our connection as a community. . . . A single voice has the power to move the entire community to reason and is always given the opportunity to do so. You can't argue compassion to a voting booth . . . When we lose Town Meeting to a voting booth we lose our voices.*

* * *

SB 2 in Northwood

Ironically, as I was writing this book, Northwood's town meeting tradition ended. SB 2 was voted in on March 8, 2011, achieving the three-fifths super majority by just a few votes. School meeting went the same way. Those who pushed for SB 2 used an effective strategy of framing the question this way: Wouldn't it be better if more people got to vote? SB 2 = Fairness.

More is always better, right? Fairer? Instead of wasting a whole day at town meeting, voters could, at their leisure, visit the polls on election day and vote yea or nay on all articles.

Who could argue with that kind of efficiency?

Nobody did. Town meeting appreciators were taken by surprise. We never thought Northwood, *our Northwood*, would go SB 2. Our town meeting was well attended, spirited, and our decision-making, if not perfect, reflective of the views of the town. Many points of view were represented,

many people spoke up. Debate could get intense, but remained—for the most part—civil. Sure we complained about high taxes, but so does virtually every other town in New Hampshire. Since New Hampshire has no sales or income tax, the burden falls on property owners. There was no evidence to show that an SB 2 system lowered taxes. So those who loved town meeting, i.e., those who participated (with a few exceptions), were taken aback. We just couldn't believe it when SB 2 squeaked through.

Getting town meeting back after SB 2 has been voted in seems nearly impossible. Many towns have tried and failed. It's that pesky three-fifths super majority again—and who's voting? Why, it's the people at the polls who enjoy that convenience and may not understand the importance of the discourse that goes on at the sit-down town meeting. The virtues of town meeting are so much more complex than the simplistic: "More voters good; fewer voters bad." How to explain the *quality* of the vote, the power of face-to-face discussion, the importance of all segments of a town's population being represented, all sides being given the opportunity to speak, all sides being informed at the same time in the same place, so that the Mind can find compromise. This doesn't fit on a campaign sign.

Many were deeply saddened by the loss of town meeting in Northwood. At the suggestion of a fellow mourner, I wrote an obituary, which appeared in two local papers, the *Forum* and the *Concord Monitor,* as follows:

An Obituary for Town Meeting

Northwood Town Meeting, born March 23, 1773, died March 8, 2011, gone too soon at the age of 238, deeply mourned by those who loved her. She guided her town through peacetime and wartime, beginning in 1779 when she sent three of her native sons to fight for freedom. She built roads and bridges and schools and, of course, the Meeting House so her folks could gather each spring and decide together what was best for their community in the coming year. She was committed to education, at first building several one-room schools, and then, as transportation improved, a more centralized school system. She supported libraries, too, knowing that democracy thrives when people are educated and informed. Ever compassionate, she took care of the poor when they couldn't care for themselves.

Yes, she could be feisty. Better, she thought, to get our differences out in the open and settle them with as much civility as could be mustered. And she was a good listener. In her presence all were welcome to speak their minds. When ideas clashed, she always found a way to quell the furor, quiet the discord, bridge the differences. Town Meeting proved again and again that good decisions don't depend on how many vote, but on how well-informed those voters are. Town Meeting believed deeply that on a given day intelligent people could be persuaded to shift their points of view through honest and spirited debate. And at the end of that day, the town would benefit. President James Garfield called town meeting "the vital force, the informing soul of the town."

With the loss of town meeting, Northwood has indeed lost its soul.

Some say Town Meeting died of old age and natural causes. But those who knew her best understand that she remained strong, vital, and, yes, essential to the thoughtful implementation of true democracy in our town. Those who knew her best, and those who have studied her unique and astonishing life history, know for certain that she did not die of natural causes. She was assassinated.

A graveside service will be held on Saturday, March 12, at Coe-Brown Academy in Northwood, beginning at 9:00 a.m. In lieu of flowers, please contribute to a worthy civic organization of your choice.

A flurry of response followed publication of the obituary. At town meeting, many people approached me to share their sorrow. A few dressed in funeral black. I received at least four hugs from surprising sources (Yankees are not big huggers). In letters to the editor and comments online, many lamented the passing of town meeting in Northwood and other towns. Some, however, celebrated the implementation of SB 2:

- Prior to the March 8, 2001 elections, 73 school districts in NH had adopted SB 2 in their communities. . . . Although I did not vote this time to support SB 2 for either the school or town, it is something that has worked well in many communities. The last time I checked the sky had not fallen.

- Here's a toast to the majority of Northwood voters formally acknowledging and empowering those citizens who cannot or choose not to spend a day each year for the school meeting and the town meeting respectively.

- Reports of the death of the Northwood Town Meeting have been greatly exaggerated. Now called a deliberative session, she will continue to build bridges, roads, and libraries. She will continue to allow us to get our differences out in the open. She will continue to welcome all of us to speak our minds. She wasn't murdered—she got a new lease on life.

- I have come to the conclusion that all the "whiners" who stage last rites for the SB 2 transition are really upset about the "loss of control" they maintain with their clique behavior, clique traditions, clique domination, and simply getting their way over ordinary folks.

- You mean one can spend 15 minutes to vote instead of wasting the better part of a Saturday listening to 4–6 hours of malcontents spouting conspiracy theories and/or picking fights over interpretations of budget numbers? And people with kids and no childcare, or jobs that require them to work on Saturdays, now have an opportunity to research the issues at home and have some control over the town's decision-making process? How horrible.

Linda Smith—active public servant and citizen volunteer—objected, rightly, to my assertion in the obituary that Northwood had lost its soul. She wrote:

> Town Meeting may be missed by many; to say that Northwood has lost her soul is error. Attend any one of the meetings where town citizens give up the comfort of their home life to drive to town hall or community center or school library to help steer the decisions of their community and you will see the soul of Northwood. She may be going through a transition period but she still has a strong pulse. Whether it is the Scouts, Lions Club, NALMC, the Food Pantry volunteers, the VFW or the many other organizations, there is much going on with the people who give life to our community. Northwood is alive and well. We may shed a tear to say goodbye to Town Meeting as we know it, but this

Saturday we can celebrate all it has been and be ready to work within the framework of the future.

Tears were shed, that's for sure. Here are some comments from those who saw the demise of town meeting as a significant loss.

- As a town moderator, I share your affection for Town Meeting, not because of the history but because pure democracy really does work.

- I offer my deepest condolences to the Town of Northwood on the death of a wonderful tradition and the basis of our democracy here in America. We here in Deering have had the same problem several times over the last several years but have been able to hold on to our town meeting by doing the work before the vote to educate the voters of what the choices really were and what it would mean to our town.

- By 8 votes no less. Thank you for this, Rebecca. I think it's too bad that my son only gets to go to one town meeting. I credit going to town meetings for my level of civic involvement. My biggest gripe about the SB 2 campaign is the "democracy of fairness angle." I wish the supporters would come clean and admit they want to vote down budgets without explaining to their neighbors why it is not needed.

- It is all of NH that lost its soul when SB 2 came along. Deerfield has been without town meeting for several years now and she is truly missed.

- In New Boston, established in 1763, our town meeting sadly died in 1999 at the age of 236. In the past decade we've seen the "deliberative session" turn into a hollow event that has no real relevance. Gone are the days of citizens investing their time and passion for the community—working together, debating and deciding the right way for our community. It's been replaced by a culture too busy watching cable TV to take the time to meet with fellow citizens and perform their most basic civic duty in defense of democracy. Your article touched me and made me long for the wisdom of and worry about the future for Brentwood, Chester, Chichester, Deering, Dunbarton, Farmington, FREEDOM, Gilmanton, Henniker, Haverhill, Hinsdale, Hollis, Lincoln, Madison, Marlborough, Mont Vernon, Moultonborough, Pembroke, Pittsfield, Plymouth, Sanbornton,

South Hampton, Tamworth, Temple, Tilton, Whitefield, and Mason. I'd vote town meeting back in a heartbeat.

- As a native Vermonter I grew up with the tradition of town meeting. It is democracy in its purest form. A thing of beauty that is sometimes not so beautiful but nonetheless important. I'm sad to see it go from so many places.

- Welcome aboard, Northwood. It's a bus without a driver.

- Another NH tradition gone by the wayside.

- Can you say: "Default budget"?

- I had always looked forward to Town Meeting as it afforded me an opportunity to have a real say in how my tax dollars were spent. Being a California resident for the last two years and paying CA income tax, CA sales tax, and CA property tax (as well as NH property taxes) with virtually no say, you can imagine how much I miss having a direct vote in how my tax dollars are spent like I had in Northwood.

- A fitting tribute to one of the last bastions of NH liberty.

And finally, my favorite:

- Amen, Becky.

Eric Reitter gets the last word on town meeting in Northwood. He wrote from California with a perspective that puts the whole business in a different slant of light. He illuminates the big picture when he writes:

> I'm disappointed by the loss of Town Meeting. I enjoyed the give and take of the debate, and whether articles that I supported were approved or failed, I ultimately came away with the feeling that we were all in this together and that I had a chance to voice my opinion. I brought my children to Town Meeting each year and while I can't say that they enjoyed it as much as I did, they learned the importance of participating.
>
> I'm disappointed that I won't be able to show them democracy in its truest form in Northwood anymore. However, I'm looking forward to returning to Northwood soon, participating in the new deliberative sessions, and town government once again. Even with SB 2 in place, New Hampshire's form of town government affords it citizens more opportunity to have a direct voice in government than just about any other place in the country. Let's hope that the supporters of SB 2 are right and now everyone gets involved.

19 ⚖

The Future of Town Meeting

Professors Maura McNeil and Inez McDermott and their students at New England College like Chaloe Tyler give me hope. The professors teach a class on town meeting. Over two terms, the students first learned its history then went out into the broader community, attended town meetings, and did projects based on what they'd learned. Some responded through photography, others through writing, some through their visual art, some combined the three. One student printed T-shirts. All apply their creativity to explaining what town meeting had come to mean to them—and the results of their work were displayed to the public at an end-of-term celebration.

Ashley Paul and Zak Harris put together a limited edition book called *Everything . . . Or Close to Everything You Need to Know about Town Meeting*. They write:

> There is more to town meeting than the budget being raised, a fire station getting a new truck, or paving a town road. . . . Welcome to what could be, arguably, the remains of democracy as we know it.
>
> Don't believe it?
>
> Find another place where every person's voice can be heard, recognized and valued. . . . Find a place where feuds are born and extinguished. Find a place where a community has the power to collectively decide on and change the future of their neighborhoods now and neighborhoods to come.
>
> Welcome to Town Meetin'.

Most of these students didn't know a lot about town meeting when they started the course, but—through their reading, discussion, and best of all, boots on the ground at the meetings themselves—they all ended up admiring it. So it's not just us old fogies full of nostalgia who see the value in this incarnation of democracy. It's the young-uns, too.

Zak Harris interviewed a mother and son at the meeting he attended:

Zak: Do you like being here at town meeting?
Son: No, because they are boring.
Mom: Now town meeting is part of town culture. If they wanted to get
rid of baseball, wouldn't you go up and argue against it?
Son: Well, yeah, I'd argue all day.

Town meeting is a valued part of our culture, Mom says, not to be discarded lightly. And Son understands.

In these days of so much technology and social media, Ashley Paul and Zak Harris ask:

> *Where will you find a place where an individual voice can still be recognized, accounted for, and really mean something?*
>
> *Perhaps it is outdated to use a system that has been around for over 300 years, but in a developing culture where voice and individuality are so crucial, why would we even consider limiting the voice of every person? A pen is mightier than the sword, but a voice is mightier than a pen. Town Meeting's roots are historical, cultural, and influential and are symbolic to the founding of the United States of America.*

When historian Joann Bailey called town meeting *dear*, she invoked its essence. Dear means cherished, as well as costly. Town meeting costs time and energy. It demands commitment as well as our collective and individual wisdom. It taxes relationships. It tests our mettle. Yes, speaking into the mic, speaking what you believe, raising your hand among your neighbors and voting a different way, changing your position in the face of a solid argument—all these actions require courage. Town meeting requires us to reach consensus for the good of our community and it reminds us that the best discourse is civil discourse.

Susan Clark and Frank Bryan, writing about Vermont, recognize that town meeting is in danger of slipping away. The many practical suggestions they make for preserving town meeting in *All Those in Favor*—improving attendance, keeping the institution relevant and vital, publicizing it thoroughly—apply equally to New Hampshire. Respect for the past and hope for the future live at the heart of their plea to save town meeting. They write:

> *How can we live in peace?*
>
> *In our beloved Vermont at the dawn of the postmodern era, we can help answer that question. And (like it or not) we shall help answer it, either by our action or by our inaction. Indeed, we are called upon to*

answer, for we are uniquely positioned to do so. Vermonters still practice (and practice most thoroughly) the planet's single best example of the single best way to live in peace. For us this way of resolving human problems humanely, this way of combining our natural and inescapable longings for both liberty and community, this way of common enterprise—this way of peace—is a way of life.

The world calls it democracy.

We call it town meeting.

SB 2 threatens the future of town meeting. The best thing that could happen at the state level is for the legislature to repeal the law that allows the SB 2 process to be implemented in place of traditional town meeting. But as dangerous as that ill-conceived legislation is, it is not the biggest danger to town meeting.

In Gilford would more people have attended a traditional town meeting than attended the SB 2 deliberative session? Probably. Still, as the number of registered voters in these towns grows, it seems the number of people willing to actively participate in town affairs—run for office, serve on committees, attend meetings including the big one—fails to keep pace, and even declines. Town meeting takes work. Democracy is hard! The Mind must be engaged before, during, and after town meeting itself.

The greatest threat to town meeting is diminishing citizen participation and interest. For town meeting to work properly, we must turn out. We must represent *all* the varying interests and factions of our town. We must speak up. And listen. And debate. And compromise. And actively determine our community's future.

Are people simply too busy for pure democracy?

If the answer is yes, that's a devastating truth. For town meeting to thrive, we must make it a priority. If town meeting dies, it will be apathy that killed it.

"*When in some obscure country town the farmers came together to a special town meeting, to express their opinion on some subject which is vexing the land, that, I think, is the true Congress, and the most respectable one that's ever assembled in the United States.*"

HENRY DAVID THOREAU

Resources

Agran, Rick, Hildred Crill, and Mark DeCarteret, eds. *Under the Legislature of Stars: 62 New Hampshire Poets*. Durham: Oyster River Press, 1999.

Bailey, Joann. *A Guide to the History and Old Dwelling Places of Northwood*. Portsmouth: Peter E. Randall Publisher, 1992.

Barry, Kevin. *Town of Deerfield SB2 Deliberative Session, January 30, 2010 Minutes*.

Bliss, William. *Colonial Times on Buzzard's Bay*. Boston: Houghton Mifflin, 1894.

Bouton, Nathaniel. *Town Papers, Documents and Records Relating to Towns in New Hampshire, Volume IX*. Concord: Charles C. Pearson, 1875.

Bryan, Frank M. *Real Democracy: The New England Town Meeting and How It Works*. Chicago: University of Chicago Press, 2004.

Callum, Roberta; Marjorie Coe, Martha Fellows, Perley Newton, and Albert Reed. *Highlights in the History of Unity, N.H.* Unity: The Historical Committee for the Bicentennial,1964.

Chase, Sidney M. "Town Meetin' Day," *Scribner's Magazine*, November, 1910.

Chase, William C., ed. *The American Winston Churchill*. n.p., 2003. http://www2. mcdaniel.edu/History/awc.html (accessed 2010).

Churchill, Winston. *Coniston*. New York: The MacMillan Company, 1906.

Clark, Susan, and Frank Bryan. *All Those in Favor: Rediscovering the Secrets of Town Meeting and Community*. Montpelier: RavenMark Press, 2005.

Curren, Thomas S., and Kathy Neustadt. *Home to the Mountain: A Bicentennial History of Wilmot, New Hampshire*. Wilmot: Town of Wilmot, 2007.

Daniell, Jere, "Town Meeting: Symbol for a Nation." Unpublished manuscript, Dartmouth College.

deToqueville, Alexis. *Democracy in America*. Translated by George Lawrence, edited by J. P. Mayer. New York: Harper and Row, 1969 (from the orginal 1845 and 1850 texts).

Della Fera, Michaeline. *Women at the Table: 40 Intimate Profiles of Political Women of the Northeast*. Spring, TX: L & L Dreamspell, 2008.

Dubrulle, Elizabeth. *Goffstown Reborn*. Charlestown: The History Press, 2009.

Gould, John. *New England Town Meeting: Safeguard of Democracy.* Brattleboro, VT: Stephen Daye Press, 1940.

Hale, Sara Joshepha. *Northwood.* Boston: Ingraham and Hewes, 1827.

Harris, Marie. *Weasel in the Turkey Pen.* New York: Hanging Loose Press, 1993.

Hebert, Ernest. *The Dogs of March.* Hanover: University Press of New England, 1979.

Holmes, Richard. *Chester Revisited: A History in Honor of the Town's 275th Anniversary.* Portsmouth: Peter Randall Publisher, 1998.

Humphrey, Zephine. *A Book of New England.* New York: Howell Soskin Publishers, 1945.

Jackson, Shirley. "Biography of a Short Story," in *Come Along with Me.* New York: Penguin Books, 1967.

Jackson, Shirley. "The Lottery," in *The Lottery.* New York: Farrar, Straus, and Giroux, 1976.

Jager, Ronald. *Last House on the Road: Excursions into a Rural Past.* Boston: Beacon Press, 1994.

Jager, Ronald, and Grace Jager. *Portrait of a Hill Town.* Warner, NH: R. C. Brayshaw and Company, 1998.

Kingsbury, Frank Burnside. *History and Genealogical Register of the Town of Langdon, Sullivan County, New Hampshire from the Date of Its Severance from Walpole and Charlestown from 1787 to 1930.* White River Junction, VT: Right Printing Company, 1932.

Knowing the Territory: A Survey of Municipal Law for New Hampshire Local Officials. 2010 Edition. Concord: New Hampshire Local Government Center.

Laufman, Dudley. *She Plumb Ned, She More'n Plumb.* Center Ossipee, NH: Beech River Books, 2011.

Mansfield, Howard. *In the Memory House.* Golden, CO: Fulcrum Publishing, 1993.

Nottingham 250—Anniversary Commemorative Edition.. Nottingham Historical Society, 1972.

Paul, Ashley, and Zak Harris. *Everything . . . Or Close to Everything You Need to Know about Town Meeting,* published in small numbers as part of their coursework at New England College, 2011.

Richardson, Roxanne Spiller. *History of Northwood, NH 1878–1946.* MA thesis, University of New Hampshire, 1946.

Rule, Rebecca. *The Best Revenge*. Hanover: University Press of New England, 1995.

Rule, Rebecca. *Could Have Been Worse: True Stories, Embellishments and Outright Lies*. Concord: Plaidswede Press, 2006.

Sanborn, Edwin David. "Early Settlers of New Hampshire," in *The Granite Monthly*, 1877. http://www.seacoastnh.com/Places_%26_Events/NH_History/Early_Settlers_of_New_Hampshire/.

Sellers, Frank M. *History of the Town of Langdon from 1787 to 1987*. Sellers Publications, 1987.

Sheldon, Ken. "Heaves, Hoops, and Earl Hadley," *New Hampshire Magazine*, March 2011.

Stradley, Linda. *What's Cooking America*. http://whatscookingamerica.net/History/Cakes/ElectionCake.htm.

Town Government in New Hampshire, The New Hampshire Historical Records Survey Project, 1940, sponsored by the University of New Hampshire.

Town Meeting and School Meeting Handbook. 2011 Edition. Concord: New Hampshire Local Government Center.

Town reports and websites for Allenstown (2010 report, allenstownnh.org), Bow (2009 report), Colebook (www.colebrook-nh.com), Dalton (www.townofdalton.com), Gilford (www.gilfordnh.org), Gilmanton (gilmantonnh.org), Newbury (www.newburynh.org), and Northwood (2009 and 2010 reports).

Webster, Clarence M. *Town Meeting Country*. New York: Duell, Sloan & Pearce Publishers, 1945.

Whitaker, Deborah. "Town Meetin': A Darius Wherry Story," *Yankee Magazine*, March 1936.

Zimmerman, Joseph F., *The New England Town Meeting: Democracy in Action*, Westport, CT: Praeger Publishers, 1999.

"As a transplant, I think town meeting is what makes New Hampshire New Hampshire. It's the only place where you feel like you can really have your say. In New York it's on the ballot and you can vote yes or no. That's not having your say."

LORI FISHER

Addendum

When is Town Meeting Not Town Meeting? When It's a Play

In 1994 I wrote a play called *Town Meeting*, inspired by the many town meetings I'd attended in my adopted town of Northwood. ("Lived here all your life?" "Only since 1978." "Newcomer, eh?" "You bet—and always will be.") It had to be done. Town meetings are plays. Every one of them. The New Hampshire State Council on the Arts awarded me a New Works Grant to develop the show. In March of that year, the Ann White Northwood Theater Workshop performed my play to sold-out houses. It was *long*. Almost as long as real town meetings—well not quite, but close to three hours, saints preserve us. Too long. Audience members got the full experience of sitting too long on hard seats. Still, people seemed to enjoy it. (We are a patient bunch, us Yankees, with bottoms well adapted to hard seats.)

I remember opening night, sitting behind a couple of selectmen and their spouses, worried about their reactions. Relieved when they laughed. A lot. At one point in the show, a spouse turned to me and whispered: "Becky, you don't know how true this is!"

Oh, but I did. I'd created a composite based on various true, true-ish, and highly fabricated stories (as well as rumors) I'd heard over the years. Of course, for dramatic purposes, I upped the ante, using the fiction writer's old trick of "What if?" Maybe the town clerk wasn't actually smitten with the moderator. But she might have been. Maybe the chief of police didn't actually shoot a hole through the roof of the cruiser during a romantic liaison—but he might have. Maybe a PTA lady didn't really give birth under the refreshments table; it's not completely outside the realm of possibility.

Perhaps what the select-spouse meant was that an awful lot of behind the scenes planning, prodding, prompting, and manipulation goes on in small-town politics. Maybe she recognized the stories behind the stories, like grudges that simmer for decades just under the surface, then rear their gnarly heads: "I wouldn't vote for him if he was running against a rabid coyote from Massachusetts." Maybe what she meant was that our small towns are chock full of characters doing their own idiosyncratic things, and driving other characters nuts. Maybe she meant that human nature is a given: we are who we are, part stereotype and part unique individual, whether we live and work in Woodford, New Hampshire, or Washington, D.C. Maybe she recognized her neighbors and herself in the characters portrayed on stage.

Since that premiere, *Town Meeting* has been revised, rebuilt, reconsidered, and resuscitated. Thankfully, it's gotten a lot shorter. It's been performed as a full production and as a staged reading in a number of towns, including Boscawen, Bradford, Hillsborough, and Nottingham.

In 2000, with help from John Rule, lyricist, and Chris Cote, composer, the show morphed into *Town Meeting: The Musical.* It had to be done. I envisioned the selectmen dancing. And in the musical version, they do—as do the town clerk, the moderator, the dumpmaster, the PTA ladies, the police chief and deputy, Esther Crawford Fox (holder of the Boston Post Cane), and even Bigfoot, in a cameo appearance. The musical version has been done in Northwood by the Ann White Northwood Theater Workshop and in Strafford by the Lakeside Players. It's a lot harder to cast though—and harder to put together what with all that singing and the need for musicians and such. The police chief plays bongo drums in one number.

The short, nonmusical version is more straightforward to stage. A flag, a lectern, chairs for the legislative body (which is also the audience), a table for the selectmen, one for the PTA, a voting booth, and that's about it. It's a comedy, of course, and directors have enjoyed casting against type— dumpmaster as selectman, librarian as hard-boiled lawyer, or vice versa. They've also enjoyed casting *to* type. In Nottingham, a bit of imaginative casting gave the real police chief the role of Chief, and the deputy the role of Dicky the Deputy. Each performance can be tailored to the particulars of the town in which it's being performed—different names for the characters, different street names or business names to match the town, references to controversial issues, inside jokes. Sometimes the play is done with extensive rehearsal, sometimes without much at all. It's even possible, in a staged reading, to recruit characters from the audience, hand them scripts, props, point them to a chair, and say, Go for it.

Here's the play for your reading, and if you're part of a theater group, performing pleasure. Down with apathy! Town meeting lives!

TOWN MEETING

by Rebecca Rule

Cast of Characters

Town Officials

MODERATOR—town meeting veteran

GLADIE B.—town clerk

MAXINE MARSH—1st selectman

REVEREND HOLLY— 2nd selectman, sleeps through
   most of meeting

TURTLE TUTTLE—3rd selectman

PTA Ladies

JULIE

MEG

Police Officers

CHIEF

DEPUTY DICKY JELLY

Goodys

MA GOODY

OLD GOODY—Ma's father

ED GOODY—a cousin

BABY GOODY—Ed's little sister

STELLA GOODY-ENRIGHT—Ma's daughter

The Fugitive

MICKEY ENRIGHT—estranged husband of the beautiful Stella

Others

ROBERT (or ROBERTA)—the dumpmaster (or mistress)

ESTHER CRAWFORD FOX—oldest person in town, knitting
   a very long scarf

ATTORNEY CHRIS GOODIE—working for Mickey.

Set

Chairs for all, grouped as follows: three Selectmen, two PTA ladies, five Goodys, Chief and Dickey, Moderator and Gladie, Esther and Robert plus empty chair for Chris in ACT II. One chair set off to the side with a microphone for Mickey. More elaborate sets may include tables for Selectmen and Gladie, lectern for the Moderator, voting booth for Mickey to hide in. PTA table with goodies (food goodies, that is) to be served at Intermission.

*** Brief Interludes indicating time passing—some lively music!

Act I

TIME: Town Meeting About to Begin

AT RISE: ALL (but CHRIS GOODIE) on stage, frozen in place. They become animated as each name is mentioned; they speak or become engaged in conversation.

ROBERT

(*Reflectively.*) It is possible that the large boil on the town of Woodford's . . . ahhem . . . will burst—or be lanced—at this town meeting. The Moderator will try to maintain order, but there will be controversy. Should the cemetery fence be repaired? Does the police department need a new cruiser? And who blasted the hole in the roof of the old one? Should the town accept the skating pond from the Daughters of Illustrious Yankee Patriots? Will Esther Crawford Fox, ninety-seven years old and counting, accept the Boston Post Cane as Woodford's oldest citizen?

Course the Goodys have problems of their own. Mickey Enright's out of jail. No, he's not technically a Goody—he's an in-law. And an outlaw. Arrested last month for disorderly conduct at the Frothy Mug. Some say Mickey wa'n't any more disorderly than usual. Some say our chief of police has eyes for Mickey's bride—the beautiful Stella Goody-Enright.

Well, Mickey served his thirty days, but he wa'n't happy about it, and no sooner was he sprung then he was right back at it—stirring up trouble in Goodyland. Last night, Dicky the Deputy chased him into the Grisly Swamp, but Mickey escaped. Now Mickey is at large.

Between you and me, he hiding over in the voting booth and Town Meeting about to start. Mickey never was the brightest bulb on the tree.

Meanwhile, here's your crash course in Woodford politics, where grudges are held long and hard, retribution is both art and entertainment, and once in a while (despite our best efforts) good sense and compassion prevail.

Let the festivities commence.

                              ESTHER
Is this where I collect my town report?

                              GLADIE
Why Esther Fox, I have one right here with your name on it.

                                ED
What'll be the signal, Turtle? Gotta have a signal.

                              TURTLE
How 'bout I ding this jelly doughnut, Ed, and hit you side the head?

                                ED
(*Troubled by that idea.*) Huh?

                              TURTLE
How 'bout you scratch your armpit? Like this. Scratch your left armpit when
the time is right.

                                ED
(*Practices his scratch.*)

                              MAXINE
"What's going on out Goody way," the people want to know. "Heard sirens in
the night. What's with the roadblocks?" I didn't know a thing. When the first
selectman doesn't know a thing about a thing like a manhunt, looks like she's
not on top of things.

                              CHIEF
(*Shrugs.*)

                              MAXINE
What the hell did you think you were doing, Chief, chasing Mickey Enright out
through the swamp in the middle of the night? Siccing the Rottweillers on him!

                              CHIEF
No Rottweillers—just Dicky's little cocker spaniel. Hey, the man hadn't been
out of jail twenty-four hours and he's right back into it with the Goodys. What's
he think he's doing nosing around that house in the middle of the night?

                              MAXINE
He lives there.

MICKEY

I live there!

CHIEF

The beautiful Stella Goody requested police assistance. And I felt obliged
to assist.

MICKEY

(*Whips out cell phone, dials.*) Oh geez—a machine. I hate machi—ok, this is
Mickey Enright. We talked last night on the telephone. I'm at the Woodford
Town Hall. Just get yourself to the village, can't miss it. I'll be here—if you're
still willing. I'll be wearing . . . (*Describe what actor is wearing.*)

ED

(*To GOODYS.*) Who wants a coffee? (*Finds thermos.*) Stella? You want a coffee?

MICKEY

Sweet Stella.

STELLA

(*Coldly.*) No, Ed. I don't drink coffee. I never drink coffee. I hate coffee. Why
do you always ask me if I want a coffee when you know I never drink coffee?

ED

I thought you might like a coffee this one time, Stella, on account of you were
up so late last night—you and the chief, *conferring.*

ROBERT

Mornin' Turtle—I mean, Mr. Selectman, sir.

TURTLE

"Sir" is it? You never used to be so polite, Robert. Budget committee—as I
recall—you gave me nothing but lip, called me everything but "sir."

ROBERT

Well sir, budget committee, that's one thing. But selectman, that's entirely different. You're in charge now. Got your own desk at town hall.

ED

Got your own swivel chair.

ROBERT

Key to the file cabinet.

MAXINE

Access to confidential town records.

MICKEY

And police records and court documents and tickets and fines and warnings and who knows what all. Which don't seem right.

STELLA

Push-button telephone.

BABY

Shiny nameplate reads: Turtle Tuttle, see-lect-man.

JULIE

That fudge looks so good. But I resist. I'm resisting. (*Stretches, rubs tummy.*)

MEG

(*To Julie.*) You sure you're all right? If you had a contraction, would you know it?

JULIE

Of course. I graduated Lamaze. Second in my class. (*She winces.*) Just a twinge.

TURTLE

Better watch yourself, Robert. You're working for me now.

ROBERT

Oh yuh? Evidently Maxine thinks I'm working for her. Down to the landfill all hours, finding fault, telling me where to put it.

OLD

(*Amused.*) Maxine tell you where to put it, Robert?

ED

She's told me where to put it several times. But I refused.

ROBERT

God it's tempting, though. Nosing around the compactor: "There's glass in there, Robert? Isn't that a beer bottle I see down in there. I believe it is. What's it doing in the compactor instead of the bottle pit? You should snag that out of there." She's leaning way over, peering down in. One little slip—

ED

One good shove!

ROBERT

She'd tumble.

BABY

(*Diabolically.*) Flip the lever—

ED

Smush.

ROBERT

"How that selectman get down in the crusher?" I'd say. "That's no place for selectmen. They belong over in compost."

ED

(*Earnest.*) Can't do it, Robert; she'd clog the gears.

* * * *Music* * * *

MODERATOR

At Budget Committee Turtle raised the sensitive matter of the shotgun hole in the roof of the cruiser.

GLADIE

Which is why there's a new cruiser up for vote on the warrant. Dicky Jelly says, no, they needed a second vehicle anyway on account of the rising crime rate.

DICKY

That's right. And it's Richard. I go by Richard.

ESTHER

Mafia!

MICKEY

Around here you don't even have to commit a crime to get in trouble—that I know for a fact. Got outta jail and all I wanted to do was see Stella, my wife. But the chief said no. He said Stella didn't want to see me, something about some Restraint Order. He said he had her "personally protected." Which I don't much like the sound of *that.* So I head out to the Old Goody Place, under cover of darkness, expecting Stella would be real glad to see me, and the next thing I know I'm running out through the swamp being shot at and chased by Dicky's cocker spaniel.

JULIE

(*Thoughtful.*) Once a cruiser has a hole that size in the roof—I shouldn't think it would ever be quite the same.

OLD

Why don't they just patch it up with chicken wire and Bondo?

MODERATOR

It is a large hole, as I understand it. Squirreled the damaged vehicle away, right quick, down the town shed. But Norman at the Sunoco says it's a great gaping thing. He says glue in a sheet of Plexiglas and call it a sun roof.

GLADIE

Wouldn't it be apt to leak though in a hard rain?

MODERATOR

Norman says a certain town official associated with the police department phoned him up, in the middle of the night, offering Norman financial incentive if he could get the hole patched up by morning and keep his mouth shut about it. Which of course he couldn't do either.

STELLA

You people don't even know what you're talking about!

MICKEY

Stella's not particularly cordial in the morning. She improves as the day progresses.

MODERATOR

Gladie, I, uh, I had an idea you and I might drive upcountry to that new restaurant after the meeting, that Hill House of Pizza and Seafood.

GLADIE

People might have something to say if we went out to a restaurant, just the two of us. They might think we were out on a date or something. Tongues might wag.

MAXINE

Imagine it: the Moderator and the Town Clerk (*gasp*) out on the town, scarfing clams—

TURTLE

(*Blazing.*) In cahoots.

BABY

In love.

JULIE

(*In distress.*) Indigestion!

DICKY

(*Alarmed.*) I just had a call on my Official Police Radio.

MAXINE

What is it now, Dicky? Mafia? Gang wars? UFOs? Somebody steal another box of spaghetti?

DICKY

An important message just come through. The fugitive may be armed.

BABY

(*Mimicking.*) The fugitive may be armed.

DICKY

Road blocks have been established.

CHIEF

All necessary precautions have been taken to apprehend said fugitive—

DICKY

Mickey Enright.

MAXINE

(*Scornfully.*) Mickey Enright. Harmless. I've known him since he was a baby. Bald, drooly little toothless baby.

MICKEY

(*Sweetly.*) Harmless.

DICKY

Maximal precautions have been taken to protect the safety of the Woodford citizenry from the alleged criminal actions of the alleged criminal currently at large.

MODERATOR

Yes, yes, yes, right, right, right. Since there seems to be no immediate danger, maybe we should get on with the meeting. Now, I realize there's strong feelings about some of the issues coming up, particularly some of the larger money items. And that's all right. That's fine. That's as it should be. But I give you fair warning, *I will not tolerate personal attacks.*

GLADIE

He will not tolerate personal attacks.

MEG

Damn! They're the best kind.

MODERATOR

(*Surveying the room.*) I will not tolerate it. I will cut you off and you will stay cut off. We've got a good lot of business to plow through today. Open under Article 1, to raise and appropriate the sum of $1,000 for purchase of the so-called skating pond from the Daughters of Illustrious Yankee Patriots. I await your pleasure.

TURTLE

He's gonna cut me off, is he? That shetpolk. He wants to try it just once.

ROBERT

He'll gavel ya, Turtle. He'll have ya hauled out of here by that string of wispy hair on the top of your pick-ed head, and then Dicky'll beat you to a quivering pulp in the town hall yard.

DICKY

Richard.

ED

What's a shitpolk?

ROBERT

Ed. Shetpolk. You know. Big ugly poky bird lives in the marsh.

DICKY

Sounds like a Goody to me.

ROBERT

Makes a noise like a stake being drove into the mud with a maul. Flaps its big old wings—flap, flap, flap—over your head and you better watch yourself, misterman, or you'll get a surprise from the skies. A shetpolk's aim is deadly.

ESTHER

Mafia.

ED

(*Brightening.*) You mean a mud hen!

MEG

Same old "democracy is a privilege, let's behave like grownups" speech. But it won't do any good. No grownups here. Can you feel it?

JULIE

What?

MAXINE

Controversy.

BABY

(*Enthusiastic.*) Conflict.

MAXINE

Confrontation.

MEG

A creeping fog. Up to our ankles and rising . . .

MODERATOR

Article 1, to raise and appropriate the sum of $1,000 for the purchase of the so-called skating pond from the Daughters of Illustrious Yankee Patriots having been moved and seconded—

OLD

Table it!

GLADIE

But Mr. Goody, your daughter's illustrious.

OLD

And my Aunt Poo and my Cousin Dib. Don't make no difference.

MAXINE

There's already a motion on the floor.

MODERATOR

Did I hear a second?

MICKEY

Second.

GLADIE

Who made that second?

HOLLY

Second.

MODERATOR

I'll open the floor to discussion. Who wishes to speak to Article I, to raise and appropriate the sum of $1,000 for purchase of the so-called skating pond from the Daughters of Illustrious Yankee Patriots? I await your pleasure.

OLD

(*Pointing to a page in town report—i.e., his script.*) A new cruiser!

MA

Didn't we just buy a cruiser for them people?

OLD

What's this gonna do to the tax rate?

MICKEY

If I paid taxes, I wouldn't be able to afford them.

OLD

They whine and cry. Crime escalating. Gotta have a new cruiser so we can chase them criminals around, eighty miles an hour on the old back roads, shake the balls (*pause*) right out of the ball joints.

ESTHER

Mafia!

MICKEY

And if them police dogs get after you, better scamper right along. Dicky's Cocker Spaniel's a quick little fella.

MODERATOR

Motion on the floor to raise and appropriate the sum of $1 to buy the body of water known as the skating pond behind Patriots Hall from the Daughters of Illustrious Yankee Patriots. Now we've had a thorough discussion of the issue— acreage, insurance, liability. We've heard all about how Norman's truck fell through the ice last winter plowing and some little dite of gas leaked into the water and the Conservation Commission sent in the SWAT team, and all that uproar nothing ever came of, and the turtles and frogs and wogs and snakes and so forth survived.

ED

I'm voting no.

BABY

I'm telling Aunt Poo and Cousin Dib.

ED

I'm voting yes.

ESTHER

I read the obituaries, you know. I'm old, but I'm not oblivious.

MEG

Esther, I haven't heard anything about the passing of the Boston Post Cane. I really couldn't tell you. I didn't even realize Willard Willie had died—that's how on top of things I am. (*Of scarf.*) It's beautiful, Esther. Is it almost done?

ESTHER

Who knows? Who ever knows when a thing is done? People thought I was done twenty years ago. But I wasn't. Some wished it. Didn't do them any good. Maybe I'll finish this scarf up today, if I don't get too irate. When I get irate my hands shake. It's for my nephew, that knucklehead Robert.

JULIE

You always seem so serene.

ESTHER

I do get irate. I certainly do. It's good for my arteries. My blood gets heated up, shoots through and reams me right out. Some people, I'd get irate just looking at 'em. Most of them are dead now though. I outlasted 'em. Get irate and stay irate. That's my advice. Nobody dies irate.

MODERATOR

Now I know some of you prefer a ballot vote on issues about which there are strong feelings—and where you might be inclined to vote in opposition to your neighbor, or your wife, and (*joking*) nobody, course, wants to vote in open opposition to those spirited Daughters of Illustrious Yankee Patriots.

ROBERT

Not if you're in range.

MA

Vote however you want. I don't give a hoot.

JULIE

(*Pained.*) Is it time to vote? How should I vote?

MODERATOR

I understand you'd just as soon keep your vote private and not be influenced by others. I respect that, of course. Perfectly natural. On the other hand, I don't want to hear after the fact that this meeting proceeded in anything other than a fair, democratic, and timely fashion.

GLADIE

(*Hanging on his every word.*) Well said, Mr. Moderator.

MODERATOR

Thank you, Gladie. In this case, however, involving a small money amount such as it is, and time of the essence, I'm of two minds, so I've decided the ballot vote will be held only at the will of the house if the house so wills. I await your pleasure. (*Annoyed.*) How many of you wish to determine this matter by ballot. I'll ask for a show of hands. (*Counts.*) Sufficient number. I find sufficient number desiring a ballot vote. We'll proceed in an orderly fashion—

OLD

God sakes, we're talking about a dollar. One stinking dollar to take that mud hole off those Illustrious Yankee Patriot hands. Let's use our heads.

ROBERT

Be a pleasant change.

DICKY

If some want a ballot vote and some don't feel they can exercise their democratic rights without one and on the other hand, at the same time, some want to get this article over quick and move on, well then how about—this could work, Mr. Moderator—how about we vote on whether or not we should have a ballot vote?

MA

What the hell are you talking about, Dicky?

DICKY

Richard.

ESTHER

What is that young Dicky talking about, Robert? Is he all right in the head?

MA

Shoot me now and put me out of my misery.

CHIEF

(*To STELLA, cup in hand.*) Coffee, Ms. Goody.

STELLA

No! (*Then sweetly.*) No, thank you, Chief. It's very kind of you to think of me, but I never drink coffee.

OLD

Never knew a Goody didn't drink coffee. Hot coffee, cold coffee, sweet or bitter. Got me through the war. Gets me through the storms, plowing all night and most the day. Keeps me sharp, so I can knock out snotty folks' mailboxes and look like I wa'n't even trying, block them driveways in good and solid. Ha. I drink a gallon on a night like that, and piss two.

TURTLE

(*Adamant.*) Indefinitely postpone.

* * * *Music* * * *

MODERATOR

(*Testy.*) I have explained to you people, several times—

BABY

You cannot indefinitely postpone an article once the article is on the floor.

TURTLE

Then I propose an amendment.

HOLLY

Second.

TURTLE

Amend down from $1 to zero. Leave a dollar on that line, those in the majority of the board of selectmen, which is not me, can shift moneys from another line onto the pond line and buy it irregardless.

OLD

They'd do it too, better believe it.

JULIE

(*Agonized.*) They wouldn't.

MEG

They should.

GLADIE

If it's in the town's best interest.

ESTHER

Which they wouldn't recognize if it struck them between their squinty eyes.

MA

Or any other tender spots for that matter.

MODERATOR

I'll ask for a show of hands. Those voting in the affirmative raise their hands on the first call. Those voting in the negative on the second. All those in favor . . . Hold them up there until you're counted. Keep them up. (*Counts.*)

OLD

Skating pond my . . . Nothing but a puddle beside the road.

GLADIE

The kids like it for skating in the winter. They slide their little pucks around. And in warm weather it's a haven for ducks.

ESTHER

Willard Willie used to enjoy feeding the ducks.

JULIE

Who's Willard Willie?

MEG

He is . . . he used to be the oldest man in town. Holder of the Boston Post Cane.

ESTHER

(*Eyeballs town officials.*) They gave him the Boston Post Cane at town meeting and now he's dead. What's that tell you?

ROBERT

Calm down there, Auntie. Don't get yourself all worked up now.

ESTHER

If they try to stick me with that Boston Post Cane, Robert, I'm going to get worked up. I may become irate.

MA

You sit right there, Stella, where I can keep an eye on you. You've caused enough trouble for one day, you and that chief of police getting all the tongues in town wagging. You and that Mickey, too, causing all sorts of trouble, bothering my chickens in the middle of the night with your goings-on, then Mickey running off through Grisly Swamp. . . .

ROBERT

He's a good fella, Mickey. Goodhearted. Known for it. Smart too. You ever see him take a motor apart and put it back together, just the same way—no parts left over or nothing. He can recite all the counties in New Hampshire, backwards in alphabetical order. Learned it in fourth grade and never forgot it. He's practically a genius.

MICKEY

(*Recites NH counties, backwards in alphabetical order.*) Sullivan . . . Strafford . . . Rockingham . . .

MODERATOR

All those opposed . . . (*Cards go up.*) The vote being manifestly in the negative we will dispense with the ballot vote and I'll call for a show of hands on the main motion.

MICKEY

Merrimack . . .

TURTLE

Are we discussing the chief of police here, 'cause if we are—

DICKY

I didn't say anything about the chief. And I'm not going to either. So don't ask me, 'cause I don't have anything to say on the matter of the hole in the roof of the new cruiser and how it might have gotten there. No knowledge of any alleged goings-on in the back seat of the cruiser that night between any two people engaging in any goings-on neither of who was me.

ROBERT

(*Amused.*) Thanks for clearing that up, Dicky.

DICKY

Richard.

MICKEY

Hillsborough . . .

MAXINE

Mr. Moderator. Point of order.

MICKEY

Grafton . . .

MAXINE

If you'll all look at your warrants, you'll see that Article 1 is written for $1,000 to be paid to the Daughters of Illustrious Yankee Patriots. The $1 is an amendment, made and seconded half an hour ago.

ESTHER

Since the daughters talked it over among themselves and decided to donate the pond.

MAXINE

We're voting on the dollar to show the town accepts, or doesn't accept the donation.

MODERATOR

It may be that with all the talk about Norman's accident and pollution and liability and turtles, along with the vote about how to vote, we've strayed.

MICKEY

Coos . . . Cheshire . . . Carroll

STELLA

Who said I called the cops on Mickey anyway? It wasn't necessarily me called the cops. Could have been anybody.

ED

Mickey meant well. He was trying to make up with you.

STELLA

Mickey always means well. When he chain-sawed the pine tree and dropped it on Ma's bob house, he meant well. He meant for it to fall in the other direction. Good intentions didn't help Ma's bob house.

MICKEY

Belknap!

MODERATOR

You can't amend an amendment, Mr. Selectman.

GLADIE

You have to vote first on the amendment to amend the main motion. Why, if we don't proceed in an orderly fashion, how can we proceed at all?

MODERATOR

If the amendment passes, then the house can amend the amended motion if the house so desires. If it fails, we're back to the main motion and the house can amend that.

MEG

You can't amend an amendment before it passes.

GLADIE

Good grief, no. Unless the one who made the amendment and the one who seconded both withdraw their motions.

MODERATOR

You've got it right down pat, Gladie. Next thing I know you'll be after my job.

ESTHER

(*Suggestively.*) That's not what she's after.

TURTLE

Move the question.

JULIE

(*Desperately.*) What's the question?

MEG

(*To JULIE.*) You feeling all right? You're looking a little peak-ed. You're not . . .

JULIE

Oh no. It's just . . . gas! Little Bundle's not due for thirteen days, much too well-behaved to interrupt my first town meeting. I've registered to vote. I'm voting and I'm going to keep on voting. I like voting.

(*ATTORNEY CHRIS GOODIE enters wearing a suit, carrying a briefcase, strolls the length of the hall. This causes a stir.*)

MA

What's she all dressed up for?

GLADIE

Could be lost, poor soul.

OLD

Who in the particular hell is that?

ESTHER

(*Awed at the sight of CHRIS.*) Mafia!

*** Music ***

INTERMISSION

ACT II

TIME:Later that day

AT RISE:Characters grouped in animated discussions as lights come up. CHRIS wandering the hall looking for somebody. But who?

OLD

Fifteen hundred dollars to scrape the g.d. rust off some g.d. cemetery fence, but they can't spend fifty g.d. cents to fix the g.d. washouts on Goody Road. Oh no, that road is perfectly fine. Just drive the high ground. That's what the Reverend Holly told me. That son of a—

MA

I don't believe he's a reverend, either. I don't believe he ever reverended a thing.

BABY

He couldn't reverend his way out of a sock.

ESTHER

Mafia!

MA

If they gotta have a fence, we got some chicken wire out back the shed—

(CHRIS takes seat next to ESTHER.)

ESTHER

You're sitting on my knitting.

CHRIS

Excuse me. (Disentangling herself.) I'm looking for someone, who's supposed to be here looking for me. (Checks watch.)

ESTHER

They come and they go.

JULIE

(Screams out in agony.) . . . Sorry, just a twinge.

TURTLE

Disturbing the peace. Disturbing the peace, he says. Neighbors complained. "Chief," I says to the man, "I been target practicing in this g.d. gravel pit since 1954. My own g.d. gun, my own g.d. gravel pit on my own g.d. land. You gonna come in here and tell me I can't shoot my own g.d. gun in my g.d. own gravel pit on my own g.d. land at two o'clock on a g.d. Sunday afternoon?" "Hey," he says, "neighbors complained." "What neighbors?" I says. "Nearest one's a mile away and he's my g.d. brother-in-law." That's when I decided I better run for selectman. Had to. The man was harassing me.

MODERATOR

Having been moved and seconded that the town raise and appropriate the sum of $1563 to repair the Victorian cast iron fence around the Meadowbrook Cemetery, the first selectman has made a request to give a brief explanation of this article in order to enlighten the house. House be enlightened.

ROBERT

Don't seem possible.

JULIE

(*In distress.*) *Move the question.*

MAXINE

The fence in question has deteriorated over the years to the point where if repairs aren't done right away, it may—come another winter—be beyond repair. The cemetery trustees—

ROBERT

Representing the largest constituency in town.

OLD

Too bad they can't vote.

ED

Why not?

MA

They're dead, Ed.

ROBERT

Scratched from the checklist.

ESTHER

Like Willard Willie.

MAXINE

The cemetery trustees collected estimates as follows: $305 for labor to remove the damaged sections; $148 for black rustproof paint. And . . . I can't read this writing. Reverend Holly, what's that say?

MA

Can't read.

ROBERT

Can't write.

OLD

Can't talk.

DICKY

That's why we elected them.

MODERATOR

(*To GLADIE.*) Long day, rate we're going.

GLADIE

Perhaps you'll be too tired to drive up to that Hill House of Pizza and Seafood?

MODERATOR

Oh no. I could moderate all day and half the night without so much as a bead of sweat breaking out.

GLADIE

That's what makes you such a fine moderator, Mr. Moderator.

MODERATOR

Matter of fact, I find it kind of stimulating.

* * * Music * * *

CHIEF

Can you hear me In the back?

OLD

No.

CHIEF

Early this morning your police department engaged in the pursuit of a fugitive within town limits.

DICKY

The manhunt continues at this hour.

MICKEY

The Mickey man hunt.

CHIEF

Private citizens such as yourselves would be well advised to take precautions. Doors should be locked. Vehicles secured. Children and valuables should not be left unattended. Don't be surprised if you come across roadblocks.

DICKY

They are in place for your safety.

CHIEF

Please cooperate with the cadets and Civil Defense volunteers assisted by several deputized members of the Lions Club manning those roadblocks at no cost to the town.

MA

You didn't give 'em guns, did you, Chief?

ROBERT

You didn't give them ammunition?

ESTHER

Mafia!

MAXINE

No Esther, the Lion's Club.

ESTHER

We'll have to take the back way home, Robert.

CHIEF

Three of our part-time officers are tracking down leads as they become available. If anyone has information as to the whereabouts of said fugitive—

BABY

Is there a reward?

CHIEF

—so-called Michael Paul Enright, a.k.a., Mickey Enright, last seen at 2:37 a.m. in the so-called piney woods behind the Old Goody Place, let us know immediately. This man is unpredictable, potentially dangerous, and probably still in the vicinity.

*** Scary Music ***

ED

It'd have to be a large reward to get me to wander around Grisly Swamp in the middle of the night.

STELLA

Ed's afraid Bigfoot will get him.

DICKY

Tear him limb from spindly limb.

OLD

I didn't hear you volunteer to run out through the swamp last night, Dicky.

DICKY

Richard.

BABY

Dicky's afraid of swamp ghosts—oooooo. He's afraid a big fat bear might eat him up. Or Bigfoot.

MICKEY

Must have been the old man called the cops. Stella wouldn't have turned me in. Stella wanted me home. She loves me. She married me, didn't she?

MEG

She threw Mickey out on his ear.

ROBERT

Mickey got to fighting down to the Frothy Mug.

MICKEY

Just funnin' with my friends.

ROBERT

Which was not unusual. But for some reason, the police got after him. Mickey resisted arrest—so the chief claimed. Course Mickey says he was all willing.

OLD

Slapped him in the pokey for thirty days. Ha!

MAXINE

Nobody would post his bail. Especially not Stella. That would have defeated the purpose. Look at them, look at Stella and the chief, they're all over each other.

ROBERT

In for thirty days, and Stella gets a restraining order—though he seemed pretty well restrained to me, being in the pokey and all, but what's the first thing he does when they let him out? Sneaks back to see the beautiful Stella Goody.

DICKY

Mickey said: "Stella, I love you." And, "Stella, take me back."

MICKEY

Stella, put down that can of pepper spray! Stella didn't bail me out because she wanted to give me a chance to think things over. Which I did.

MODERATOR

Norman down to the Sunoco claims Mickey gave Dicky his black eye, but somebody else said the stock of Old Goody's 12-gauge nicked Dicky when he tried to stop Old Goody firing into the bushes to make sure Mickey was good and gone.

DICKY

Richard.

OLD

Dicky run into a tree in the dark and gave himself that shiner.

GLADIE

Sometimes it's hard to see a tree coming at you in the dark.

(*CHRIS circles hall looking for her client during this conversation.*)

MEG

Sometimes you don't even know what's going on in your own family. Take Maxine (*pause*)—it got so her husband was going to wetlands meetings every other night. Very concerned about your mallard ducks, your pollywogs, your purple loosestrife.

MA

And they were running late, those meetings.

MEG

It took her from January to June to figure out that he and that wetlands woman were holding private meetings. And they weren't keeping minutes.

TURTLE

(*Of CHRIS as she passes.*) Ed, that's our woman. Got to be. Why didn't you alert me, Ed? Why didn't you scratch your g.d. arm pit, then? You were supposed to scratch your g.d. arm pit and give me the g.d. signal.

MODERATOR

Order! Order please!

MAXINE

That's $263.46 for granite posts. And that figure includes the digging of the holes.

OLD

Who's gonna dig 'em?

ROBERT

Oh, they'll put it out to bid. Put an ad in the paper costs $40 to get somebody to dig $2 worth of holes.

TURTLE

(*Loudly.*) I have something to say and I'm going to say it. I have here a petition to present to the legislative body on behalf of the undersigned citizens of Woodford. I'd like to be recognized, Mr. Moderator—

MODERATOR

Hold on to your petition and wait your turn, Mr. Selectman. We're discussing holes here.

ED

I'll dig the holes.

MA

Ed likes to dig.

MAXINE

Ed is not an employee of the town and is not insured under the town policy. If he digs the holes and is hurt, for example, if he should fall into a hole and—

GLADIE

(*Alarmed.*) My goodness, how big do those holes need to be?

TURTLE

(*Loudly.*) Mr. Moderator! My constituents and I would appreciate it if you didn't cut me off again.

MODERATOR

Did I say it was your turn to talk, Turtle? Gladie, did I give Turtle Tuttle the floor? Check your notes.

GLADIE

(*Checking notes.*) You know, on second thought, I might enjoy going out to supper tonight, Mr. Moderator—up to that Hill House of Pizza and Seafood. Why I'm a little peckish now—and I'll probably grow hungrier as the day wears on. I believe I will accept your invitation, Mr. Moderator.

MODERATOR

(*Passionately.*) So moved.

ROBERT

Pay attention, fellas. We're all headed for Meadowbrook Cemetery, sooner or later.

OLD

When I go, stuff me and lean me in the corner.

MA

I thought we'd stew you and feed you to the dogs.

OLD

It'd be cheaper to rip the damn fence down and be done with it—

MODERATOR

Goody, is this a question?

OLD

Paint won't stick. Rust flakes right off in your fingers.

MODERATOR

Goody, I've opened the floor to questions and questions only, questions for the selectmen or cemetery trustees so that the people can understand the issue and the costs to the town. If you have a comment, I will call on you later, when the floor is open for comments. Do you have a question? If you have a question, ask it. Otherwise, sit down.

OLD

No, I don't have a question. I have a comment.

MODERATOR

Hold your comments.

OLD

Hold your own comments!

GLADIE

I have a question, Mr. Moderator, just between ourselves.

MODERATOR

And what would that be, Gladie?

GLADIE

Do you prefer the pizza or the seafood?

MODERATOR

Pizza gives me heartburn.

GLADIE

I like clams, but just the necks—or your clam strips, like you used to get at the Howard Johnson's. I like my seafood firm.

MODERATOR

I prefer stomachs. The juicier the better. Ninety percent of the flavor's in the stomachs, Gladie.

GLADIE

But they squirt so.

MODERATOR

Say we order a quart of clams. You eat the necks. I eat the stomachs.

GLADIE

Okay.

TURTLE

Wouldn't it be cheaper to take the whole thing down? Isn't it true the back side's rusted right through? What's the sense in buying ten gallons of paint to pretty it up if you know damn well it'll peel in a month? Was this work put out to bid? Three bids as required by law?

MODERATOR

Would the other two selectmen care to address Selectman Tuttle's questions?

MAXINE

Not particularly.

CHRIS

If I could interject—

MODERATOR

I'll allow none of that.

MAXINE

You know Mr. Moderator, it would have been nice if Mr. Tuttle had raised his questions at the budget hearings held in the month of January for the purpose of thrashing through these very issues. I wonder why Mr. Tuttle chose not to raise his questions at that time. Certainly, as chairman of the Budget Committee he could have.

JULIE

(*Feeling poorly.*) What's the Budget Committee?

ESTHER

Them that know and can, do. Them that don't know and won't do, but want to criticize everybody else, run for Budget Committee.

(*BABY discovers MICKEY's hiding place.*)

BABY

You're going to jail. That's what the Chief told Stella. I heard him.

MICKEY

Stella's going to jail? How come? What'd she do? Stella won't like it in jail.

BABY

Not her. You.

MICKEY

I already been.

BABY

You're going back. The Chief's gonna make sure of that and Stella's glad. The Chief said: "Mickey's going back to jail and this time he's going to be there a long long long long long long time." And she said, "I'm glad." And then she gave him a long long long long wet smack right on the lips.

* * * *Music* * * *

STELLA

(*To CHIEF.*) Meet you after? To discuss my husband's case?

CHIEF

I'll give you an update at that time, yes, I will.

BABY

He's gonna give her an update.

MICKEY

(*Angry.*) He is, is he?

TURTLE

I run on a simple platform, and won for the simple reason a majority agreed with me that taxes are too high.

MA

How's the old people supposed to live?

TURTLE

I've been saying right along something's got to be done about the *fat* at town hall.

MAXINE

(*Rises from her seat, dangerous, expanding.*) Was that comment addressed to me, Mr. Tuttle?

TURTLE

Town hall is being run by a gang—Same Old Gang, I call them, S-O-G, sog—who don't give one hoot how the old people supposed to live. They say: Can't pay your taxes, tough luck—

ESTHER

That's right!

ED

Get out—

OLD

Drop dead—

MA

Make room for somebody who can.

TURTLE

If the new police chief wants a big raise, give it to him.

ROBERT

Hey, he's worth it.

STELLA

He certainly is.

TURTLE

If the new police chief wants a spanky new cruiser—

ROBERT

Well, he better have it then.

TURTLE

Carpeting in police headquarters? Make it thick and squishy. We can't have officers wearing out their shiny shoes—paid for by the town—on that hard old linoleum.

ED

Course not.

MA

Why can't they just wear regular shoes like the rest of us?

TURTLE

Did you know that we pay—we the people pay for having the chief's uniforms cleaned?

MEG

Is that in the budget?

GLADIE

Fine print.

TURTLE

That's right, everything except his undershorts and his socks. Maybe them too. Check the books.

MAXINE

Some people, you can't satisfy them. You try to save a little money, cut a corner or two, do all you can, but are they happy?

ROBERT

Hard to tell, with some of 'em. Some of 'em being miserable makes 'em happy.

JULIE

(*Shaky.*) High taxes really hurt. They hurt people just starting out like Kinny and me, and Little Bundle and old ladies like Esther.

ESTHER

Who you calling an old lady?

MAXINE

Turtle Tuttle. Look at him. So pleased with himself. What does that man know about—

JULIE

(*Clutching her stomach.*) Fat.

MA

Hasn't lived here long enough to say so.

ESTHER

Not a native.

ROBERT

By rights a man ought to live in a town two decades before he's allowed to open his mouth at town meeting, say nothing about running for selectman.

MAXINE

If we came in to Town Meeting and announced we were going to run the town for nothing this year, so you don't have to pay any taxes at all, Turtle and his gang, they'd complain about that. They whine and complain and curse and moan.

MA

Where they come from that's all they know to do.

JULIE

Where do they come from?

ALL

Massachusetts.

MODERATOR

Does anyone else wish to speak? (*Hands raised all over the house.*) Does everyone understand the question before the house? All those in favor manifest by saying Aye?

CROWD

Aye.

MODERATOR

Opposed? The ayes have it. Close under Article 5, open under Article 6 to raise and appropriate the sum of $1,393,842.57 for general town operations as listed in your town report. I await your pleasure.

MAXINE

So moved.

HOLLY

Second.

MODERATOR

All those in favor manifest by saying Aye.

CROWD

Aye.

MODERATOR

Opposed.

OLD

No.

MODERATOR

Close under Article 6, open under Article 7 to raise and appropriate the sum of $17, 826 for a new cruiser for the police department. I await your pleasure.

JULIE

What just happened?

ROBERT

We just spent a million dollars.

JULIE

I didn't vote. I didn't know we were voting. (*Groans.*) I was waiting all this time to vote and (*gasp*) now, I can't believe I (*wails*) missed it.

ED

What do we need a police department for anyway? Nothing going on. And if something did happen, the state police would cover. You call the state police, they *have* to come. Call 'em up: "Hey state police, the bank's being robbed." What they gonna say, "Sorry, we're busy, catch you later." No, sir. They'll send a squadron right down, right off quick.

ROBERT

We got no bank, Ed.

TURTLE

Indefinitely postpone.

ED

Second.

MODERATOR

It's been moved and seconded to indefinitely postpone Article 7, to raise and appropriate the sum of $17,826 for the purpose of purchasing a new cruiser for the Woodford police department. I await your pleasure.

DICKY

The Woodford Police Department would like the Moderator's permission to make a brief presentation on this article to the voters.

MODERATOR

(*Sigh.*) Denied.

STELLA

Mr. Moderator—I think it's only fair we should hear some explanation. Would these cutbacks impair the ability of our police department to perform their official duties in an efficient and timely manner?

ROBERT

You mean, could they do any worse?

DICKY

Yes, we could, and I'll tell you why.

TURTLE

Mr. Moderator—I have a petition that I'd like to present at this time on advice of counsel.

MAXINE

What counsel?

TURTLE

(*Indicating CHRIS.*) This counsel right here! Said petition calls for the immediate removal of the chief of police from office, revokal of all said chief's power—

ED

—and take away his gun, too.

STELLA

(*Alarmed.*) You can't take away his gun. They can't take your gun, can they Chief?

TURTLE

We the undersigned are calling for an investigation into certain matters involving a cover-up and conspiracy with the other two selectmen, so-called Maxine Marsh and Reverend Holly. And a large hole in the roof of a certain police cruiser that rendered it inoperable and who put that hole in the roof of that police cruiser—

ED

And who lied about it, huh?

MODERATOR

We are not proceeding here according to *Robert's Rules* or my rules or anybody's rules. I cannot and will not permit this contravention to continue.

TURTLE

We're calling for an investigation by the state Attorney General's office into—

CHIEF

I stand on my record.

DICKY

Me, too.

TURTLE

You can stand on your record or your head, don't make no difference. I got proof. (*Pause.*) Ms. Lidbecker? (*He walks to CHRIS, extends his hand.*) I'm Turtle Tuttle, selectman for the town of Woodford. We spoke several times on the phone. You brought the papers?

JULIE

I think I may have just had a contraction. I think I may have had more than one contraction.

MEG

I'll take you right home—no, I'll take you to the hospital? No, I'll call an ambulance. No, I'll call Kinny. No—

JULIE

I think I'll lie down for a minute. (*Collapses behind the PTA table.*) I don't want to miss the vote on the (*gasp*) cruiser.

ROBERT

Are you insinuating, Mr. Selectman, that the chief shot that hole in the roof of his own cruiser? Are you suggestion a cover up because the chief don't want anybody finding out who was with him that night, down on the Gully Road, in the back seat testing the springs?

CHRIS

Sir, my name is not Lidbecker. You've made a mistake.

TURTLE

Lidbecker. Lidberger. Liddinger. Almandinger . . .

CHRIS

Goodie. (*Goodys rise as one, mouths open.*) G-O-O-D-I-E. With a silent E. No relation. Now if I may clarify—

OLD

Not a resident. Can't talk at Town Meeting if you ain't a resident.

MODERATOR

At the discretion of the moderator, nonresidents may be allowed to speak.

CHRIS

I'm here on behalf of my client Michael Enright.

MICKEY

(*Steps out of voting booth.*) Been hiding out. Had to. Chief's out to get me, for no good reason.

CHIEF

Michael Enright. (*Hand on gun.*) You are under arrest. Cuff him, Dicky.

DICKY

Richard.

CHRIS

One moment, officer. If you cuff my client, Michael Enright, you'll be cuffing the wrong man. I have here a warrant for the arrest of your chief of police; Mr. Enright having persuaded me via telephone in the night and me having persuaded the NH Attorney General that Mickey Enright had been unjustly accused and incarcerated. This court order authorizes the selectmen to strip the chief of police of his powers, and, if they so desire, to authorize a duly endowed deputy to take him into custody.

ROBERT

How do you feel about that, Chief?

CHIEF

Not good.

DICKY

Who should I cuff?

CHRIS

(*Pointing to the CHIEF.*) Him! (*DICKY cuffs the CHIEF.*)

STELLA

I wanted to put up your bail, Mickey, but *he* said no. He said a little cooling off would be good for you. He said it was for your own good.

CHIEF

Shut up, Stella.

STELLA

You shut up! Did you hear that, Mickey? That man told me to shut up.

MICKEY

He's not a nice man, Stella.

STELLA

I can see that now. I can see that I have been cruelly deceived and taken advantage of.

MICKEY

If we could just sit down quiet together—talk it out, Stella—over a cup of coffee—

STELLA

Coffee! I never—(*Sweetly.*) Well, okay, Mickey. A cup of coffee would be nice.

* * * *Music* * * *

MODERATOR

I await your pleasure.

OLD AND JULIE

Move the question.

MODERATOR

All those in favor . . . All opposed . . . We seem to be deadlocked. Half of you want the cruiser; half don't. Now is there anybody here entitled to vote who has not yet voted.

BABY

Mickey didn't vote.

MICKEY

Abstain.

TURTLE

Abstaining is not voting.

GLADIE

Yes it is. Three kind of votes. Vote yes, vote no or abstain.

MODERATOR

In the instance of a tie vote, the motion fails. As Moderator, I could break the
tie, but I ain't going to. Close under Article 7, open under Article 8, to raise and
appropriate $124 to install a street light at the intersection of Pig Lane and the
Old Stage Road.

MAXINE

Mr. Moderator, point of order. When we voted on Article 7 we were voting
on Turtle's motion to indefinitely postpone. The vote failed in the tie so the
motion to indefinitely postpone failed, which means, I believe, the original
motion passes—

CHIEF

And I get my cruiser after all. Ha!

TURTLE

You mean the chief gets his cruiser after all?

ROBERT

But, Turtle, he don't get to use it.

MA

Motion to recess for the lunch hour—

(*JULIE screams, she's delivering under the table . . .*)

GLADIE

Wait! We can't forget the happiness article! In this long-standing tradition, the
Boston Post Cane, our symbol of longevity, is awarded to the oldest living resident. Esther Crawford Fox, would you come forward? (*Applause, cheers.*)

JULIE

(*Pops her head up.*) Is it time to vote?

ESTHER

I don't want that old cane. I won't have it. (*Pause, glare.*) All right. (*Long pause.*) I'll say this and this is all I'll say. (*Pause.*) You can take your Boston Post Cane and . . . give it to the Historical Society. Put the damn cane in the damn museum—

(*Cry of newborn from under the table. JULIE rises with the baby in her arms.*)

MA

My heavens, a baby born at town meeting—and a cute little mite at that.

CHRIS

It is a boy or a girl?

ROBERT

Well, either way, it's a native.

SEVERAL

A native!

ESTHER

A baby born at town meeting. I never thought I'd live to see the day!

*** Music ***

All Stand and Bow

THE LYRICS

For a taste of the musical version, here are John Rule's lyrics for the opening number, "You're at Town Meeting," followed by Chris Cote's music. Feel free to sing and play along!

If the rigors of democracy leave you a little weak
and palpitating
or foaming on the microphone even before you speak,
it's stimulating
you're at town meeting where
we calmly discuss all the facts.
The moderator never tolerates
personal attacks.

Robert's Rules *requires some kind of education*
elementary
but every native comprehends a situation
parliamentary.
When the motion before the house
is a crisis about to unfold
the entertainment value is
worth its weight in gold.
You're not alone if you're concerned
that simple honesty my be in decline
but town reports give the real scoop
for those who carefully read between the lines.

For some to crack the budget is truly their cup of tea
it's mathematic.
For others, local gossip sets imagination free
they're diabolic.
Our hidden motives differ,
but on one thing we agree:
Town officials paid their worth
are working for free.

So bundle up the kids
and bring Auntie
and her old cane.
The coffee's waiting.
Be careful in those
front row seats
spilled blood might
leave a stain.
We're percolating.
You're at town meeting
and if we get a little irate
just try to see it our way
(you better see it their way)
We may negotiate, oh yes, we may negotiate.
Town meeting!
Let's all settle in.
Town meeting!
Motion to begin.

Chris Cote   1

/1/ You're At Town Meeting

Chris Cote / You're At Town Meeting 3

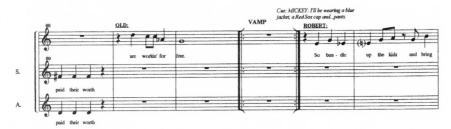

Chris Cote / You're At Town Meeting   6

Index of People and Places